MADAME DE LAFAYETTE

By Constance Wright

Madame de Lafayette

by CONSTANCE WRIGHT

HENRY HOLT AND COMPANY

NEW YORK

For Mary Lee, with all good will
—and a few doubts

AUTHOR'S NOTE

Recently, in 1956, Count René de Chambrun, one of Adrienne de Lafayette's descendants, took possession of the chateau of La Grange-Bléneau, where she spent the last years of her life; there he discovered a treasure trove of documents. Until these have been sorted over and made available to scholars, no absolutely definitive life of Adrienne can be written. So much material is already available, however, that her story is told here with the hope that only a few minor details are lacking—and with the conviction that the last word can never be spoken of a person of whom there is abundant record, and who lived so abundantly.

Contents

PART ONE

January, 1782—October, 1791

CHAPTER I

Heroic Homecoming

Pᴀʀɪs, which today is a city of light, of broad boulevards, of endless vistas, was at the end of the eighteenth century still a walled town. It was surrounded by field and woodland and by sprawling suburbs, some of them as hideous slums as one could find anywhere in Europe.

The streets of the city proper were narrow and crooked. In winter they were thickly smeared with mud and sewage, but on the day preceding January 21st, 1782, a miracle of municipal house cleaning was brought to pass. The entire city was swept clean; thousands of firepots were distributed for after dark illumination—for January 21st was to be a day of fête, of fanfare. At Versailles, Queen Marie Antoinette of France had borne a son. In the morning she would come from La Muette, a royal hunting lodge on the edge of the Bois de Boulogne, for her churching in Notre Dame. Later in the day, the King would join her for a state banquet at the Hotel de Ville.

The weather on the 21st was clear and bright. Everyone was out; everyone wanted to see the royal processions as

3

they entered and left the city. In the afternoon, however, sensation seekers discovered that there was a counter attraction. In the Rue St. Honoré, which was off the expected line of march, a crowd gathered in front of a large, handsome house, which, with its wide forecourt, its pillared façade, and beautiful formal garden that stretched as far as the Tuileries and what is now the Rue de Rivoli, was one of the showplaces of Paris.

This was the city mansion—a hotel in the primitive sense of the term—of a very important family that for generations had held high positions in the government of France. The Duc Maréchal de Noailles was the patriarch of the clan; his eldest son, the Duc d'Ayen, was Captain of the King's bodyguard. The Hotel de Noailles had always been admired, but for the past five years passers-by had stopped to gape at it in wonder. It was widely known that this was the home not only of the Noailles dukes and duchesses but of a Noailles son-in-law, the Marquis de Lafayette.

All knew the life story of this remarkable young man. In 1774, at the early age of sixteen, Gilbert du Motier, one of the richest boys of noble blood in France, was married to Marie Adrienne Françoise, the second of the Duc d'Ayen's five daughters. Three years later he left abruptly to fight in the American War for Independence. In 1779 he returned a universal hero, the darling of the court and of the nation, only to depart for another long campaign across the Atlantic which had recently ended in victory. Three days ago, Lafayette had landed at Lorient and word had just been spread about in the capital that he might arrive at any moment.

Among those who waited at the gate of the Hotel de Noailles were some women who sold fish in the Paris market. Dressed in their Sunday best, they had brought with them sheaves of laurel to present to the conqueror. That Lafayette had routed the British almost single handedly at Yorktown they were sure; they were also sure that in some way, not yet revealed to them, he would be the champion of liberty—*their* liberty—at home.

Presently a carriage appeared; cheers and cries of "long live Lafayette" went up. The tall young man of twenty-four who emerged from the post chaise, with his broad shoulders, his great beak of a nose and his reddish hair, was no Prince Charming, but the crowd had not expected that he would be as pretty as a porcelain doll. In his uniform of an American Major General, Lafayette was an impressive, a soldierly figure.

As always, his manners were equal to the occasion. He accepted the fishwives' offering gratefully and without the slightest hint of condescension. He made a little speech of thanks and waited patiently until all had had a good look at him before entering the house.

It seemed as if the show was over. The servant who opened the door to him, and even the fishwives, could tell the Marquis that his wife, the person he had wanted most to surprise, was not at home. She and all the adult members of her family—her father, her mother, and her sisters—were at the reception at the Hotel de Ville. When they would return was anybody's guess. By this time the town hall dinner must be over, but protocol demanded that no one should leave before the Queen had been bowed into her coach. After her would come the King, the Princes of the Blood, and all the high dignitaries of the realm in slow moving, well-established order of precedence. This might mean a wait of several hours, and the crowd began to thin out soon after Lafayette had disappeared from view.

A short time later, however, those who lingered got their reward. A fresh wave of sightseers began to pour in from the direction of the Hotel de Ville, filling the street and the courtyard of the Hotel de Noailles and lining the steps of the parish Church of St. Roch across the way. First, distant shouts and the blare of trumpets, then, the thud of horses' hoofs and the jingle of harness announced that there had been a change of royal plan. The Queen's coach, with its mounted escort and outriders, all decked out in their be-ribboned birthday finery, came lurching down the Rue St. Honoré. It ground to a halt before the house of the Duc d'Ayen.

Again a shout went up, a double-barreled shout, for the Queen was not alone in her jewel box setting. Beside her on the velvet cushions was seated a young woman, elaborately dressed, elaborately jeweled, but not as resplendent as the Queen, for no one was permitted to out-glitter royalty. Dark haired, white skinned, with delicately chiseled features— what one noticed first about Adrienne de Lafayette were her very large, her very expressive eyes, deep set under thick, dark eyebrows. Because she was so small and slight, Adrienne —who had recently celebrated her twenty-second birthday— looked almost like a school girl; her youth, her pallor were perfect foils to set off the triumphant, full-blown beauty of her carriage-mate.

That the Marquise de Lafayette should be riding in the royal coach was due to a generous impulse on the part of Marie Antoinette. Just as the dinner party at the Hotel de Ville was breaking up, the news of Lafayette's return was passed from mouth to mouth, from ear to ear, until it reached the Queen. She realized Adrienne's predicament. All the ladies at the dinner were expected not only to wait their turn here but to follow the coach as far as La Muette for another round of curtseying, a second ceremonial fare-well.

Marie Antoinette sent word to Adrienne to leave at once and to hurry home to her husband. When Adrienne demurred, the Queen offered to alter her route and invited— in fact, commanded—the young wife to come with her. There was kindness in the invitation; there were also showmanship and a consideration for popular sentiment with which the

Queen was seldom credited. She saw, no doubt, that on this day of days the people of Paris would like to view the mother of the Dauphin, but they would also like to see the wife of their favorite Marquis.

Lafayette himself, when he heard the noisy overture to the Queen's arrival, hurried out of the house and pushed his way through the crowded courtyard. He was standing bareheaded at the gate when the coach drew up. The Queen leaned out; she extended a hand for him to kiss; she smiled. She knew Lafayette far better than she knew Adrienne. He had been one of the rather fast and foolish set that revolved about her in the early days of her marriage. At that time she had not thought too highly of him—an awkward, tongue-tied youth, a clumsy figure on the ballroom floor. Once Marie Antoinette had laughed at the Marquis when he was chosen as her partner in a quadrille and had made a few blundering missteps that spoiled the pattern of the dance. When he became a hero she learned to be more gracious.

And she was very gracious now. She congratulated him on the American victory and on the part that he had played in it. "As you see," she said, "I have brought you Madame de Lafayette. Her place today is not with me, but with her husband."

Lafayette murmured his thanks. All eyes during this brief and largely one-sided conversation were fixed upon the Queen. When the signal for the coach to move on was given, all eyes were fixed on Adrienne, who had not spoken a single word. She had been helped out on the farther side of the carriage and stood staring speechless at her husband.

If possible she had become more pale; all color had drained from her lips and cheeks. She took a step forward, stumbled, and would have fallen if Lafayette had not sprung forward to catch her. Sweeping her up in his arms, her head against his shoulder, her voluminous skirts trailing to the ground, he carried her toward the house, much impeded by the curious who pressed about him and followed to the very doorstep.

The crowd was enthralled. Those who couldn't get near enough to see plainly, shoved their neighbors, craned their necks, and stood on tiptoe. Those who had handkerchiefs took them out to wipe their eyes. There were enthusiastic ululations, ohs and ahs of commiseration and delight.

For a legend had grown up about Adrienne, just as it had grown up about her venturesome husband. She was his faithful, virtuous wife; she was Penelope to his Ulysses; she was the mother of his only son, who had been named George Washington Lafayette after the American general. When the treaty of alliance between the colonies and France had been signed, the American envoys went to pay her their respects. It was even said that when Voltaire—the great Voltaire—returned to Paris from exile in 1778, he sought out Adrienne and fell on his knees before her. "I wish," he cried, "to present my homage to the wife of the hero of the New World; may I live long enough to salute him as the liberator of the old!"

Closely identified as she was in the public mind with Lafayette, it seemed altogether fitting to the onlookers in the courtyard of the Hotel de Noailles that the poor little woman should faint at sight of her husband after years of separation. Fainting was much in fashion, particularly among fine ladies —and Adrienne was, after all, the daughter of a duke. In losing consciousness she had behaved just as her audience had hoped she would, and it went away well-satisfied after the door had closed upon her. What it had just witnessed was as good as the finale of a stage play, and soon a popular ballad was being sung in the music halls of Paris that told how Lafayette had come home from the wars to offer to his wife "a heart of flame."

It so happened that the little drama of Lafayette's return

had been judged correctly, though across the footlights, so to speak, only its crude outlines could be grasped. Its finer points were known to none but the principal actors.

Adrienne was indeed a good and faithful wife—and her faint had been quite genuine; she was not given to swooning for stage effect. When she came to herself in the privacy of her father's house, she was dissatisfied with the part she had played. This was not the greeting she had intended for her husband. She had been overwhelmed as much by the publicity of her meeting with Lafayette as by the sudden release from long tension.

During the past eight years Adrienne had known moments of exquisite happiness, but she had also known much sorrow, much frustration. The history of her marriage to Gilbert du Motier was—and would forever after be—the history of her life.

CHAPTER II

A Red Tapestried Room

EVEN BEFORE SHE first saw him, even before she had heard his name, Adrienne de Noailles became aware of Gilbert's existence. She was a child then, not yet entered on her teens.

In the mansion of the Rue St. Honoré, Adrienne had had an unusual upbringing. Most children of noble families were put out to nurse and might pass their early years in a peasant cottage, or even in one of the ugly slums that surrounded Paris. If they were girls, they were sent away to a convent as soon as they could toddle and little more notice was taken of them until they were ripe for marriage.

Not so the daughters of the Duchesse d'Ayen. Though convent-bred herself, she could not bear to be separated from her children. Her five little girls had a governess and masters who came in to teach them music and dancing, but the Duchess herself was their most effective teacher.

Every afternoon they would assemble in her crimson tapestried bedroom. Before they settled down, the smaller ones on stools, the larger ones on chairs, there was an argument as to who should sit closest to their mother in her high-backed *bergère* beside the fireplace, or by the open window if the weather was warm. Her snuff box, her work bag, and a pile of books would be spread out on the table beside her.

The Duchess read aloud to her children from religious works—she was deeply and sincerely religious—from books of history and mythology, from books of the classic poets and dramatists. Sometimes—even before they could write themselves—she would have them dictate letters to her so that they could learn to express themselves clearly and eloquently. But this was not a formal study hour. Most of the afternoon was given up to conversation; in the eighteenth century, conversation was a serious business, an art in itself. The Duchess and her little flock talked about the day's happenings, about what they had done or seen, about what they should or should not do in a given situation.

The Duchess, though naturally impatient herself, always allowed them to express their own ideas. Once she complained that they were not as obedient as children of their age ought to be and Adrienne spoke up wisely. "That may be, *maman*," she said, "because you let us argue and raise objections. You will see that when we are fifteen we will be as obedient as other children."

Already Adrienne was thinking of marriage. Fifteen was the accepted age of female consent—of consent, that is, of a girl to the will of her parents—for she could take it for granted that her parents would select her husband and well in advance might wonder what their choice would be.

The day for obedience came earlier for Adrienne than she had expected. She was twelve, and her older sister Louise was thirteen, when they noticed that a coolness had arisen between their father and mother. This was not unusual. The Duke, a gregarious man, a born courtier, and an atheist, was very different in temperament from his devout, home-loving wife, who would rather dine with her children and their governess than with the King and Queen at Versailles. The girls saw little of their father. He was so often away from home that they never felt at ease with him.

For a year the strained relationship continued. Then Adrienne, when she and Louise went occasionally with their mother to Versailles, began to meet a tall, red-haired boy, a young Marquis who was living with his tutor in her father's house. Gilbert du Motier was an orphan. His childhood had been spent in the country, in Auvergne. For the past three years he had been at a fashionable boy's boarding school, Le Plessis, in Paris, where the younger brothers of the Dauphin, the future Louis XVI, were also pupils.

The meetings were always casual and always chaperoned. They generally took place, as if by chance, out of doors in the garden. Another boy, somewhat older than Gilbert, was frequently present. He was the Vicomte Louis de Noailles, a cousin once removed, the son of the girls' great uncle, the Duc de Mouchy. In the autumn of 1773, Louise, aged fifteen, was married to her cousin. At this time Adrienne's mother broke the news to her that she was promised to the Marquis de Lafayette. The marriage contract had been signed months ago in February, not only by the two families involved but also by the King.

This explained the presence of Gilbert at Versailles and also the long, undeclared war between Adrienne's parents that preceded it. When, almost two years earlier, Lafayette's guardians had proposed him as a husband for one of her daughters—which one was immaterial to them—Henriette d'Ayen refused her consent. Her reasons seemed fantastic to the Duke. Her chief objection was that Gilbert du Motier was much too rich; she didn't want greater wealth for her children than they already possessed. That the Marquis was so young and an orphan, with no one to guide him, was also unfortunate.

It had taken many heated discussions behind closed doors,

many conferences with Lafayette's proposers, before Madame d'Ayen yielded, and then only with the proviso that the young people should have an opportunity to become acquainted before anything was said to Adrienne. In the interval the Duchess had met Gilbert and had taken an immediate liking to him. She told Adrienne that she had come to love him as if he were one of the two sons she had lost in infancy. She was sure that he would make her daughter very happy.

Adrienne accepted this prediction as trustfully as she would any other arrangement that her mother might have made for her.

Before the wedding that took place on April 11th, 1774, when Adrienne was five months past her fourteenth birthday, there were nightly receptions in the Hotel de Noailles. All of Paris came in rainbow review to offer their congratulations to the fiancée, who, frizzed and curled, laced within an inch of suffocation, sat bolt upright on a tabouret beside her mother's chair. As each guest appeared, Adrienne rose and was led forward to be introduced, often a mere formality, since many who came to the Rue St. Honoré were relatives she had known since early childhood. To each of the deep bows that were made to her she was expected to return a curtsey in the grand manner, her left leg doubled under her to support her slim young body, her right foot extended to make a point beneath her satin petticoat. The wedding gifts that accompanied or followed these visits were magnificent and consisted chiefly of jewelry.

On April 11th, the bride was led by her father to her *prie-dieu* in the crowded, candlelit chapel of the hotel. After the Nuptial Mass was performed, Adrienne was allowed to retire upstairs for a few hours, to take off her veil and relax a little before she was re-dressed in yet another costume, even more elegant than her wedding gown of silver tissue. She then went downstairs to join the wedding guests as a married woman, a marquise.

The festivities were long drawn out and ended with a feast, the young couple being seated for the first time side by side at the head of the table. Honeymoons had not yet been invented. The good old folkway custom of helping to undress the bride and groom and seeing them get into bed together was nowadays considered crude, but about midnight a procession formed to lead the newlyweds to the door of the best bedroom in the house, the same red tapestried room with which Adrienne was so familiar. There she and Gilbert spent their wedding night.

*   *   *

Did she already love her husband? Years later, looking back, Adrienne could smile at the question and say no. She had only a childish, tepid liking for this overgrown boy, whom most people thought glum and shy. He had never been shy with her. Even in their early encounters he had let her see how affectionate he could be, how eager he was for her affection.

Madame d'Ayen, moreover, had impressed upon her daughter the necessity of making a great effort to endear herself to her husband. She herself, alas—she admitted it with a sigh—had never studied the art of pleasing a man. In the early days of her own marriage she had let the Duke see all too plainly that she had a mind of her own!

In the year that followed the Lafayette-Noailles wedding, the Duchess exerted herself to make home attractive to her son-in-law, for a clause had been inserted in the marriage contract that Gilbert and Adrienne should live with her until they were old enough to have a home of their own. The Duchess overcame the physical inertia that in part accounted for her retired way of life and, much to the Duke's satisfaction, took Louise and Adrienne to the Queen's balls at Versailles and gave dinner parties for them there and in Paris. Because she had no social ambitions of her own and was so kind and cordial to everyone who came to her house, she developed a belated reputation for being the perfect hostess.

A few weeks after Adrienne had turned sixteen, she gave birth to her first child, a frail little girl whom she named Henriette for her mother. The baby should, of course, have been a boy, a marquis-to-be, but Lafayette was not unkind enough to press the point. He was delighted, he said, to be a *père de famille*—a real family man—and took much notice of Henriette when he was at home.

He was, unfortunately, often absent. Even before he left boarding school Lafayette had set his heart on a military career and, as a prospective son-in-law of the Duc d'Ayen, had been able to buy a commission in the Noailles Dragoons, a crack regiment that the Duke himself commanded. Each summer Lafayette went for four months of war manoeuvers at Metz. When he was in Paris, he led the conventional life of a gay and chic young officer, going often to the races, the masked balls at the opera and the Cabaret of the Wooden Sword, a roadhouse halfway between Paris and Versailles, where there were nightly contests in seeing who could consume the most wine without disappearing beneath the table. One did not take a wife to such resorts—particularly a wife who had been as carefully brought up as Adrienne.

Each time that Lafayette left her for one of his tours of military duty, Adrienne found the parting more difficult; each return was more rapturous. That Gilbert might go farther than the garrison town of Metz, that he might spend years away from her instead of weeks and months, never crossed her mind until a day in April of 1777.

Adrienne was pregnant for a second time. Gilbert had gone to England for a few weeks' visit to one of the Noailles uncles who was Ambassador to the Court of St. James. Instead of coming home directly from London, as was expected, he was next heard from at Bordeaux. He had heard of the revolt in the American colonies. Like many other young enthusiasts who longed to twist the British lion's tail, he had enlisted in the American army and had bought a ship to take him and a group of his fellow officers across the Atlantic.

The Duke, who had not been consulted, was outraged. He was sympathetic to the American cause in principal, but not in practice for members of his family. He ordered the scapegrace to return—and was disobeyed. Fearful of arrest, of being dragged back ignominiously to Paris, Lafayette disguised himself as a postillion and galloped across the border into Spain. Shortly after, word came to the Hotel de Noailles that Lafayette's ship, *La Victoire,* had sailed from a Spanish port.

Adrienne was stunned. In his letter of farewell, Gilbert apologized for shrinking from a goodbye that he knew would be so painful to them both, but that was the only excuse he gave for keeping his intentions secret.

How little she had known him! How little they had shared, one with the other, their most perplexing problems! At the time of her marriage, Adrienne had had a secret sorrow of her own. Like many adolescents who have outgrown their nursery conception of religion, she was plagued by religious doubts, doubts so strong that she had not yet—after two years of seeking—received her First Communion. She said nothing to Gilbert, knowing that he, like most men of her acquaintance, was not a practicing Catholic. After she became his wife, however, and knew that she was going to bear him a child, her misgivings suddenly vanished. The revelation that she was in a state of grace came peacefully, without further struggle and she was able to receive the sacraments in all sincerity. Gilbert, too, it now seemed, had had his inner, hidden conflict, a conflict between luxuriating in a pampered, too thickly cushioned, way of life and proving himself in what he thought to be a noble enterprise.

She quickly came to his defense in the only way that was

possible—by saying nothing. Harsh words were spoken by the elders of the Noailles clan of Gilbert's folly, of his disobedience, and lack of consideration for his wife. Adrienne hid her grief and preferred to be thought childish or unfeeling rather than to swell the chorus of disapproval. She found a firm support in her mother, who also refused to speak ill of her much loved son-in-law.

During that first long, two-year absence, Adrienne bore a second daughter, who was christened Anastasie. She saw her little Henriette sicken and die. When Lafayette returned to her in glory—his wife's family had long ago come around to the widely held opinion that he was a hero—another child was begotten who proved to be the son for whom both Adrienne and Gilbert had longed. George Washington Lafayette, born on Christmas Eve of 1779, was two years old, his sister, Anastasie, was four, on the day in January when their father was crowned with laurel by the fishwives of Paris and their mother rode home in the royal coach beside the Queen.

For Adrienne, the past two years had been, if possible, more trying than the first separation. Long, affectionate letters had come from America during the earlier campaign, but, with British cruisers patroling the Atlantic, communication had been difficult recently and she had gotten most of her news from English newspapers that gave as gloomy a view as possible of the American war.

Adrienne had had time to assess her marriage and to make certain difficult resolutions for the future. She had accepted the fact that she was married to an ambitious man; Lafayette had made it very plain that with him, his career would always come first. What he had undertaken in a spirit of adventure had become a serious mission and he had let her see how strong a hold the democratic ideas he had absorbed in America had upon him. They were ideas that she herself could assimilate, since they coincided so closely with the

Christian concept of the brotherhood of man that she and her sisters had learned at their mother's knee.

What plans Gilbert might have in mind, what new dangers he might court in carrying them through, she could only guess. She would help him if she could, but foresaw that her part in the years ahead would be passive. She would have to continue, as in the past, to stand aside, to make few demands. That Gilbert loved her she could not doubt; when he was with her she was sure of it. But he did not love her exclusively, passionately as she had learned to love him. Just as she once had hidden her religious strivings from him, so she would hide her deepest feelings from him now; otherwise, he might come to resent a wife who was overpossessive, who clung about his neck.

And yet at their first encounter she had fainted in his arms! For long after Lafayette's homecoming, Adrienne kept a careful watch upon herself, though every time that Gilbert left her, even if only for a very few moments, she had a definite feeling of malaise. Her heart contracted as if again he were gone beyond recall, or as if she might have lost him in some more subtle but no less cruel, manner.

The sternest task Adrienne had set herself was to show no jealousy of the admirers, male and female, who flocked about Lafayette, or even of anyone in particular—a woman—to whom his fancy might have strayed.

CHAPTER III

The House in the Rue de Bourbon

HONORS CAME THICK and fast upon Adrienne's husband in the early months of 1782. The King, whom he visited promptly at La Muette on January 22nd, promised to make him a Maréchal de Camp, a military distinction that came usually only to men who were twice his age. Lafayette was invited to dine in company with the gray-haired immortals of the French army, one of whom was Adrienne's grandfather, the Duc Maréchal de Noailles, and another, Adrienne's great-uncle, the Duc Maréchal de Mouchy. Later Lafayette was to receive the most rarely awarded French decoration, the Cross of St. Louis.

In the meantime he was feverishly busy. The American war was over, but the treaty which would recognize the independence of the colonies and put an end to hostilities between England and France would take months—more than a year, as it turned out—of negotiation. There were frequent conferences with the French cabinet and with the American commissioners in Paris. Lafayette was also much in demand socially. "I had the honor," he said later of this halcyon time, "of being consulted by all the ministers—and, what is much more worth while, of being kissed by all the ladies."

A gallant man could say no less. There were some—and they were not altogether friendly—who suggested that the Marquis was more interested in politics than in women, but when he had first gone overseas the gossips of Paris and Versailles had wondered if there was not a romantic motive for his flight. Lafayette might have been crossed in love.

Love, in a society in which young people were expected to do as they were told and marriages were made by parents, guardians, and lawyers, was a deliciously personal and uninhibited affair. As long as certain conventions were observed, it need not be kept a secret. Everything concerning Lafayette, including the state of his affections, was now newsworthy. While the honors he had received from the King were being talked of and envied, word was also being passed about that the Hero of the New World and the Old had found himself a mistress, and that she was a lady whom he had once courted unsuccessfully before he had become so famous.

At that time Lafayette had often gone with his brother-in-law—Louis de Noailles, Louise's husband—to the Palais Royal, the home of the Duc de Chartres, son of the Duc d'Orleans, the King's cousin. Chartres had introduced horse racing into France from England, was a mighty pursuer of women, and an organizer of parties of pleasure that were sometimes held informally in the public amusement places of Paris. The King's brothers, the Comte de Provence and the Comte d'Artois, took part in these expeditions and sometimes also the Queen, who was bored by the dull and pompous routine of Versailles and by her dull, but virtuous, husband.

Lafayette at this early stage of his career had none of the social graces he later developed. He was diffident and proud, self-consciously aware of his country upbringing and of the fact that he was received into smart society only because he had married a daughter of the Duc d'Ayen. He tried to assert himself by doing exactly as his companions did, by drinking more wine than he could stomach, by trying unsuccessfully to provoke his friends into fighting duels with him, and by making a few timid advances to one of the prettiest women of the Duc de Chartres' coterie.

This lady's name was Aglaé de Hunolstein. She and her husband were members of the Duke's household. Madame de Hunolstein was somewhat older and far more sophisticated than her admirer and she was not particularly flattered that this bumpkin from Auvergne should have singled her out. She didn't actually laugh in his face, as Marie Antoinette did when he failed so miserably as a dancing partner, but she snubbed him nevertheless.

Like the Queen, however, Madame de Hunolstein took a different view of Lafayette when, almost overnight, he became a national figure. At the time of his first return from America, she was proud to let the world know that he was her "friend" and that she saw him frequently. She was also one of the first to greet him with open arms in 1782 and was ready and eager to give him more, much more, than a ceremonial kiss on either cheek.

During that spring and summer, while the trees were in leaf and the fountains played in the courtyards of the Palais Royal, Lafayette became the accepted lover of Aglaé de Hunolstein. He could visit her whenever he chose, and his comings and goings were noted by the Palais Royal group.

Soon, however, the affair began to run a wavering course. Lafayette had little time to devote to romance. Aglaé, at first so receptive, became moody and apprehensive; she several times suggested a break in their relations. Her life, which had been so pleasant and light-hearted hitherto, was becoming complicated. There were good reasons for her uneasiness, which she hid from Lafayette. Trouble was in the making.

In the autumn, when the Marquis went to Spain for five months on business that concerned the American peace, a barrage of ill-natured talk was directed at his chosen lady.

It was said that Aglaé had dismissed Lafayette five years earlier to America because she saw her way to a more important and profitable liaison with the Duc de Chartres. The Duke was tired of her, it was said; by the time of Lafayette's return he was glad to be rid of her. And it was just as well that her present cavalier was rich because Madame de Hunolstein wheedled her suitors into buying her expensive presents. A Russian nobleman, for example, had given her a handsome set of furs. It was even said that Aglaé had become thoroughly promiscuous and at night went scouting for lovers in the dark arcades of the Palais Royal, a part of which, open to the public, was given over to shops, restaurants, and a theater.

Some of this malignant gossip was due, no doubt, to jealousy of Lafayette. He had risen so fast in the world and was so universally caressed that he had made a few enemies. But part of the mischief Aglaé had brought upon herself. She had committed the serious blunder of breaking one of the conventions by which the game of dalliance was played. It was permissible for a married woman to have a lover only as long as she remained officially a married woman—and the Comte de Hunolstein had openly repudiated his wife. He would have nothing more to do with her.

When Lafayette came back from Spain in the early spring, he was in Paris only a very short time before going to his birthplace, Chavaniac, in Auvergne. There, on March 27th, 1783, he wrote a letter to his mistress, a sorrowful letter of farewell. He had not seen her while he was in Paris, but he had heard from her and she had asked him to give up all claim upon her. She wanted written proof that their affair was at an end.

Aglaé was frightened; she was burning her bridges behind

her. Her family, scandalized by the bad reputation she had acquired, was trying to force a reconciliation with her husband. If that failed, she would have to leave the court and live a retired life away from all temptation.

A woman faced by such a dilemma was in need of comfort and this Lafayette generously supplied. He had heard the stupid slanders, he said and dismissed them all as contemptible lies. He was doing now what she asked only because he realized that he had had all the pleasure from their connection, she the pain. It was he who had always taken the initiative; he had been the pursuer, she the pursued. In his final sentence he slipped into the second person singular, the thee and thou that in French denotes a very special tenderness. "But at least my heart is my own, dear Aglaé. All that you are, all that I owe you justifies my love, and nothing, not even you, can keep me from adoring you."

They did not meet again. The efforts to patch up the de Hunolstein marriage came to nothing. Lafayette no longer visited the Palais Royal and in June, Aglaé left the palace to live in a convent.

Her disappearance caused only a minor ripple of interest. The gossips, putting two and two together, said that Lafayette had deserted her. His heart could not have been broken because he was often seen in the more sedate salons that he now frequented with yet another lady whom he had met even before he went to Spain! She was a sister of one of his Franco-American officers. She was even more beautiful than Madame de Hunolstein and, unlike poor Aglaé, was witty and intelligent. There was a kind of magic about Madame de Simiane; when one met her at a social gathering she was so charming, it was said, so ready to be pleased, that one felt like giving another party especially in her honor. Though she had been much courted, no man could claim to be her lover, and for Lafayette to have won her heart was yet another triumph.

He had his magic too, it seemed, for he was able apparently to enjoy his intimacies with other women and at the same time remain on excellent terms with his devoted little wife. Not by a word, not by the flicker of an eyelash, did Madame de Lafayette notice the attentions that her husband paid Madame de Simiane. Earlier, when he was in pursuit of Aglaé, she had turned a deaf ear to all malicious talk. Though no one who observed her could believe that she was indifferent, no one, least of all her husband, suspected the full cost to her of her forbearance.

When, years ago now, Lafayette's guardians were looking about them for a suitable match for their ward, one of them claimed that "if he doesn't make his wife happy he will be the first man of his family to have failed." Lafayette had had every intention of living up to this tradition. He would have liked to make the whole world happy—and why not Adrienne, of whom he was so very fond? However far he might be from her, however absorbed by other loves and other preoccupations, she remained the stable center of his restless life; she was the one to whom he could always return and find unchanged.

He was soon to discover how useful she could be to a man whose career was about to enter on a new phase.

*   *   *

Lafayette had been pleased, if not surprised, when shortly after his return from America Adrienne told him that she was again pregnant. A brother for George Washington Lafayette was on the way, the prospective father wrote to George's august namesake across the ocean. But this was only wishful thinking. The "brother" was to be yet another sister, a seven months child, born in September of 1782.

The baby was christened Marie Antoinette Virginie—the third of her names, the name by which she would be known, representing a compromise. Adrienne had wanted the name of a saint, Lafayette a name that was peculiarly American and Virginie fulfilled both requirements.

In the same month in which Virginie was born, her father came of legal age. A noble might be married in his teens, he might even become a Major General before he was twenty, but he was not thought capable of controlling his business affairs until he was twenty-five.

During Lafayette's minority his estate had been managed by an agent, a Monsieur Morizot, who groaned over the lavish sums that, unknown to him, his client had borrowed to spend on the American war. Morizot had had to sell various properties to cover these debts. He now had to make another cut into capital, for Lafayette's first move after reaching his majority was to commission Morizot to find him a suitable house in Paris.

The house that the agent bought was in the Rue de Bourbon, on the left bank of the Seine, across the river from the Hotel de Noailles. It was not as spectacular as Adrienne's childhood home, but it was on a large scale and, what with the furniture and the necessary alterations, cost more than a quarter of a million *livres*.

The family moved into the Rue de Bourbon in 1783. They had barely settled in when Lafayette was off for a third voyage to America that lasted seven months, followed by a tour of Germany and Austria to inspect the might of France's most powerful neighbors.

Adrienne had looked forward to having a home of her own. She and Gilbert had often talked of a place where they could sit cozily by their fireside and be able to entertain a few friends without asking permission of their elders. But there was little coziness in the Hotel de Lafayette; their friends were legion now. During the seven years that the hotel flourished as a social center, guests by the score sat down daily at the long banqueting table in the dining room.

There was such a constant stream of visitors that the host and hostess were seldom alone.

Many of the visitors who came to the Rue de Bourbon were, of course, Americans. Lafayette continued to be active in behalf of his adopted country. In getting the youthful nation on its feet economically, he worked closely with the first American minister to France, Thomas Jefferson. If an American was ill, in trouble, or in debt, or if he merely wanted an admission card to Mass at Notre Dame at which the King would be present, Lafayette came to the rescue. If the Marquis was not at home, as was often the case, Madame de Lafayette acted for him.

Every Monday evening Adrienne presided over American dinners at which Virginia hams were sometimes served, hams that had been cured in the smokehouse at Mount Vernon, presents from General and Mrs. Washington. French guests were also invited to enjoy this exotic fare and in so doing, make personal friendships that would strengthen the bond between France and her new ally.

The prim American ladies who sat down at Adrienne's board—Miss Abigail Adams of Quincy, Massachusetts was one of them—thought that the mistress of the house was "very agreeable and pleasing." She was not quite as beautiful as they had expected, but they were gratified to find one French marquise who was not over-rouged and overdressed and one French home in which children were seen and heard and cherished. The little Lafayettes learned to speak English almost as soon as they learned to speak French. They were sometimes allowed to come downstairs after dinner to sing American songs for the company. That the children's mother seemed more anxious than their father to have them perform only added a homely touch to this scene of domestic harmony in the midst of Old World splendor.

But was it a good thing for the children to be exposed to all the attention they were getting? Adrienne asked herself this question and decided that a little flattery and caressing would not hurt her girls, but that it might have a bad effect on her boy. He would soon be old enough to realize that he was the son of an important personage and might become vain or bumptious. He would be distracted too, from his lessons by the constant coming and going. When George was six-years-old Adrienne, with Lafayette's concurrence, rented a small apartment in the Rue St. Jacques, not far from the Hotel de Lafayette. Here George could live quietly with his tutor, a young man named Félix Frestel, and she could visit him every day.

Her days were very full. Every charitable organization in Paris wanted her support and the prestige of her name in soliciting funds. She became increasingly involved in her husband's activities.

On the walls of the study in his new house, Lafayette had had engraved the Constitution of the United States, with an empty frame beside it for the Constitution of France that— he told his visitors—he hoped to have a hand in writing. Until that day should come, he devoted himself to reforms that tended towards democracy, one of them being the extension of civil liberties to Protestants and Jews. Lafayette went to the desolate sections of the country where the few Huguenots left in France were living and brought the leaders of the outcast sect to his home in Paris for secret conferences with government officials and for Adrienne to entertain. She was glad to cooperate, for she, a convinced Catholic, believed firmly in liberty of conscience. Any infringement of that liberty was a denial of the freedom of will that God had given to man.

Certain welfare projects that Lafayette undertook were handed over almost entirely to Adrienne's management, for he had found that, though inexperienced, she had a surprisingly good head for business. Lafayette had a scheme for relieving the grim poverty that existed in his native hill country of Auvergne. He established a school on his estate at St. Georges d'Aurac to teach weaving to sheepherding peasants and to give much needed winter employment. It was Adrienne's job to ask for gifts of money from individuals and from the government to keep the school running.

More work for Adrienne resulted from her activity, and her husband's, in the antislavery movement. At Cayenne in French Guiana, Lafayette bought a plantation, *La Belle Gabrielle* and a large number of Negro slaves, who were to be freed as soon as they had been educated and given a means of supporting themselves. Adrienne conferred frequently with the priests of the Seminaire du Saint Esprit in Paris, who had a mission at Cayenne and who were willing to supply teachers for the plantation school; she spent long hours in correspondence with the plantation's manager. At this time she also visited the prisons of Paris to investigate the horrible conditions that existed there, one of Lafayette's aims being a reform of the penal code.

Reform—reform on an even more far reaching scale—was the subject of eager talk, not only in the Hotel de Lafayette but also in clubs and in the political salons where Lafayette frequently met his beautiful friend, Madame de Simiane. The feeling that something was basically wrong in France had been growing for a generation—and now was the time to set it right. There was a brief period, a delicious moment, when it seemed as if the whole world might be rebuilt according to the blueprints of wise men and philosophers. None would suffer, all would gain.

In 1787 an "Assembly of Notables" was called to the Palace of Versailles to make recommendations to the King that would solve the staggering financial difficulties that confronted his government. In this Assembly Lafayette brought to the fore his civil liberty program and bluntly suggested that one way to meet the national deficit was to drastically reduce the expenditures of the royal household. He had in mind the huge amounts spent on pensions, sinecure appointments to favorites, and the extravagances of the Queen.

"The millions that are being dissipated are raised by taxation," he said, "and taxes can only be justified by the true needs of the state." There was a shocked silence around the long, green conference table as he added that, "the millions given over to depredation and cupidity are the price of the sweat, the tears and even the blood of the people."

At a later session, presided over by the Comte d'Artois, the King's brother and Lafayette's fellow playboy of Palais Royal days, Lafayette asked that a National Assembly, representing all classes in the kingdom, should be called. Again a silence of stupefaction; such a body had not met in France for more than a hundred-and-fifty years.

The royal Count leaned forward in his gilded armchair; his plump cheeks had crimsoned. "What, Monsieur—you demand the convocation of the Estates General!"

"Yes, Monseigneur, and *even better than that*," Lafayette replied, with significant emphasis on the final words.

"You are willing, then, that I say to the King, 'Monsieur de Lafayette makes the motion to convene the Estates General?' "

"Yes, Monseigneur."

From that time forward, Lafayette was looked upon as a dangerous man by the court party, the clique that surrounded the Queen. Marie Antoinette, who had smiled on the Marquis so graciously when she brought home his wife to the Rue St. Honoré, saw to it that he was stripped of his title of Maréchal de Camp.

Nevertheless, within a year, so desperate was the government's need for money that the Estates General was summoned. The very nature of the archaic Assembly had been forgotten; decaying manuscripts were searched to define its powers and composition. Hopes for what it could accomplish, however, were high—and there was always the hope for "something even better."

The meeting of the Estates was scheduled for the spring, but before it met, France was devastated by a series of unforeseen calamities. The harvests of 1788 shriveled under a scorching sun; hailstorms destroyed orchards and vineyards as well as fields of standing grain. The price of bread rose steeply; restrictions were put upon its sale, so that even guests in great houses were expected to bring their rolls with them to a dinner party.

The population of Paris and its environs swelled alarmingly. Unemployed workers from the cities, and peasants from the ravaged countryside, poured into the capital. Some of these people came from distant provinces and spoke strange dialects; with their hairy faces and tattered clothing they seemed barely human.

The winter that followed was colder than any living man could remember. Great bonfires were kept alight on the banks of the Seine to keep the poor from freezing to death and the ranks of the poor increased from day to day. Here, close at hand, in the very heart of the city, was a new force to be reckoned with, the blind, unreasoning thrust of hunger and nakedness. As yet the men of good will, reformers such as Lafayette, had not guessed or felt its power.

CHAPTER IV

The King's Jailer

D URING THAT COLD WINTER of 1789, Adrienne must often
have seen the fires that burned along the river bank as
she drove back and forth between her house in the Rue de
Bourbon and her mother's house in the Rue St. Honoré.
Madame d'Ayen was alone there now. All of her little girls
were grown and married and one of them, the sister next in
age to Adrienne, had died in the spring of 1788, leaving a
baby daughter.

In January, the Duchess herself came close to dying of
pneumonia. She made a slow recovery. One day when her
daughters were gathered about her bed in the red tapestried
room she spoke sadly of the troubles that might lie ahead for
France and for her children, in particular for Adrienne's
husband.

Gilbert du Motier was, and had always been, Madame
d'Ayen's favorite son-in-law. She was not politically minded
and could not fully understand all of Lafayette's "American
ideas," but she applauded all that he had done to break down
the barriers that divided man from man and to mitigate

poverty. These were ills that should be fought unceasingly, but the battle might be long and bitter. Gilbert would be in the forefront of events—suppose he failed, or came to harm!

At the time Adrienne did not take these words too seriously. They were only a by-product of illness, she thought, of Madame d'Ayen's tendency to worry, of her dread of change and conflict. Later, however, Adrienne would remember her mother's prophecy and when it had been made.

In the spring, Madame d'Ayen was so much better that she went to recuperate at her husband's villa at Versailles, taking Adrienne and her family with her. In May, the Estates General convened in a blaze of medieval pageantry, more thought having been given as to how the representatives of the various orders in the state should dress than to how they should vote or carry on their business. Adrienne saw her husband walk in a procession that included not only the clergy, nobles, and commoners but the King, the Queen, and royal pages and royal falconers, with hawk on wrist. As a noble delegate from Auvergne, Lafayette was costumed in cloth of gold, with a plumed hat in antique style that might have been worn by a courtier of the seventeenth century.

At first it seemed as if the will of the King and of the majority of the nobles and high ranking clergy would prevail, and that the three orders would each form a separate chamber. But the commoners, the Third Estates, demanded that there should be a single assembly in which all votes had equal value. Lafayette felt so strongly on this subject that he was ready to rush off to Auvergne to stand for re-election as a representative of the Third Estate, when the difficulty was swiftly resolved. The commoners, locked out of their meeting hall, refused to disband except at the point of a bayonet, and the King, who was always unwilling to go to extremes, gave ground. France's first parliament, her first National Assembly, came to birth.

Within a matter of weeks the constitution that Lafayette

had dreamed of was being written. It was not a republican constitution. No one, not even he, thought that that was possible in a country where royalty had been so long established. The most workable form of democracy, the best that could be hoped for, was a limited monarchy such as was already in existence in England.

During the long, hot summer months mighty changes in taxation and government were voted into existence and all feudal privileges, titles, and prerogatives were outlawed. Lafayette was elected vice-president of the new Assembly, and on July 11th made his maiden speech, suggesting that a Declaration of the Rights of Man, closely modeled on the American Bill of Rights, should be written into the constitution.

The Assembly was debating the proposal when on July 14th news came to Versailles that the Bastille, the Paris prison into which so many unfortunates had disappeared without trial, had fallen before the attack of an unarmed mob. When King Louis was told by one of his courtiers of what had happened he asked, "Then this is a great riot?"

The answer was, "No, sire, this is a great revolution."

Lafayette, and all who thought as he did, rejoiced that the old symbol of despotic power was gone, but he was horrified by the savage, wholesale massacre of the prison's defenders after they had surrendered and by the days and nights of mob slaughter and destruction that followed. He went back to Paris at the head of a delegation sent by the King to investigate and at once was given the difficult and dangerous job of keeping order in the city. Adrienne, leaving her children with her mother for safe keeping until the autumn, soon joined him in the Rue de Bourbon.

There, a new routine had been established. She saw even less of her husband than of old. Her house was even more crowded, even more of a public place. Uniforms and epaulettes appeared in the Hotel de Lafayette; spurs jingled across its highly polished floors.

Lafayette had been put in command of the Paris militia, and under his direction what had been a local, amateur police force became the well-paid, the well-equipped National Guard of France. He often worked round the clock, his days given up to active duty, his nights to administrative detail. Lafayette was immensely popular with his men, but they were an undisciplined, headstrong lot, eager to follow him to battle, as he told one of his American friends, but very reluctant to stand sentry when it rained.

It was raining dismally on October 5th, 1789, when a ragged army of women—and men disguised as women—marched on Versailles, demanding bread and the return of the King to Paris. They were on their way before Lafayette was aware that they had left the city. An even larger, a more menacing crowd had gathered before the Hotel de Ville and threatened to follow. Lafayette and his guardsmen marched with them, hoping to keep some sort of order and to prevent bloodshed.

Night had fallen before the marchers reached the royal palace. A muddy, bedraggled multitude surrounded it. Camp fires had been lit in the Place d'Armes. Over one of them a horse which had been accidentally shot was being roasted and devoured.

Except for the horse, there had been no casualties, though throughout the day there had been much wild talk, much drunkenness, and threats made against the Queen. In the popular mind the "Austrian Woman" had become a witch, the source of all the evils that afflicted France. Lafayette, however, thought that there would be no further demonstration that night; the long march and the rain had had a subduing effect. He posted guards, found quarters for his troops in the city churches, and toward morning, exhausted by having been on his feet continuously for almost twenty-four hours, went to bed in the now empty Noailles mansion.

He had less than an hour's sleep. At dawn an orderly was

leaning over him, shaking him and shouting in his ear that the mob had broken into the palace and had tasted blood. Two of the royal guards had been killed. The Queen's bedroom had been invaded. She had escaped, just in time, by a secret staircase to the King's apartments.

Lafayette rushed to the scene. The lower floor of the palace was awash with a flood of whirling, frenzied folk, while above, on the upper floors, the royal family and their attendants were marooned. Lafayette and his men managed to flush and sweep the invaders out of the building and to barricade the doors.

He went out on a balcony and tried to harangue the crowd, but his voice could not be heard above the hubbub below. There was a moment's silence when the King appeared and in his dull, lethargic manner announced that he would do as his good people of Paris wished; he would go back with them to the city. There were cheers at this; there was a call for the Queen. She started to go out with the Dauphin and her daughter, but a howl went up: "The Queen alone—no children!"

Marie Antoinette was pale; she hesitated. Lafayette held out his hand to her. "Madame, will you come with me?"

There were tears of rage and humiliation in her eyes as she put her hand in his. He led her out into the sunlight—a strangely disheveled figure, still half-dressed. A petticoat and a yellow striped wrapper had been thrown over her nightgown; her hair hung loose on her shoulders. As if they were at the head of a line of stately dancers, Lafayette led her forward where she could be seen by the crowd. He then bowed elaborately and fell on one knee to kiss her hand.

The pantomime, the touch of theater, had just the effect that he had hoped for. There was enthusiastic applause from those who only a moment earlier had wanted to disembowel the Queen and tear her limb from limb. There were cheers again when Lafayette went out on the balcony with one of the palace soldiers, presented him with the tricolor cockade, the insignia of the National Guard, and kissed the man fraternally on either cheek.

Later in the day the royal family, escorted by Lafayette and the ever present mob, went back to live permanently at the Tuileries—and the court party had its bitter say on the subject of Lafayette. He was nicknamed "General Morpheus" because he had been asleep when the mob broke into the palace. He was accused of being the King's jailer.

There was only a grain of truth in the charge but appearances were against him. The removal of the seat of government to Paris—for the Assembly soon followed the King and Queen to the capital—had raised the Commander of the National Guard to a position of supreme importance. Government of any sort was impossible in the midst of riot and confusion, and preventing riot and confusion was Lafayette's business. He not only protected royalty whenever it appeared in public, but in private he tried to persuade the King, and especially the Queen, to accept the new dispensation.

Sometimes he despaired. Madame de Simiane, who had been influenced by the anti-Lafayette diatribes, urged her friend to be more respectful to his sovereigns but Lafayette replied that, for their own good, he was only trying to tell them the truth. Louis and Marie Antoinette were like naughty children who would not take their medicine unless told that the werewolf would eat them. "Believe me," he said, "they would have been served better by a harder man."

Though sometimes he felt that "all hell was conspired against him," his self-confidence, his inborn optimism, bore him up against all discouragements. And, on one occasion, he felt that he had triumphed. On July 14th, 1790, the first Bastille Day, there was a glorious rally in the Champ de Mars, the great open parade ground on the left bank of the Seine, not far from the Rue de Bourbon. In the presence of 400,000 civilians and 60,000 troops, the King and the entire nation swore to support the constitution that the Assembly was so busily writing that it could give little attention to governing the country. Adrienne witnessed the ceremony. With her was her son George, who, usually kept in the background, was allowed for once to see his father riding on his famous white horse, Jean Le Blanc, at the head of his guardsmen and taking the oath at a great Altar of Liberty, twenty feet high, which had been set up in the middle of the field.

To a ten-year-old boy, it was a holiday from school and a thrilling spectacle—to Adrienne a solemn moment. With pride, but with dismay, she saw her husband at the head of a revolution that was daily becoming more complex and unpredictable. She completely shared Lafayette's principles and saw in them a fulfillment of the Christianity she so fervently professed. Nothing in her training or her experience, however, had prepared her for the violence of deed and the violence of opinion in this time of upheaval. Many aristocratic doors were closed to her now. There were members of her own family who failed to recognize her in public and who no longer came to the Rue de Bourbon.

Lafayette had no sooner made it plain that he took his new position seriously and was determined that law should prevail, than attacks began upon him from the extreme left as well as from the right. Certain members of the Jacobin Club were beginning to see that the mob of Paris could be a useful tool for their own ends; certain radical journalists undertook to destroy Lafayette's popularity by a fusillade of newspaper articles and pamphlets that ridiculed everything about him, from his patriotism to his red hair.

He was said to be the Queen's lover—certainly a shot that was wide of the mark. His love affair with Aglaé de Hunolstein was disinterred and given as the reason for his hostility to the Duc de Chartres, now the Duc d'Orleans, whom Lafayette suspected of having instigated the hunger march on

Versailles and other outbreaks in the hope that the King might be deposed so that he, the Duke, might seat himself upon the throne. Adrienne herself was brought into the limelight when a lurid account was given of the loose morals—as well as of the overzealous piety—of "General Redhead's Wife."

In policing the city, Lafayette was often called upon to protect priests and church property. The church had been nationalized; the clergy were forced to take an oath of allegiance to the state and many of them resisted on grounds of conscience. Adrienne strongly sympathized with these rebels to an authority that they would not recognize. She was willing to discuss the matter with those who had conformed and would let them state their views, but she made a point of being present at her parish church of St. Sulpice when a nonjuring priest denounced the oath from the pulpit. She and her mother took part in a correspondence with the Vatican in a vain attempt to prevent a break between France and the Holy See.

Once Adrienne felt that she had to take a stand that might seem disloyal to Gilbert. Lafayette had invited the Bishop of Paris to dinner. Adrienne was sure that the bishop, who had just conspicuously taken the oath, was coming not as a private individual nor as a churchman, but as a politician seeking to identify himself with Lafayette. That day Adrienne spent in the Rue St. Honoré, though her empty place at the head of her own table was noticed and unfavorably commented upon.

Above all, throughout these troubled, swift-moving weeks and months, Adrienne feared for her husband's safety. Lafayette had to deal constantly with crowds that were very different from the good humored, sentimental folk who shed tears in the Rue St. Honoré when they saw him greet his wife. Sometimes he was able to talk to them, or even to trick them, as at Versailles, into good behavior; more often he and his men had to use the forward rush of their horses and the flat of their swords. Each time that he was called out on an emergency—and he was on call at all hours—Adrienne felt that he was in far greater danger than when he was fighting the British three thousand miles away in America.

She had a brief respite from her worries when, in April of 1791, Lafayette gave up his command of the National Guard.

It had been announced that the King was to go to St. Cloud for Easter Mass. There was a rumor that he might be leaving the city, or even that he might be leaving France. When Lafayette arrived at the Tuileries to escort the royal carriage he found a noisy crowd packed so closely in the courtyard that the carriage could not move. Again the King yielded to popular demand and gave up his expedition, though Lafayette urged him to persist.

Disgusted by Louis' weakness and by the insubordination of his troops, for some of them had sided openly with the mob, Lafayette sent in his resignation to the Hotel de Ville. He quitted his house in the Rue de Bourbon to escape being asked to reconsider, and Adrienne was left to deal with the contrite delegation of officers and officials of the Paris Commune that tramped into her salon.

She knew how each of the guardsmen had behaved at the moment of crisis. Some she greeted cordially, to others she was only coldly polite. As she listened to their arguments, she hoped that her husband would stand firm against their pleas, but four days later Lafayette again took up his burden and Adrienne hers, of being constantly alert to danger. Familiar sounds could make her tremble; the clatter of horses hoofs in the courtyard of the hotel, a midnight knock upon the door, the hurry of footsteps down a corridor.

Her fears gave her no rest. They reached their climax on

July 17th, 1791, when yet another, a more disastrous riot
occurred on the Champ de Mars.

*   *   *

Again it was the position of the King and Lafayette's
guardianship of him that was the cause. On June 20th, Louis
and Marie Antoinette had actually tried to slip out of the
country; they were arrested, at Lafayette's command, and
were brought back to the Tuileries. On July 17th, a petition
was laid on the great Altar of Liberty in the center of the
Field of Mars, calling for Louis' dethronement.

The day was Sunday. A crowd gathered. A few people had
come to sign the petition and many more to see what would
happen next, for the Mayor of Paris had forbidden the demonstration.

Suddenly a woman screamed. She was standing on the
wooden platform beside the Altar and felt something sharp
prick through the sole of her shoe and pierce her foot. The
point of a gimlet protruded from the flooring. Excitement
soared as two men were dragged out from the hole under
the Altar. They had a keg with them which they protested
had nothing in it but drinking water. They were apparently
making a hole in the floor so that they might take turns in
squinting up for a worm's eye view of the undergarments
of female signers of the petition.

No one believed their bizarre story or gave them time to
prove it. The keg, someone shouted, must be full of gun-
powder; the hole was a duct for the fuse that would set off
the bomb just when it could do the most damage. The two
men, both of them were old and unable to defend themselves, were buffeted about by the crowd. They went down
under blows from every side. In a few minutes all that was
left of them were some shreds of clothing, some bloody frag-
ments of trampled flesh—and two heads bobbing about on
pikes.

This happened early in the day. Lafayette was summoned. By the time he reached the Champ de Mars the heads had been carried off the field and the affair seemed to be over. He returned to his home, but at eight o'clock in the evening he was again sent for.

And from eight o'clock onward, Adrienne was in torment. Earlier in the day a bullet, fired by a sniper, had whizzed past Gilbert's ear and now she expected that there would be further gunplay. Recently a law had been passed by the Assembly that in case of serious disturbance, a red flag should be hung from the Hotel de Ville, the riot act should be read aloud three times, and then, if the crowd did not disperse, the troops were to fire.

As she waited anxiously in her quiet house, its windows open to the warm summer air, Adrienne heard the sound of distant firing—a single volley, then, after an interval, a second. Later she was to learn that the first salvo had gone over the heads of the crowd, which stood its ground and answered with catcalls and a shower of stones. The second volley took effect, and at least a dozen people, but probably more, fell. Looking out of the window, Adrienne saw—for it was still light—people running wildly through the street. She judged rightly that the mob had been deflected from the Champ de Mars and that the danger there was over.

But the danger had only shifted ground. The street filled rapidly from end to end with a shrieking, jostling crowd that pressed about the closed gates leading into the courtyard. The terrified servants came flocking to Adrienne from all parts of the house. Anastasie and Virginie followed their mother's small, determined figure as she hurried about, reassuring the more hysterical members of her household and seeing that doors were barred and windows closed and shuttered. Even so, one could hear the tumult from without and soon one of the most terrible of all sounds—a crowd shouting with a single voice, shouting for revenge and the head of the wife of Lafayette.

Before he galloped off that evening, Lafayette had posted a double guard at the doors of the house. The men—how pitifully few they now seemed!—were drawn up in battle line in the courtyard, but they could not protect the entire building. The windows of Adrienne's private sitting room on the ground floor looked out on a garden and beyond it to the Square of the Palais Bourbon. It was here that the first assault was made. Some of the rioters had climbed over the garden wall and were advancing on the house when a little troop of cavalry swooped into the square and charged the crowd, which dispersed as quickly as it had gathered. The Rue de Bourbon was cleared, the attacking force in the garden melted away, and in a very short time all that was to be seen of it were a few flying figures disappearing into the dusky side streets leading off the square.

The threat to the house had come and gone like a whirlwind, but it had left its mark on Adrienne and even more deeply on her youngest child. Virginie—little Virginie—who was not yet nine years old, would remember to the end of her life the terrible cries she heard from the street and the way in which her mother reacted to them. Tears, tears of relief and almost of joy, were trickling down Adrienne's cheeks as she threw her arms protectively about her little girls and cried, "At least your father is safe! At least he is safe!"

*   *   *

Oddly enough, a period of peace followed the riot in the Champ de Mars, which the radical press promptly magnified into a massacre. The Jacobins who were chiefly responsible for laying the petition on the Altar—Marat, the journalist, Danton, Desmoulins, and Robespierre—disappeared from Paris and went into hiding. They soon returned, however, to blacken the name of Lafayette. In the Jacobin Club he was branded as an "assassin of the people." A pamphlet detailing his crimes—"only since the Revolution"—was circulated, as well as caricatures of him hanging from a lamppost.

On the other hand, the Assembly publicly thanked him and the National Guard for the action it had taken and, unperturbed, went back to putting the final touches to the constitution which had been so long in the making. On September 13th, the document was submitted to King Louis, who, in chastened mood, declared that he would accept it, maintain it at home, and defend it from attack abroad. On the 24th, he went before the Assembly to take the oath, not from a throne, but from an ordinary armchair placed to the left of the presiding officer.

Again the constitutionalists exulted. They felt that at last their goal had been reached. The King was not an ideal monarch, but he was better, they said, than any other in Europe—he had learned his lesson. Royal power had been curbed; all Frenchmen were now equal before the law; prosperity would return and disorders would gradually die away. So deeply ingrained was the idea of kingship in the French mentality that shouts of *"vive le roi"* were heard once more in the streets of Paris and even Robespierre said in a speech before the Jacobin Club that the revolution was over. The Club, however, must continue its work of keeping patriotism at a high level in the country.

Lafayette had long thought that this would be the proper moment for him to retire from public life, or at least to take an extended holiday. He had never accepted any remuneration for his work and he had never aspired to office. He would again resign his command of the National Guard and this time the severance would be lasting. He would go to spend the winter at his boyhood home, Chavaniac in Auvergne.

Adrienne was overjoyed. She, too, was in need of a holiday, for her years in the Rue de Bourbon had always been strenuous; of late they had been harrowing. She would be sorry to say goodbye to her mother, but their parting would be brief. The Duchess promised to come soon for a visit at Chavaniac. Adrienne also contracted for a visit from her dearly loved sister, Louise de Noailles.

On October 8th, Lafayette said a formal farewell to his troops at the Hotel de Ville. There was a flurry of speech-making and testimonials. His men gave him a sword, the hilt of which had been forged from metal salvaged from the ruins of the Bastille. The Commune of Paris ordered a gold medal to be struck in his honor and gave him a bust of General Washington by Houdon.

That same afternoon the Lafayettes, all but George, who would follow a few weeks later with his tutor, Monsieur Frestel, left Paris. Adrienne had been busy, as any housewife would, in making arrangements for a long-term shift from city to country living. The baggage vans were packed. The great house in the Rue de Bourbon was shrouded and handed over to a small staff of caretakers.

Adrienne left it without regret. She saw ahead of her something that she had always yearned for: a quiet family life, away from murderous crowds, away from politics, and the endless round of social obligations, away, in short, from everything, including the fascinating Madame de Simiane, that kept her husband from her. Nine years and more had gone by since Lafayette's return from America. Adrienne would soon be thirty-two, and it seemed as if she might at last have Gilbert—not entirely, but a little—to herself.

PART TWO

October, 1791—October, 1792

CHAPTER V

The House in the Hills

THE JOURNEY TO AUVERGNE was to be made in a fleet of light carriages, better suited to the rough provincial roads than a heavy, cumbersome coach. In the first carriage rode Adrienne and Lafayette, in the second Anastasie, Virginie, and a little pinched, dried-up elderly lady, Mademoiselle Marin, who had once been governess to the Duchesse d'Ayen's children in the Hotel de Noailles and who was now in charge of Adrienne's daughters. Other carriages followed, filled with all the servants who could be persuaded to leave Paris for a winter in the country.

Chavaniac is only some four hundred miles to the south and slightly to the east of Paris, but the Lafayettes took a full ten days to get there. They passed through Fontaine-bleau, skirted the rich valley of the Loire, and soon were moving through the hills that were familiar to Lafayette as a boy. Auvergne is a beautiful, an eerie region, with its forests, its deep-cut river gorges and towering rock forma-tions. On the cliffs above the winding road perched frag-ments of ruined castles that had been destroyed more than a century earlier when the power of feudal robber barons was broken by the crown.

In towns along the way, there were frequent halts for festivities. Auvergne was proud of its illustrious son and gave him the sort of wholehearted welcome that recently had been lacking in Paris. Lafayette had to listen to elaborate, laudatory speeches, to walk bareheaded in ceremonial processions, and to drink ceremonial draughts of wine. The carriages were forever filled with flowers. When they left the city of Clermont it was after nightfall, and ahead of them moved a long, glittering line of mounted National Guardsmen, swinging torches. At Brioude, the nearest large town to Chavaniac, a triumphal arch had been raised.

On the 18th of October, the end of the pilgrimage came in sight. The chateau of Chavaniac stood—and still stands— on the slope of a hill, commanding a view of distant mountains, a long, massive building, with turrets at either end. Beneath it nestles a village of some forty or fifty houses. Adrienne knew it well, for she had traveled this way more than once and, while Lafayette was in America in 1784, had spent an entire summer at Chavaniac.

She was well-acquainted therefore, with the doughty old lady who was now the sole occupant of the chateau, an aunt of Lafayette, who had helped to bring him up and who was the mother of the little girl cousin with whom he had played in childhood. Madame de Chavaniac—she, like Louise de Noailles, had married a near relative and so had preserved her maiden name—was long a widow and long childless. Her daughter had married and died in childbirth soon after Lafayette left for his first adventure overseas. All her emotions—and they could be violent when aroused—were centered on the male members of her family, living and dead: on Lafayette and his son George; on Lafayette's father, her brother, who had been killed thirty-two years ago at the Battle of Minden.

The old lady's greeting to the travelers was fervent. She thanked God for all his mercies. As she embraced her adored nephew, she cried out in her deep and far from feeble voice, "I never thought that I would live to see you again!"

Two weeks after the Lafayette carriages drove into the courtyard of the chateau, the Duchesse d'Ayen arrived, followed soon by Louise de Noailles. They had not traveled together because Madame d'Ayen had stopped at Plauzat, not far from Clermont, to visit another of her brood, Pauline, the Marquise de Montagu. A few days later—to Madame de Chavaniac's great delight—George and his tutor appeared. The family circle was complete. Not for years had the old house in the hills been so full of people and activity.

The children were enchanted to find themselves free to roam wherever they would, unsupervised. The Duchesse d'Ayen was always happiest when she was with them and with her daughters; she found Madame de Chavaniac congenial. At Plauzat one could no longer go to Mass, and there was a hall close to the chateau where meetings of a club, affiliated with the Jacobin Club of Paris, were held. The excited shouts of debate were plainly audible in Pauline de Montagu's sitting room. Here at Chavaniac, the Duchess was pleased to find that the village curé was living in the chateau and that the little church at the foot of the hill was full of worshippers on Sunday.

A strong feeling of good will existed between those who lived in the village and those who lived in the castle. As a boy, Lafayette had accepted all the riches that came to him without question, but later he had learned to be a good landlord. One year when the crops failed in Auvergne, he distributed his grain *gratis* instead of holding it for a high price. He had established a doctor in the town and had built a good road leading to it so that weekly market fairs could be held. Nearby, at St. Georges d'Aurac, was the weaving school he had founded. From England, Lafayette had imported blooded cattle and hogs to improve the local breed, as well as a trained agriculturist to superintend his farms.

He wrote to Madame de Simiane that the changes he found in Chavaniac were all for the good. In the old days when he, the lord of the manor, walked abroad, everyone took off their hats to bow to him. Now it was he who bowed to the representative of constituted law, Dr. Guitandry, the village mayor.

There was much for Lafayette to do beside write to Madame de Simiane. He had sent an architect down from Paris who was already at work with his assistant on plans for remodelling the chateau. It had been built originally as a fortified place, with small concern for comfort. There was a great vaulted guardroom on the ground floor. A spacious circular staircase led up grandly to the second floor, where the family would live and try to keep warm during the winter months when snow lay thick on the roofs and cold winds blew down through the crevices of the hills. There were already many family portraits in the house, but Lafayette had ordered nine pictures to be painted of the principal scenes of the revolution. Eventually they would hang in what he was pleased to call "the Washington Gallery."

Seeing her husband so absorbed in his projects and apparently so contented, surrounded herself by so many people whom she loved, Adrienne felt that it was time to relax and enjoy herself. She was surprised to find how difficult that was. She was not often troubled by haphazard moods of depression. Perhaps it was merely physical fatigue that accounted for her low spirits—or was it a presentiment that this blissful state of affairs was too good to be true or lasting?

Adrienne was relieved when Lafayette gracefully declined a position on the Council of the Haute Loire to which he had been elected, on the grounds that it would take him away too often from his home. Less reassuring was a speech he made to a large contingent of the National Guard that visited the

chateau. Lafayette said that he was charmed to find himself
a private citizen; the only thing that could draw him out of
his retirement was the possibility of France being attacked
by some foreign power. This remark echoed an incident of
the trip from Paris that at the time had troubled Adrienne
and accounted in part, for her present sense of insecurity.

She, as well as her mother, had expected to visit Pauline
de Montagu on her way to Chavaniac. Devoted though she
was to Louise, Adrienne was also fond of her two younger
sisters, and particularly of Pauline, who was seven years her
junior. One could not help loving Pauline. She was as caress-
able and impulsive as a child. Like all the d'Ayen daughters,
she was devout and was almost absurdly concerned with
scruples as to right and wrong doing that had once been
discussed by young philosophers in the red tapestried bedroom of the Hotel de Noailles.

The two sisters had seen little of one another lately. Since
her marriage in 1783, Pauline had lived with her father-in-
law, the Vicomte de Beaune, an irascible gentleman of the
old school. He was an uncompromising royalist and, like all
of the breed, had come to disapprove violently of the constitution and of Lafayette, the King's jailer. Even when
Adrienne went without her husband to see her sister in Paris,
the Vicomte would stalk from the room without speaking to
her, banging the door behind him.

The old gentleman was well out of the way now. He had
left for Coblentz in February, following in the footsteps of
so many other nobles who had bolted across the Rhine immediately after the fall of the Bastille. Pauline and her husband,
Joachim, had been staying all the spring and summer in
Auvergne, and it had seemed the perfect moment for a reunion. Before leaving Paris, Adrienne wrote suggesting that
she and her family should stop for a few days at Plauzat on
their way south.

The letter that had come back to her was tear-stained.

Tears came easily to Pauline. Except for her baby daughter, Noemi, she wrote, she was alone at Plauzat, Joachim having gone on a brief trip to Paris. There was nothing that she would like better than to have a visit from Adrienne and Gilbert, but she still lived in fear of her trigger-tempered father-in-law. If the Vicomte de Beaune should ever hear that she had entertained the renegade Marquis de Lafayette in his chateau, he was quite capable of putting her out on the doorstep and having nothing more to do with her.

But Pauline couldn't bear to have her sister pass her by. She had an urgent reason for wanting to see Adrienne, even if it was only for a very few minutes, and said that she would come to meet the Lafayettes at the posting station at Vaire, near Plauzat, where they would have to stop to change horses.

When the travelers drew into the town, however—their journey then was nearly over—there was no sign of Pauline. Vaire was so small that it could be taken in almost at a glance. A servant came out of the inn to tell Adrienne that there was a lady inside who wanted to speak to her.

Adrienne and Lafayette entered. They found Pauline waiting for them in a dark little private room into which she had popped directly from her carriage, not wanting to be recognized. Even smaller than Adrienne, Pauline closely resembled her sister; they both had inherited their mother's white skin and her beautiful dark eyes.

Pauline's eyes were wet as she rushed into Adrienne's arms. How sad it was, she cried, that they should have to meet in this fashion—and who knows when or where they would meet again! Pauline had a confession to make that she knew would distress her sister and brother-in-law. It was this that had brought her to the posting station. She herself would soon be leaving the country. She and Joachim were about to emigrate.

Emigrate—the very word had taken on a new, an emotional significance even before the King's attempt to escape from France. The number of Frenchmen who had gone to the Rhineland since the fall of the Bastille was not large in proportion to the total population, but among the emigrants were the King's two brothers, the Comte de Provence and the Comte d'Artois, who were loudly demanding the armed help of the sovereigns of Europe in restoring absolute monarchy in France. The military forces that had been gathering at Coblentz and Worms were a threat to the new regime that Lafayette and his friends had struggled to create against so many internal difficulties—a threat of which they were only too well aware.

It was some comfort to learn that the de Montagus were not going to the Rhineland but to England. All last winter, to emigrate or not to emigrate had been a smouldering question in the household of the Vicomte de Beaune. Joachim had taken the view that the royalists should stay at home; if they sought foreign aid in solving their domestic problems they might have to pay dearly for it later. There were many painful scenes, the old man violently abusive, the young man pale with anger but trying to keep a curb on his temper and maintain the respectful tone that every French son should use in speaking to his father.

Pauline had been much too timid to express her own opinion, but secretly she agreed with her father-in-law. Without sharing his personal hatreds, she, too, was a royalist and, with the noisy shouts of Jacobins continually in her ears at Plauzat, thought it was high time to leave France. For months she had been gently trying to sell the idea to Joachim.

She had read aloud to him all the discouraging news in the Paris newspapers. He had begun to weaken a little after that dreadful affair in the Champ de Mars that might have cost Adrienne her life, but he didn't really succumb until word came from Germany that his poor old father might die of a broken heart because of his son's stubbornness. Joachim felt that in quitting the country he was a martyr to filial duty, but that in going to England he was sticking by his principles. He was now in Paris making preparations for a quiet trip across the Channel with his wife and child.

All of this was briefly told in the dark little inn at Vaire in the short time it took to take one set of horses out of the carriages and harness up another. Lafayette said that he disapproved entirely of what Pauline and her husband were doing, but he would always continue to love his little sister-in-law. He kissed her very affectionately at parting.

Adrienne, more profoundly stirred, clung to Pauline until the last moment. She promised to write as often as she could. Pauline promised too, for, though they were now definitely on opposite sides of the fence, they must try to keep in touch with one another.

Remembering later that brief rendezvous at Vaire, Adrienne realized how easily, how inexorably, Lafayette might be swept out of this quiet backwater of Chavaniac. She could not unburden herself to her mother because she discovered that her mother knew nothing of Pauline's plans. Pauline apparently could not bring herself to tell her news a second time.

But the autumn days continued to pass peacefully; the first snow had fallen, and Adrienne was just beginning to regain confidence in the future when the blow fell, the blow that had fallen so often in the past. In mid-December a courier, wearing the royal colors, arrived at Chavaniac with a dispatch for Lafayette. Lafayette had been put in command of a section of the regular army. No war had been declared, but France was mobilizing.

There was no question of refusing to answer this call to arms. Lafayette, as always when action lay ahead, was full of enthusiasm. War had no terrors for him. He felt that a sense of emergency might unite the nation. Just before Christmas of 1791, only two months after his arrival, he left the chateau, taking with him his valet, Chavaniac, who was the son of the village tailor, and a boy named Félix Pontonnier, the coachman's son, whom Lafayette had educated to be his secretary.

*   *   *

All over France there were similar partings. At almost the same moment, Pauline de Montagu was writing to Adrienne and her mother on the eve of her departure from Paris. The snow was falling there also. For the last time Pauline went to Mass with her younger sister, Rosalie de Grammont. Many of the churches in Paris were closed, the pulpits of the few that were open being occupied by priests who had taken the required oath. The sisters went to a private house where services were being held in secret, hoping that their footprints in the snow would not betray them.

The following day, very early, before it was light, Rosalie came, her cloak powdered white with flakes, to say goodbye. She and Pauline took care to be very casual in the presence of the servants, who thought that the young master and mistress were just going away for a few days and would soon be back.

When Joachim had gone downstairs, carrying the baby Noemi, who had been taken out of her crib and was still asleep, Rosalie drew Pauline aside and in a whisper asked if she was sure she hadn't forgotten something. "Of course, you are taking your diamonds with you."

"Why should I?" Pauline asked. "I wouldn't wear them. We won't be going to any grand parties in England."

"Poor darling—all the more reason why you should take them!"

Pauline saw that Rosalie was more realistic than she, that this might be a long absence, that some day she might need the money that the diamonds represented. Picking up her jewel box, she hid it under her cloak as she went downstairs to join her husband in the carriage that would take them to Calais.

CHAPTER VI

❧

A Waiting Time

FOR A SHORT WHILE after Lafayette's departure, the
Duchesse d'Ayen and Louise de Noailles stayed on at
Chavaniac. It meant much to Adrienne that her mother
should be with her at such a time, her mother who had
comforted her all during the years that Gilbert spent in
America. Louise's presence was also a consolation. Louise
was gentle and serene—the angel of the d'Ayen family. In
childhood she and Adrienne, being so nearly of an age, had
shared all the pleasures and pains of their growing years.
Their marriages had drawn them even closer, for Louis de
Noailles, Louise's husband, went to America with Lafayette
in 1780 and came home an ardent liberal—a fayettist, as
Lafayette's sympathizers were sometimes called.

Unless they were willing to take the risk of being snowed
in for days at a time, however, Adrienne's guests could not
linger indefinitely. The Duchess began to be restless so far
from home and was anxious to be in Paris because her
youngest child, Rosalie de Grammont, was pregnant and
close to term. Louise had also to get back to her husband,

who would soon be called into service, and to her three small children, Alexis, Alfred, and Euphémie.

Adrienne saw first her mother and then her sister go. Again she expected that the separation would not be long, for she hoped that in the spring she would go to Paris, or perhaps to join her husband somewhere in the north.

There was a sense of loneliness, however, of isolation in this remote and mountainous region, after the last carriage had driven off. Adrienne was on the best of terms with Aunt Chavaniac, but the old lady's views on almost every subject were positive and antiquated. Her horizon was limited; for years she had gone no farther from the chateau than to the village church. The youngest members of the family, George and Virginie, were cheerful folk to have about the house, but they were absorbed in the world of childhood, which is a world apart. For adult companionship, Adrienne turned to her older daughter Anastasie. Anastasie was fourteen now, almost a young lady. An observant, imaginative girl, she was proud to be made her mother's confidante. She and Adrienne had always been intimate, but now a very special, a woman-to-woman relationship developed.

This was to be a time, a slow moving time, when one waited from day to day, from week to week, for news that letters from Paris and the Paris journals might bring. Adrienne heard from her mother and sisters frequently, and from Lafayette. He was sometimes in the capital, camping out in the deserted house in the Rue de Bourbon, and sometimes moving about from one army post to another.

On Christmas Day of 1791, Lafayette rode out of Paris on his way to Metz, escorted to the barrier by cheering National Guardsmen. He was as gay, one of Adrienne's correspondents wrote, as if he were going to a wedding.

But his new command, he soon discovered, was far inferior to the fine military force he had himself built up. The line soldiers were poorly clothed and poorly armed. Discipline was slack. France had been so long at peace that fortifications near the frontier were in bad repair and there was a great shortage of trained officers, fully a third having gone across the Rhine.

In Paris the situation had deteriorated. The Assembly which had written the constitution had dissolved itself and passed a law denying to its members the right to stand for reëlection in the new Assembly which began its sittings in October. This body was dominated by members of the Jacobin Club, and even more so by a group of fiery representatives from the Gironde, disciples of Rousseau, with a lively antipathy to all aristocrats. Girondists were soon given ministerial rank. Lafayette was under frequent attack in the Assembly and in Marat's sheet, *The People's Friend*. His popular following had steadily declined since the "massacre" in the Champ de Mars.

The drift toward war was constant and compelling. All factions, except the extreme radicals led by Marat and Robespierre, looked to it as a solution rather than a catastrophe. Throughout the winter, administrative and economic affairs were allowed to run to ruin as the debate on foreign policy rose and fell, and rose again.

A demand was made that the Austrian Emperor should withdraw his troops from the borderline of France and that the émigré forces should be expelled from the Rhineland. It was disregarded. At last, prodded by his advisers, King Louis appeared before the Assembly and in a feeble voice asked that war be declared on Austria, the homeland of his wife. The vote on the motion that followed was almost unanimous.

By that time, April 20th, the winter was over. There were a few skirmishes with the enemy, a brief and unhappy excursion into Belgian territory. Adrienne read with horror that a high officer, a general in Lafayette's division, had been killed. After the French forces had retired there came a lull in hostilities—but how long would that continue?

Because of his lack of military success, the cry was raised that Lafayette was holding his fire and was dallying with the enemy. Just how far this Jacobin hate propaganda had spread was demonstrated to Adrienne when, in the early spring of 1792, a battalion of volunteers from the Gironde on its way to the front appeared in the village. Some of the townspeople came to her and told her that the troops were in an ugly mood. When they learned that the chateau up there on the hill belonged to Lafayette there was talk of burning it to the ground.

Adrienne took prompt action. She sent word that the men were to be well fed at her expense and invited the officers to dinner at the chateau. The dinner was so pleasant and harmonious, the hostess so tactful and charming, that there was no more anti-Lafayette talk while the Girondists remained in the town.

And now it was June, June 20th, 1792. In Auvergne, summer was ripening, in Paris, the weather was already sultry. A demonstration took place, unpremeditated, perhaps—half ludicrous, yet altogether sinister in its implications. A crowd from the poorest sections of Paris and its suburbs frisked through the Assembly hall, just across the garden from the Tuileries. The proceedings of the Assembly were halted while the *Ça Ira* was sung and danced about a pair of breeches swinging from a pole and a calf's heart skewered on a pike and labelled "the Heart of an Aristocrat." Greetings were shouted to leftist members and threats and insults to the right. A speech was made, complaining that the French army was not fighting as it should and that the King was not living up to his end of the constitution.

Then why not visit the King himself? Toward four in the

afternoon the crowd streamed across the garden to the palace. The gate, for some mysterious reason, was unbolted and unguarded. The mob surged in and up the great staircase, carrying, along with various crude, homemade weapons, a full sized cannon. For hours Louis XVI and Marie Antoinette were trapped, he standing on a bench in the embrasure of a window, she and the little Dauphin wedged in a corner behind a table. No harm was done them, but they were freed only when the demonstrators were worn out with the heat and acrobatics of the day and drifted off to visit other sections of the palace.

As soon as he heard of this affair, Lafayette left his camp at Sedan and hurried back to the capital. On June 28th, he appeared unexpectedly before the Assembly to protest the insult to the crown and to the governing body. He demanded the closing of the Jacobin Club. There were a few cheers when he strode into the hall, but a motion was brought by the left—and lost—to censure him for having quitted his troops even for a few days without permission.

That night the house in the Rue de Bourbon was again picketed by National Guardsmen. Lafayette intended to appear at a review that was scheduled for the following day and to make a speech that would recall the Guard to a sense of responsibility for keeping order. But morale in the corps had declined. So few appeared at the rally that the review was cancelled.

Lafayette, during this brief visit to Paris, also had an audience with the King and Queen, in a last attempt to gain their confidence, to save them from the werewolf that threatened to devour them, the Paris mob. He urged them to leave the city and to go to Compiègne, well to the east of Paris, where they would be under cover of his army.

But he might have saved his breath. The Queen had never forgotten her humiliation at Versailles. She was reported to have said later that she would rather die than owe her life a second time to Lafayette.

Adrienne learned of all of these events, not only from the newspapers, but from the repercussions in her own family. Soon after the outbreak of June 20th, the Duchesse d'Ayen moved out of the Hotel de Noailles, so dangerously close to the Tuileries, and went to stay with Rosalie de Grammont in a little house in the Faubourg St. Germain. The Duc d'Ayen, who had been in Switzerland, ostensibly for his health, hurried home—a quixotic gesture; he had formerly been officer of the King's bodyguard and felt that it was his personal duty to protect the King. Word came from England that Pauline de Montagu and her husband, who were sorrowing for the death of their baby Noemi, had gone to the continent. Joachim had at last decided that the time had come for him to join his father and the émigré army on the Rhine.

For Adrienne herself there was a difficult decision to be made. Lafayette wrote to her to come to him at Sedan. The impulse to bundle herself and her children into a carriage and to set off at once was almost irresistible. But a family—and even a wife, if she went alone—would be an encumbrance to a general who might go into action at any moment. Adrienne, also, had been stung by the attacks on her husband's patriotism in the press. Fresh ammunition would be supplied if it became known that Lafayette was taking special precautions for his nearest and dearest. And there was Madame de Chavaniac; it would be brutal to leave her here at the mercy of the next band of incendiaries who happened to visit the village.

For weeks Adrienne could not bear to say a definite no, and during those weeks the collapse of all that Lafayette had worked for in his country first loomed and then became a certainty. On August 10th, another day of intense heat in

Paris, the Tuileries was invaded for a second time. There was nothing slipshod about this attack. It had been well organized—and even well advertised—in advance.

At an early hour the streets were flooded with people. The poor folk from the suburbs were there again, but many of them were well armed, and among the insurgents was a little band of patriots who had marched up through the heart of France from Marseilles, shouting a new, a magnificent battle song that spoke of a day of glory, of tyranny affronted, and a blood red flag.

The royal family, forewarned, left the palace and took refuge with the Assembly. The birds having flown, it seemed for a moment as if this affair might fizzle out, as if this might be another June 20th. Again the crowd swept into the palace. The men from Marseilles rushed up the staircase, but this time their way was blocked. At the top of the stairs the palace guards were stationed—Swiss mercenaries, but brave. A hand to hand struggle began and soon became a slaughter, in which nine hundred and fifty armed men and even the lackeys and the cooks in the royal kitchen were butchered. The streets surrounding the palace were littered with corpses. Smoke billowed from the stables which had been set ablaze. Until ten o'clock in the evening firing continued.

Several of Adrienne's near relatives were at the Tuileries on that terrible day of August 10th, and all miraculously escaped. Her father had followed the King into the Assembly hall. Her brother-in-law, Theodule de Grammont, Rosalie's husband, was given up by his family for dead until late in the day. He had spent several hours hiding in a chimney when the massacre was at its height and after dark arrived unhurt at the house in the Faubourg St. Germain.

Letters from Rosalie and her mother, written that very night, told Adrienne of these escapes, but from Lafayette she heard nothing then, or in the days that followed. For news of him she had to rely on the printed word—and the time lag in communication was cruel. There were reports that Lafayette was organizing a counterrevolution in the Ardennes, that he would march on Paris to restore the constitution. The King and Queen had been imprisoned in the Temple. The Assembly, now completely under the control of the Jacobins, had declared Lafayette a traitor to the new-born French Republic, soon to be proclaimed. Commissioners had been sent to Sedan to arrest him and to bring him back to Paris for trial. A price had been set upon his head.

For more than two weeks after the 10th of August, all at Chavaniac were kept in ignorance and Adrienne in a blinding agony of suspense.

CHAPTER VII

The Best of News

THE 26TH OF AUGUST was a Sunday. After dinner all the family were gathered in Adrienne's sitting room, one of the few rooms in the chateau that had been completely redecorated and refurnished with modern furniture that had come from Paris. The room was very quiet. Conversation had died a dwindling death. All eyes were fixed on Adrienne. That morning she had sent a man to Brioude to ask for letters, and any moment now Michel could be expected to appear.

Madame de Chavaniac, very gloomy, sighed occasionally. Close beside her was her faithful handmaiden, Mademoiselle Maillard and next to her was Mademoiselle Marin, Anastasie's and Virginie's governess. Virginie and George were whispering softly to one another in a corner. Monsieur Félix Frestel, George's tutor, was stretched out in an armchair, absentmindedly turning over an old book of riddles. Also present, and also silent out of respect for the lady of the house, was Monsieur Vaudoyer, the architect; his assistant,

Monsieur Legendre; and Mr. Dyson, the English farm superintendent.

Father Pierre Durif, the curé of Chavaniac, quietly entered
the room. A plump and, ordinarily, a cheerful man, the
priest was still out of breath from having played shuttlecock
with the children. He whispered to Mademoiselle Marin to
ask if the papers had come. She shook her head and whispered back that it was almost time for vespers; he mustn't
keep the whole village waiting for Michel. After looking out
of the window several times and several times comparing his
watch with the clock on the mantelpiece, Father Durif tip-
toed out again.

Anastasie sighed. She had been playing shuttlecock also—
and was ashamed of herself. It was childish, she thought. It
might seem as if she didn't care that her father had not been
heard from and might have met with some terrible misfortune. She saw her mother get up from her chair and go into
the next room.

Adrienne had not been able to sit still a moment longer.
She felt that she must be alone when—and if—the mail arrived. Only a few minutes later Félix Frestel came in and
handed her a letter. She could see that it was not from Lafayette; it had been written by Louise de Noailles. Adrienne
tore it open and had barely skimmed it through when Aunt
Chavaniac appeared on the threshold.

"Well—is there any news of my nephew?" she asked im-
periously.

"Yes, Aunt, the best of news!" Adrienne was radiant. "He's
safe. He has left the country!"

"He has left the country—you tell me that, Madame!" The
old woman's face was haggard, her eyes wide with horror
and indignation. She sank down in a chair by the door and
began to keen, tearing at her clothes and beating with her
fist and knee against the wall.

ill never see him again," she cried. "He is gone! I never see him again!"

Mademoiselle Maillard rushed in, followed by others of the household. The servants were never very far away at Chavaniac. They expected, as a matter of course, to take part in every domestic crisis, comic or tragic. Mademoiselle Maillard loosened the kerchief that swathed the old lady's neck and tried to quiet her, but it was almost half an hour before Madame de Chavaniac was coaxed out of her chair and led away, still loudly sorrowing, to her bedroom.

Adrienne could not offer first aid because she herself was surrounded. The moment she stepped back into the sitting room everyone in the chateau, including Monsieur Vaudoyer, Monsieur Legendre, and Mr. Dyson, crowded about her to kiss her hand and congratulate her as if the most wonderful good fortune had come her way.

Actually Louise had written that Lafayette's attempts to bolster up resistance to the Jacobin *coup* had failed. His troops had refused to follow him to Paris and he, and a group of his officers and men, despairing of any further effort had ridden across the frontier into Belgium.

But to Adrienne this was, for the time being, the best of news. He was safe! He had survived! She could not believe with Madame de Chavaniac, that she would never see him again. She was touched by the outpouring of good will her announcement had caused, all the more because Michel, there in the background, was loudly telling her and the others that he had heard at Brioude that many manor houses in the neighborhood had been attacked by revolutionists and they might expect something of the sort soon at Chavaniac.

As soon as she could, Adrienne sent George to comfort his aunt—he, who meant so much to her. He went rather reluctantly and quickly returned to report that everything he said seemed to make her cry the harder. Down in the village,

Father Durif was ringing the church bell—a joyful sound, but for once Adrienne intended to be absent from vespers. She asked Monsieur Frestel to stay home from church with her to help sort the papers in her desk. She couldn't take lightly Michel's talk of an attack on the chateau. There were no Jacobins in Chavaniac; Adrienne knew that every man, woman and child in the village was her friend, but even before affairs had reached their present pass in Paris there had been much lawlessness in the district and now one could expect the worst.

She and Frestel went over the contents of her desk and tossed many items into the fire. She decided to put valuables and even some of the pretty furniture from her room into an underground vault in the cellar where the family archives were stored. She decided also that the children must leave the house.

But where could she send them? Four or five years ago Lafayette had bought a large estate and, as part of it, an old mansion twelve miles away at Langeac. The house was in poor repair and had never been properly furnished. The Lafayettes had lent it to an American woman, married to a Frenchman, and she and her two children were living there temporarily. Langeac might do as a refuge for Anastasie and Virginie, but a better hiding place for George and Frestel materialized even as Adrienne was at work at her desk.

As if an angel had sent him, and before the family had come back from church, a fifteen-year-old boy named Portal arrived at the chateau after a long day's tramp from Conangles, a little village high in the mountains, not far from the great monastery of the Chaise Dieu. Portal's father had entered the priesthood after his wife's death and, unlike Father Durif, had taken the oath of allegiance to the state. He offered to hide Lafayette's son in his house.

Conangles was so remote that rioting there was unlikely. Adrienne gratefully accepted the offer. She herself saw to it that Portal was given something to eat and put to bed so that he could get a few hours sleep before he, George, and Frestel would start back that very night for the village.

When the news was broken to George that he was to make a long hike into the mountains after nightfall he was delighted, but Anastasie and Virginie wailed when they were told that they were to go to Langeac. They begged to be allowed to stay with their mother. She, however, was inexorable; they had to go—and go at once, for already the sun was beginning to slip out of sight behind the western rim of mountains. Their clothes were packed, a small carriage was brought around to the door and, still glumly rebellious, the girls climbed in accompanied by Mademoiselle Marin and a maid. A manservant rode off behind the cabriolet, and one went on ahead to warn the American lady that she might have to give up her beds to visitors that night.

There was still a great deal for Adrienne to do before she could get some rest herself. She superintended the removal of most of the furniture from her room to the hidden storage vault in the cellar. There were two of her husband's treasures that she wanted to preserve even if the vault was discovered: Lafayette's swords of honor, the one that had been given him by the National Guard and one with a gold hilt that was a gift from America. These she took out to bury in the garden.

After the rest of the chateau had gone to bed, Adrienne helped George and Frestel to disguise themselves in rough country clothes and sent George to wake his benefactor, Portal. The three young folk set off shortly after midnight in high spirits. They had renamed themselves for the journey; they would be Jacques, Jeannot, and Pierre, if they were separated in the dark and had to call to one another. Portal had a wicked looking dagger with him that he intended using if they were attacked by prowling watchdogs.

When she had let them out into the night—with her blessing—Adrienne, worn out by the day's excitement and activity, wearily climbed the stairs to her bedroom.

She was so tired that she overslept and was awakened the following morning by the distant booming of a cannon. She remembered fortunately that this was nothing unusual, for the 27th of August was the fête day of Saint Julien, the patron saint of Brioude. She felt unrefreshed, however; she had a bad headache and foresaw that she would have little chance of pampering herself.

The day was filled with alarms, false, or not so false—it was hard to say which. Adrienne was hardly out of bed when an anonymous letter was found slipped under the front door saying that the chateau would certainly be attacked by a force that was gathering at Le Puy, a larger town than Brioude, the seat of departmental government, some thirty miles distant. A little later in the morning the innkeeper's wife at Chavaniac came to Adrienne to say that a mysterious stranger wanted to meet her about dusk at a lonely spot on the road to St. Georges d'Aurac.

Though her head was still pounding, Adrienne kept the rendezvous, taking with her two men from the chateau as bodyguard. She found that the mysterious stranger was a gentleman she knew slightly at Le Puy who could tell her nothing definite of an uprising, but who urged her to come to his country house in yet another village for a few days.

Adrienne declined the invitation, not wanting to leave Aunt Chavaniac and knowing how hard it would be to dislodge her. The old lady had fully recovered from the emotional outburst of Sunday and, as far as she herself was concerned, feared neither man, beast, nor devil. She could discuss quite calmly with Adrienne what they would do if the "brigands," as she called them, actually came. If they were men from Brioude, then one might stay to parley with them but if they were from Le Puy it would be better to take to the woods—if, of course, there was time.

For the next few days Michel, the best runner in Chavaniac, was stationed on a high point overlooking the road to Le Puy but each evening he reported that he had seen nothing on the road but the usual traffic, an occasional cart or a solitary rider.

Toward the end of the week two commissioners came from Brioude, sent by the district Council to put government seals on the doors of the house as a protection against marauders. Heartened by this, Adrienne thought that it would be a good idea to go herself to talk with the district authorities. She was just about to set off when a letter was handed to her, *the* letter she had been waiting for so long. It had been written by Lafayette on August 19th at Rochefort in Belgium, where he and his companions were being temporarily detained by the first Austrian troops they had met after crossing the French frontier. They had declared themselves neutrals in the present conflict and had asked for safe conduct to the coast.

Over the years, Adrienne had received scores of letters from her far-ranging husband but never one like this. Gilbert had written to her sometimes in sorrow, as when he learned in America that Henriette, their first child, had died but he had never had to write her of a personal disaster, a personal defeat. It was he who had always been the comforter; it was she who had been in need of reassurance.

Lafayette was too close, perhaps, to the catastrophe which had driven him into exile to analyze it competently. In his heart, he said, he would have preferred a republic in France but cold logic had told him that this would be too great a break with tradition. He realized that in trying first to create the reformed government and then maintain it, he had become the target of attack by extremists in all parties. Thus he had worked steadily for his own downfall, though he did not see how he could have acted otherwise without dishonor.

"I make no excuse," he concluded, "either to my children or to you for having ruined my family. There is none among you who would want to owe his fortune to conduct that went against my conscience. Come and join me in England. Let us settle in America. There we will find the freedom that no longer exists in France, and my affection will try to compensate you for all the joys that you have lost. Adieu, dear heart."

For a moment Adrienne was so lifted out of her present concerns and worries that she thought of giving up her trip to Brioude; instead she gave the letter to Madame de Chavaniac, who slipped it into the bosom of her dress and promised to guard it with her very life. Adrienne drove off with a much more distant goal in view than the nearest large town. As soon as she could safeguard Chavaniac she would leave it—perhaps forever.

At Brioude she found a good deal to encourage her, though local elections for the National Convention that would replace the short-lived Legislative Assembly were going on and there were noisy crowds in the street. Lafayette owned a house in Brioude, but Adrienne avoided it.

She spent three days in lodgings that a young National Guardsman whom she met as she was driving into the town found for her. She was visited by leading citizens and told that she had nothing to fear at Brioude, though they could not guarantee that trouble might not come from some other direction. Various places of refuge were offered by various friends; some were fantastic—an old house that had extensive subterranean passages, a hut on the top of the Mont Dore, the highest mountain in the district. On Sunday Adrienne went to Mass, taking care to choose that of a nonjuring priest whom she felt needed her support.

On her way back to Chavaniac she stopped to have dinner with the girls at Langeac. She had sent Monsieur Vaudoyer to call on them earlier in the week and one day had ridden over herself on horseback. Anastasie and Virginie still considered themselves wretched, persecuted exiles. They had been taking turns standing sentinel all day long at a window that looked towards home. Adrienne told them that if all remained quiet for the next few days they could come to Chavaniac, at least for a visit.

She sent for them on Saturday. Anastasie rode ahead of the carriage on the return trip. She went along slowly most of the way because Evrad, one of the men, was walking beside her but when she came in sight of the chateau and saw her mother and her aunt sitting out on a balcony she gave her horse its head and galloped grandly up the hill. As she swept into the courtyard she was followed by a flock of women and children from the village who had come to welcome her home.

Anastasie was more thrilled than frightened when Adrienne told her in confidence that they must still be on the watch and described the arrangements she had made for a quick escape from the house. She had had a crude sedan chair brought down from the attic and two of the strongest men would carry Aunt Chavaniac in it to a ravine in the woods. Another man would carry Virginie, who was so small that she might not be able to keep up with the others as they ran.

"But what will we do about Mademoiselle Marin?" Anastasie asked. "She would be sure to follow Virginie—and she walks so slowly. If she was left behind no one would take her for a peasant because of those high-heeled shoes she wears."

"Well, in that case, we will just have to count on the village people taking care of her," Adrienne said with a sigh.

That evening when they were having supper, Mercier, the Chavaniac butler, kept muttering to himself as he stood behind Adrienne's chair and passed the dishes about the table.

"Things don't look good to me," he said, loud enough so that all could hear him. "Going to kill everyone—rob everything—and they're not far off. You ought to get out of here, every one of you, right away."

Mercier was one of the men who had gone with Adrienne to meet the mysterious stranger that evening on the road to St. Georges d'Aurac, and he was disgusted with her for not having accepted the gentleman's offer of an asylum.

CHAPTER VIII

❦

Soldiers From Hell

Two days later on Monday, September 10th, 1792, at eight o'clock in the morning, eighty-six armed men tramped up the hill from the village. Mademoiselle Benoite, the elderly housekeeper, who always wore a spindle attached to her belt to keep her hands busy in idle moments, looked out of the window and saw them just as she was carrying a jug of coffee up to Madame de Chavaniac's bedroom. The soldiers had encountered Monsieur Legendre, the architect's assistant, as he was crossing the courtyard. They had backed the young man up against a tree and told him not to move if he valued his life.

Mademoiselle Benoite burst into Madame de Chavaniac's room. "Get up, Madame, get up right away!"

"What on earth is the matter with you, Benoite?" the old lady asked, sitting up and pushing back the bed curtains.

"Oh, Jesus-Mary! Look out the window quick! They've filled up the whole courtyard!"

"But who *are* they?" Madame de Chavaniac asked, not to be hustled out of her bed unnecessarily.

"Who? Who? You make me tired, Madame, with your whos! Soldiers, every kind of soldier, every color and all armed to the teeth!"

"Where do they come from?" Madame de Chavaniac asked, still not to be stampeded into hysteria.

"From hell; God forgive me!" Mademoiselle Benoite cried, piously crossing herself.

At the same moment Evrad, the man whom Adrienne had deputed to carry Virginie if they had to escape from the chateau, shot into the room where Virginie was being dressed by Mademoiselle Marin. "At least we can save the child!" he shouted.

He swung Virginie up on his shoulder and started for the door.

"Wait till she gets her clothes on. She'll catch her death of cold," Mademoiselle Marin protested.

But Evrad paid no attention to her except to grumble at her for wasting time. He quickly opened the door—and as quickly banged it shut. The next room, it was the dining room, was full of soldiers.

The butler, Mercier, had gone straight to Adrienne's sitting room. She was there and in the doorway was a huge musketeer, his gun across his shoulder. He had just informed Mademoiselle Maillard that if anyone tried to leave the house there would be a general massacre but to Adrienne he said with a grin, "Don't be frightened. We're just some people who have come from Le Puy, and we have a commissioner with us."

The commissioner was an unprepossessing individual who had a split upper lip, like a hare, and looked as if he might be an escaped convict. He introduced himself to Adrienne as Alphonse Aulagnier, Justice of the Peace at Le Puy. He handed her a letter from the Committee of General Safety in Paris, dated August 19th, and signed by Jean Marie Roland, the Minister of the Interior. It ordered him to secure the persons of Madame de Lafayette and her children and to transport them to Paris.

While Adrienne was reading this document she was appalled to see Anastasie enter the room and to hear her say, "Bonjour, *maman.*" Now she could not pretend that all of her children were away from home! Madame de Chavaniac also came in.

The best thing to do, Adrienne thought, was to get Aulagnier and his men out of the house as quickly as possible before any pilfering, or worse, began. Resistance was out of the question. "I will go with you at once to Le Puy," she said, "and will give myself up to the authorities there. I will go as soon as the horses can be harnessed."

She told Mercier to see that the carriage was brought around immediately.

Aulagnier asked for the keys to Adrienne's desk. He must see if she had any letters from her husband. Unfortunately, the letter that Adrienne had received before going to Brioude was no longer wedged between Madame de Chavaniac's kerchief and her stays. It was in the desk and with it was another letter that Lafayette had written a few days later to his aunt in which he said that he supposed Adrienne had already left Chavaniac for England.

While Aulagnier was ferreting through the desk, Adrienne slipped off to Virginie's room where Virginie, in tears, was being forcibly restrained by Mademoiselle Maillard and Mademoiselle Marin. Virginie had wanted to follow Anastasie to her mother's room. Adrienne tried hurriedly to comfort the child and told her that she must stay where she was. On no account must she be seen by Aulagnier or the soldiers. If they should come here, Mademoiselle Marin could hide her inside the fireplace. This seemed more feasible than Madame de Chavaniac's suggestion that Virginie should be dressed as a peasant and turned out to run with the village children.

When she returned to the sitting room, Adrienne found the commissioner reading Lafayette's letters. "You will see by them, monsieur," she said, "that if there had been any just tribunals in France, Monsieur de Lafayette would not have hesitated to appear before them. He was sure that not a single action of his life could compromise him in the eyes of true patriots."

"I am afraid, Madame," Aulagnier replied, not too unkindly, "that the only court today is the court of public opinion."

The wait for the carriage began to seem long. Adrienne, to pass the time, spoke to one of the soldiers, whom she thought had a pleasant face and who was wearing a white uniform that she did not recognize. She asked him what was his regiment.

"I am from Medoc," the soldier said. "They sent us to Le Puy because we had a little trouble in our regiment. We killed one of our officers, but," the man shrugged, "what could you expect? The fellow was an aristocrat!"

Adrienne became increasingly uneasy as she saw that the men were beginning to wander away to other parts of the house, staring curiously at everything they discovered. They particularly admired the work that had been begun on "the Washington Gallery" where Lafayette had intended to hang his pictures of the Revolution.

"Think of owning all this," one of the sightseers said, "and then going off and betraying his country!"

Mademoiselle Benoite hobbled after them as they stopped to inspect the portraits of bygone Lafayettes in armor, ruffs, and farthingales. "Who are these people?" a soldier asked. "Some fine aristocrats, I suppose!"

"They were good people in their day," Mademoiselle Benoite said in a sepulchral voice, "and now they are no more. If they were alive today things might not be going as badly as they are!"

The soldiers ran the points of their bayonets through the canvases and later, when they invaded Madame de Chavaniac's room, they stabbed a picture of Lafayette to the heart. They also broke open the desk and smashed a jar in which the old lady kept her snuff.

But at last the carriage appeared. Madame de Chavaniac had nobly said that she would go with Adrienne to Le Puy and farther still—to Paris, if necessary. Anastasie would have to go also, since she had been recognized by Aulagnier. Adrienne was touched when Mercier, Evrad, and another servant volunteered to follow the coach on foot among the soldiers, keeping their ears open to hear if any mischief was intended before Le Puy was reached. Adrienne was much relieved that the commissioner had made no enquiries for other Lafayette children than Anastasie and that Virginie had not been discovered.

Just as she was getting into the carriage, the man whom she had sent several times to Conangles to communicate with George innocently asked, "Shall I keep on going to see Monsieur Georges while you are away?"

"Of course," Adrienne whispered, "—only keep still!"

As if this was not enough, Monsieur Vaudoyer approached to say goodbye and added in surprise, "Then Mademoiselle Virginie is staying here?"

"Oh please, monsieur!" Adrienne murmured, sinking back on the cushions.

*   *   *

It was a good thirty miles to Le Puy and since the morning was well advanced it was clear that they could not get there by night with their military escort, all of whom, except Aulagnier, were unmounted. Adrienne was cheerful. This was infinitely better, she said, than two weeks ago when she had not even received her sister's letter saying that Lafayette was safe. She thought that she might plead her cause successfully and perhaps make her captors feel a little foolish for what they had done. Madame de Chavaniac was unconcerned, although she said that it was certainly strange to be knocked out of her accustomed groove for an expedition of this kind. As they slowly jolted along, Anastasie felt sorry for poor little Virginie, who had been left behind and who was probably suffering pangs of jealousy.

At a small town, Villeneuve, they stopped so that the soldiers could eat and drink and Adrienne told Evrad to go back to the chateau to reassure them there. Aulagnier said that they would spend the night at Fix, which stood at a high point on the mountainous road to Le Puy.

It seemed as if the horses couldn't drag the carriage up the steep incline, burdened as it was with half a dozen soldiers hanging on behind it, but at last, after a struggle, the summit was reached. The women were helped out of the coach and went into the inn. Aulagnier settled with them the hour when they would leave—at two in the morning, as soon as the moon had risen.

Mercier came up to their room and said that the soldiers were not such bad fellows after all and he didn't think that there was anything to fear from them. Aulagnier, too, had been very friendly and had invited him to dinner.

Adrienne thanked Mercier, with tears in her eyes, for his devotion. He, too, was moved. "Oh, it's nothing," he said gruffly. "That was easy to do." He would sleep, he said, on a mattress in front of the door to guard them during the night.

After they had had something to eat, all but Aunt Chavaniac, who refused to take anything but some sugar water, they knelt down to say their prayers. A great scuffling broke out below—angry voices, a cry, "To arms!"

Adrienne thought that someone might have come to rescue them, that there would be a fight to the death. "Oh,

Aunt, I am afraid someone will be killed," she exclaimed in horror.

But Aunt Chavaniac had no such illusions or compunctions. It was just a soldiers' brawl. "Eh, Madame," she said contemptuously, "if they want to kill one another, let them!"

Presently the fracas subsided and sleep was possible. Anastasie dropped into complete oblivion, Madame de Chavaniac slept the uneasy sleep of old age, and Adrienne lay awake, wondering whether the soldiers would have time to get dangerously drunk before two o'clock in the morning.

At two, the travelers were aroused and given some milk to drink by the innkeeper's wife, who was sympathetic, but who prophesied that soon they all would be on their way to Paris. The journey to Le Puy was then continued by moonlight.

CHAPTER IX

The Court of Public Opinion

THE VERY ANCIENT, the very curious town of Le Puy en Velay rises in the form of an amphitheater from the floor of a high mountain valley, its steep and narrow streets paved with pebbles of lava. Twin pinnacles of volcanic rock are today crowned with gigantic statues and on a third is perched a miniature doll's house of a church. The church of St. Jean d'Aiguilhe had been in position, airily suspended, for more than eight hundred years when the Lafayette carriage approached the town on the morning of September 11th, 1792. The sun had been up for hours.

The travelers fell silent as they neared the suburb that had grown up outside the old city wall. At Fix they had been told that a prisoner who was being brought into Le Puy was set upon by a mob at this point and killed. One could not be sure how much protection to expect from Monsieur Aulagnier and his cohorts.

Adrienne saw that for the first time Anastasie was showing signs of nervousness. She whispered in her daughter's ear, "If your father knew that you were here, how anxious he would be—but at the same time he would be very proud of you!"

People stared at the carriage as it passed and shouted wordless threats; stones rattled against its sides. A few flew in at the window before it had reached the gate of the town.

Aulagnier had asked Adrienne where she wanted to go in Le Puy, and she had replied that she wanted to be taken straight to the building that housed the government of the department. The Department Council was not in session when she arrived, but the members were sent for and soon began to file in. Among them was the mayor of the town who was an old acquaintance. Adrienne remembered his having come to Chavaniac occasionally in the past.

She had had plenty of time in the long hours on the road to plan exactly what she should say when she found herself in this particular room and facing this particular audience. "I place myself confidently under your protection, gentlemen," she said. "I recognize in you the authority of the people—and that I have always respected. You may take your orders from Monsieur Roland if you choose or from anyone else. I choose to take orders only from you and I give myself up to you as *your* prisoner."

The municipal officers were surprised, perhaps, that a woman could be so reasonable and so businesslike. Aulagnier produced the letters he had found in Adrienne's desk at Chavaniac. The question was raised: what should be done with these incriminating documents? The board decided that they should be sent to Paris.

Adrienne asked that copies of the letters should be made before they were dispatched and asked permission to read some of them aloud.

Again there was a flutter of surprise. One of the men said ironically that he was afraid she might find it painful to read her husband's letters in public and to the present company.

"On the contrary," Adrienne said. "I find support and comfort in the feelings they express."

She knew that she was taking a risk to let her husband speak for himself—she might be interrupted; she might be howled down—but in a firm voice she read the passages that set forth most clearly Lafayette's patriotism and his political outlook, in particular the passage in which he stated his preference for a republican form of government, now that France no longer had a king.

While she read, there was absolute silence. Adrienne sensed, as an actor or a public speaker senses instinctively, that her audience was with her. She had touched the imagination and emotions of these coldly hostile men. Their hostility was impersonal. They were not really cold; they, too, loved their country. Other people drifted into the hall to listen. When she had finished there was applause, and the Mayor of Le Puy fervently congratulated her.

It had occurred to Adrienne that the Mayor had gone too far and might damage his position with his more radical colleagues by appearing to be so intimate with her. She would do him as good a turn as she could under the circumstances. She thanked him for his sympathy, "But why have you not been to see me, Monsieur le Maire?" she asked reproachfully. "You have not come to Chavaniac for a very, very long time."

The President of the Council, Monsieur de Montfleury, though less demonstrative, seemed also to be her friend. Adrienne urged him and his fellows to consider obeying this order of the Committee of General Safety in spirit but not to the letter. It would be unjust and pointless to force her and her children to make a long journey in these dangerous times and to go to Paris where only a week ago, as she had learned from the newspapers, there had been a wholesale murder of prisoners in their cells. No definite accusation had been brought against her. Her only possible value was as a hostage for her husband, for whom she was proud to go security and whose opinions she gloried in sharing—but why could she not be a hostage here in Auvergne?

"I would be much obliged to the department," Adrienne said, "if it will allow me to remain under house arrest at Chavaniac. If so, I will give you my word of honor not to leave my home without your permission."

It was getting late. President de Montfleury said that the matter would be discussed and decided at the next meeting of the Council. In the meantime, the three Lafayette women could stay here in the municipal building where they would be safe.

The following day de Montfleury pleaded Adrienne's cause so well that a letter outlining her proposal was written immediately to Minister Roland by Alphonse Aulagnier. Adrienne was told that she would have to remain in Le Puy, however, until a reply came back from Paris.

*   *   *

She, Anastasie, and Aunt Chavaniac resigned themselves to living as comfortably as they could contrive in the municipal building. They were prisoners, but the sentinels at their door were National Guardsmen who had asked for the assignment so that they might protect Lafayette's wife and family. Adrienne could have visitors and many people she knew in Le Puy came to offer their sympathy. She could also hear from home, from Virginie and George, and could write letters, one of which went to her mother in Paris.

She went over in her mind the people she knew who might have some influence with Roland. The list was meager, but she decided to write to Jacques Pierre Brissot, who had often come to the house in the Rue de Bourbon and had often been a guest at her table. At that time Brissot was head of the French Antislavery Society in which both Lafayette and

Adrienne were active. He was now one of the Girondist leaders in the National Convention.

"Monsieur," she wrote, "I really believe that you are a
sincere fanatic for liberty. This is a compliment I can pay to
very few people nowadays. I won't go into the question
whether your kind of fanaticism—like religious fanaticism—
defeats its own end, but I cannot think that one who has
done so much for the emancipation of Negroes could be an
agent of tyranny."

She described the circumstances of her arrest without a
warrant. She compared it to the methods that the kings of
France had once used to send prisoners to the Bastille without trial. She asked Brissot to do what he could to free her
so that she could go to England, join Lafayette, and emigrate
with him to America.

The letter was sent off at the same time as the communication of the Council to Roland. A week, two weeks, went by.
Toward the end of September, Adrienne was called again
into the assembly room to listen to the word that had come
from Paris.

The arrangement she had suggested was satisfactory, she
was informed, if the local authorities would be responsible
for her safekeeping. She had won her point, but not without
a sharp little slap on the wrist from Roland. Brissot had
shown him her letter and the minister had taken offense at
some of the expressions she had used; the style of writing she
had learned from her mother was too aristocratic. She had
said, for instance, "I consent to owe you a service;" that
smacked too much he thought, of "the antiquated pride of
what had once been called nobility." There was frenzied
applause in the Council chamber when this part of Roland's
letter was read aloud.

Adrienne could have passed over the rebuke with a smile,
if she had been in a smiling mood, but she was depressed to
realize that victory had come too late. She had had some very

disheartening news while she was at Le Puy. Lafayette was not in England, as she hoped he would be by this time. His declaration of neutrality had not been worth the paper on which it was written. It was reported in the newspapers that he was a prisoner of the anti-French coalition, made up of Austria, Prussia, and the German principalities, which considered him a dangerous revolutionary. He was on his way to a Prussian fortress—Spandau, the papers said.

Again the impulse to go to him was overwhelming. However difficult it might be to travel, or to leave France, Adrienne bitterly regretted that she had promised to stay at Chavaniac.

Perhaps, she thought, her promise might be rescinded as she listened to the Council debate how she should be guarded. It was proposed that the Commune of Aurat in which Chavaniac was situated, should supply sentinels for the chateau. "I here declare, gentlemen," Adrienne cried, "that I will not give the parole I offered if guards are to be placed at my door."

But the Commune of Aurat had no intention of posting guards. Its representative said to the Council that if Adrienne had given her word of honor that should be sufficient. "I would go bail for her myself," the man from Aurat said, "for she's a fine woman."

It was agreed that the Commune should merely check on Adrienne's presence at Chavaniac every two weeks and report to Le Puy.

Shortly thereafter, on October 5th, the three prisoners left for home. They were accompanied to their doorstep by a squad of commissioners, who were impressed by the welcome given Adrienne, Anastasie, and Madame de Chavaniac. Not only the household and the village turned out, but some of the officials from Aurat were there also. Adrienne could not resist saying in the presence of her guards from Le Puy that she was not as aristocratic as Monsieur Roland thought. She felt honored to owe a service to her country neighbors and to find herself under the protection of people who trusted her.

After the officers from Le Puy had left she invited the Aurat delegation to stay to supper. Before the meal was over she proposed her husband's health, and the toast was drunk without protest.

*   *   *

But the toast was only a flourish. Back in her own house, Adrienne's one absorbing aim was to leave it as soon as possible. The day before coming home from Le Puy she battened down her pride and wrote to Roland, begging him to release her—"I ask it on my knees," she said—so that she could go to Germany. Prisoners of state were sometimes given the privilege of having their wives with them. If she could not actually live with her husband, at least she could be near him.

She wrote in similar vein to Brissot. His only reply to her first appeal had been through Roland, but at least he was responsible for her being now at Chavaniac. "I should not write to you again, monsieur," she began—for she felt that he had betrayed her confidence—"after the use that you make of my letters. . . . Do not expect to find bitterness in what I have to say, nor even the pride of injured innocence. I plead my cause with the sole desire of gaining it."

These two letters she sent to Paris by a special messenger, an old friend whom she found waiting for her at Chavaniac. His name was Beauchet; he was the husband of one of her former maids and he had been sent to Auvergne by the Duchesse d'Ayen as soon as she heard of her daughter's arrest.

Adrienne could not wait to be free herself, however, before beginning to work for her husband's freedom. She thought at once of America. Mr. Dyson, the farm superintendent, wanted to go home to England while the going was good; one could not tell what international complications might arise in the near future. This seemed to Adrienne a good way of communicating quickly and safely with Lafayette's "adopted father," President Washington.

She wrote to him, asking that an American envoy be sent to Europe to negotiate her husband's release. If his family could go with him to the United States, so much the better; but if that was impossible, their being left behind must not be considered an obstacle. She did not mention Lafayette's name, and she omitted her signature, thinking that Dyson's papers might be examined before he was allowed to leave the country. Dyson promised to explain everything himself to the President.

Six months, however, and even more might go by before an answer came from Philadelphia. There were other American friends who were close at hand and the most obvious one to approach was the present Minister to France, Mr. Gouverneur Morris.

Adrienne knew this successor to Thomas Jefferson well, for he had often been present at the Monday night American dinners at the house in the Rue de Bourbon. Once, to please him, Adrienne had had Anastasie sing a little ditty that Morris himself had composed. Morris was not altogether to her taste, nor to her husband's. He was a snob, had identified himself with the court party, and took a rather dim and carping view of Lafayette's zeal for reform. Adrienne felt sure, however, that Morris would—and should—be concerned by her present plight.

There were others outside of France to whom she could turn, in particular Thomas Pinckney, the American minister to England, a country that thus far had maintained a hands-

30 avril 1774

Monfieur le Comte DE LA RIVIERE, &
Monfieur le Comte DE LUZIGNEM, font
venus pour avoir l'honneur de vous faire part
du mariage de Monfieur le Marquis DE LA
FAYETTE, leur arriere-petit-Fils & Neveu,
avec Mademoifelle DE NOAILLES.

From the Bibliotheque Nationale

The Lafayette-d'Ayen wedding invitation

Gilbert and Adrienne de
Lafayette at the time of
their marriage

The three children of Adrienne de Lafayette: Anastasie, George Washington, and Virginie

The chateau of Chavaniac

From a drawing by General Carbone

Madame de Simiane

From a painting by Madame Vigée-Lebrun

The Marquis de Lafayette

From a sketch by Duvivier

Lafayette and Marie Antoinette on the balcony at
Versailles: October 5th, 1789

The storming of the Bastille

From a gouache by Houël

Lafayette, as Commander of the National Guard, rescuing a victim from the Paris mob

From a contemporary print

The reunion of Lafayette with his wife and daughters—
an artist's fantasy

A nineteenth century view of the town of Olmütz

Sketch of "Cataquois," the
Olmütz jailer, by Anastasie
de Lafayette

Madame de Lafayette in
her later years

The chateau of La Grange-
Bléneau

off, wait-and-see policy in the present war. She would write to Morris, she could try to write to Pinckney; but how much better it would be, she thought, if she could speak to them herself or if she could send someone to represent her!

One night, soon after her return from Le Puy, Adrienne was roused from her bed to speak with Félix Frestel, who had stolen back from his hide-out in the mountains. He and George had been living all these weeks safely, but monotonously, at Conangles; their presence in the village unsuspected. Portal's grandmother kept house for her priestly son and his family. She had seen that the refugees were well-fed. Portal and his brother waited on the family at mealtimes and were ready to slip into the guests' places at the table if anyone came to the house and George and Frestel had to hide themselves hurriedly in the attic.

One could not live forever in an attic, however. Frestel wanted to know what was Adrienne's pleasure and was ready to carry out any program she suggested for George.

It would be best for George, Adrienne thought, if he were out of the country. If he came to Chavaniac he would be only another hostage and, young though he was, he might be useful elsewhere.

While the rest of the chateau slept, Adrienne and Frestel spelled out in whispers a plan for Frestel to go to the autumn trade fair at Bordeaux. He could easily get a license as a small time merchant and also the passport now needed to go from one department to another. He would take George with him. They would try to find a passage aboard a ship that was going to England. There they would confer with Thomas Pinckney on efforts to rescue Lafayette. They might even travel farther still to Germany.

Before daylight the plan was complete and Frestel was gone as quietly as he had come. Adrienne had told him that she didn't want to see George before they left, for at the last moment she might not be able to part with her son. She was ready to make any sacrifice herself, however, and to demand any sacrifice from her children that would serve their father. She had always been honest enough to admit to them and to herself that she was wife first, she was mother second.

PART THREE

October, 1792—June, 1794

CHAPTER X

A Net of Many Strands

E VEN BEFORE ADRIENNE was taken to Le Puy on September 10th, 1792, Lafayette's American friends in Europe had been alerted—by Lafayette himself.

A young man named William Short, who was the United States minister at the Hague, received a note that had been hurriedly written in English by the prisoner at Brussels on August 26th. It began, "My dear friend: You have been acquainted with the atrocious events which have taken place in Paris." Short had indeed heard of the atrocious events and was much perturbed. He had come to France in 1784 as Thomas Jefferson's secretary, had made many French friends and had fallen head over heels in love with an aristocratic lady, the Duchesse de la Rochefoucauld. Short was longing to hear from her and the letter in hand only added to his anxieties.

Lafayette, after telling of his arrest by the Austrians and their disregard of his declared neutrality, asked the minister to come to Brussels at once and claim him as a compatriot. "I am an American citizen, an American officer, no longer in French service, and I don't doubt of your immediate and urging [sic] arrival."

It was true that Lafayette was, technically speaking, an American citizen. In 1784, he and his male posterity had been granted an honorary citizenship by two states of the present union. It was also true that his services to the American nation had been immeasurable, freely given without thought of reward—not to mention the countless services to individual Americans, one of whom happened to be Short himself. After Jefferson went home in 1789, Short had very much wanted the post in Paris. Lafayette had written to Washington warmly recommending him and, though Morris had been appointed in his stead, Short was grateful to the Marquis for what he had done.

There was every reason therefore for Short's coming to Lafayette's aid—but go to Brussels! demand a prisoner of the mighty Austrian Empire! Short could not see himself, a representative of a small, weak country far across the globe, doing that. Lafayette also had been branded as a traitor by the present French government. There was a treaty of alliance between France and America. Looking in either direction, Short could see only an impasse. And he was very far from home. This was too great a responsibility for him to take single-handed.

Short did not reply to the Brussels letter immediately. A second, more urgent appeal arrived three days later—"depend on it, no time is to be lost." At last the harassed young man wrote to apologize lamely for not coming to Belgium. He was too busy, he said; he would come later on his way to Spain on a diplomatic mission. He hoped that all would be well by that time, for he didn't believe that Lafayette would be held for very long.

But even as he wrote, Short saw how shabby his excuses were. He salved his bruised and aching conscience by taking counsel with his American colleagues, with Morris in Paris and Thomas Pinckney in London. William Carmichael in

Madrid, the only other American representative in Europe, was too far away to be readily consulted.

In early September, a worried, three-cornered correpondence began. Both Morris and Pinckney agreed that Short had done the right thing in doing nothing. Morris thought that "the less we meddle in the great quarrel which agitates Europe the better it will be for us." Pinckney saw no use in making a request only to have it refused; he had, however, drafted an official note to the Austrian ministry and was ready to sign it if the others would cooperate.

So the matter rested when Gouverneur Morris heard from Adrienne. Her letter was delivered to him by Monsieur Beauchet, the man whom the Duchesse d'Ayen had sent to Chavaniac and who earlier had carried Adrienne's appeals to Roland and Brissot. This was only one of many trips that Beauchet made back and forth between Paris and Auvergne. He was invaluable as a means of communication now that the public mails were so hazardous and he could give the personal touch that Adrienne felt was so important.

On his first trip Beauchet had seen both Roland and Brissot and had found that, though Roland might be irritated by aristocratic expressions, he was a kindhearted man. Via Beauchet, Roland sent back word to Adrienne that he was deeply sorry for her. He would wait for a favorable moment to present her case to the Committee of General Safety and hoped that before long, he might have good news for her.

In the meantime she would have to wait, as she had so often waited before, for a letter from America and for further developments.

Again winter closed in. Adrienne could remember sadly that at this time last year Gilbert was at home, peacefully conferring with Mr. Dyson about his cattle and hogs and with Monsieur Vaudoyer about the improvements to his house. Except for one brief notice in the Paris papers that

Lafayette had been taken not to Spandau but to Wesel in Westphalia, his name had disappeared from the public press. Adrienne wondered if perhaps she might not possibly get news of him through diplomatic channels and wrote to the Duke of Brunswick, the commander of the allied armies. She sent her letter to the French Minister for War. Again Beauchet was her messenger.

When he returned about the middle of December, Adrienne learned that Roland had been successful with the Paris committee and that she was free of her parole, free to go and come as she chose within the narrow circle of her own department of the Haute Loire. She would need a special dispensation to go beyond it and Roland warned her to give up all idea of trying to join her husband; it would be very unsafe for the wife of Lafayette to travel even in France at present, and in the Rhineland there were battle lines to cross.

The first use that Adrienne made of her limited liberty was to go to Le Puy on business, for she was plagued by a new disability that threatened to chain her to Chavaniac as closely as had her word of honor. For the first time in her life she was very short of money.

In the past, money had always been there for the asking. When cash in hand ran low, one wrote to Monsieur Morizot, the man of affairs who had always been and still was in charge of Lafayette's estate. If one was in a hurry one could always borrow. Lafayette had been carelessly extravagant and had reduced his patrimony by a half, but his credit was until recently excellent. Like many husbands, he left to Adrienne the dreary routine of paying bills, and now bills were coming in and there was very little with which to pay them. Lafayette had been classed as an emigrant noble and his property had been confiscated by the state. This applied not only to his lands in Auvergne but to the much more valuable holdings he had inherited from his mother's side of the family in Brittany.

What particularly worried Adrienne was that Madame
de Chavaniac's affairs were hopelessly entangled with her
nephew's. As a result of a sale of some of his aunt's real estate
that had turned out badly and for which Lafayette felt he
was to blame, he had given her a promissory note to cover
the loss. He had thought that the interest on the note would
provide her with a safe and steady income as long as she lived.

Adrienne frequently made the long, cold journey to Le
Puy that winter to protest before the department Council
Lafayette's classification as an émigré and to consult a lawyer
who was trying to validate her claim that debts made earlier
on sequestered property should be honored. It was particularly difficult to do anything about the estates in Brittany—
there was no one in Paris whom she wanted to ask to represent her—but she could not even try to go to Germany, she
felt, until Aunt Chavaniac's future was secure and some
other long-standing obligations had been disposed of.

For she still intended, in spite of Roland's warnings, in
spite of war and passports and frontiers, to make the attempt.
It was part of her plan that George should leave the country
before she did. All during the fall and early winter she
hoped to hear that George and Frestel had got their passage
to England from Bordeaux.

She had wished that Madame de Chavaniac should know
nothing of this scheme, remembering how last August the
old lady had moaned and beat her fist against the wall because she thought that she would never see George's father
again. Somehow the secret had leaked out; it was hard to
keep a secret in the small, talkative world of Chavaniac. With
great, and uncharacteristic, self control Madame de Chavaniac said nothing to Adrienne directly, but her manner
to her niece was cold and mournful and the subject of
George's whereabouts lay, undiscussed, like a sword between
them.

Frestel was able to write to Adrienne from time to time,

but only in veiled language that was difficult to interpret. Once she thought that they were actually off, but later Frestel let her know that it was useless to try to get out of a port that was so well guarded; ships by the score were lying idle at Bordeaux. He was going with George to his parents' home in Normandy to see if there was any chance of slipping across the Channel from that point.

Then, suddenly and unexpectedly, they turned up at Chavaniac. Adrienne saw them come home with mixed feelings of relief and disappointment. She could not join at once in her aunt's and the girls' festival of joy.

Frestel told her in private that he was willing to try again if she could give him the means, for all the little supply of money she had handed over to him in October was exhausted. For several days she weighed the heavy risks against the featherweight chances of success. She finally decided that it would be hopeless; George could stay where he was, since there was nowhere else that she could send him except back to the garret of Father Portal's house at Conangles. On Christmas Eve, 1792, George celebrated his thirteenth birthday in the home of his ancestors.

*   *   *

The old year drew gloomily to its end. On December 27th, William Short was writing to Morris that Lafayette and three others who were taken with him in Belgium, all of whom had been members of the French Constituent Assembly and therefore guilty of *lèse-majesté* in royal eyes, were being treated very harshly in Wesel. Some said that Lafayette was dead, others that he had gone insane. Short did not believe these rumors, but he was afraid that Lafayette was the one "individual in all France whom both the Prussians and the Austrians hate most cordially."

Late in the year though it was for military action, all along the eastern battle front the armies of the French Republic

were delivering hammer blows. The émigré regiments that
last summer were so proud and menacing were broken and
decimated. No quarter had been given them on the field; no
prisoners had been taken. All of Belgium was in French
hands and refugees were streaming into Holland, the only
avenue of escape.

Among those who fled were Pauline de Montagu, Pauline's
soldier-husband, Joachim, and her father-in-law, the Vicomte
de Beaune. They were among the lucky few who had been
able to commandeer a carriage at Aix-la-Chapelle. They were
speeding in it down the road on the left bank of the Rhine
that led into the Low Countries. Their destination was again
England, for it seemed likely that Holland also would fall
to the French. When they came to the point where the Lippe
flows into the Rhine they saw on the opposite bank the
town of Wesel and its high-walled fortress.

Pauline leaned out of the window of the carriage, tears
streaming from her eyes. She knew that this was Lafayette's
prison. All of the émigrés had heard with glee of his downfall. Pauline, if she had dared, would have liked to ask to
stop so that she could search the windows of the fortress and
perhaps see her brother-in-law's face pressed against the bars.

Her father-in-law, no doubt, knew what was in her mind
but for once the old Vicomte, who hated Lafayette as cordially as any Austrian or Prussian could, was tactful. He
refrained from asking Pauline why she was crying. He didn't
even register a protest against the open window and the cold
air that was rushing into the carriage.

In far away Chavaniac, Adrienne, too, was thinking constantly of Wesel and its fortress and of the way thither. Over
her and hers lay coiled a net of many strands. Slowly but
surely the net would contract and she would find no loop-
hole for escape.

The Law of Suspects

IN JANUARY OF 1793, Monsieur Beauchet was again in
Chavaniac and spent less than twenty-four hours at the
chateau. Gouverneur Morris had suggested that Adrienne
might write to the King of Prussia and had sent her the draft
of a letter to sign. She thought the tone of the letter was too
humble, too crawling, and composed one of her own.

At Morris' suggestion, she also wrote to the Princess of
Orange, sister of the Prussian King, and to the Prussian
Prime Minister, Lucchessini. Adrienne had happened to see
in a foreign journal, an article by the German playwright,
Klopstock, in which he spoke admiringly of Lafayette. She
wrote to him at once, thinking that this might start a pro-
Lafayette movement among German intellectuals. All of
these letters she gave to two Italian plasterers who had been
working under Monsieur Vaudoyer's direction and who
were going home to Italy.

She was ready to snatch at any straw that drifted within
her reach. In March, not having heard from Washington,

she wrote to him again. Had her letter failed to reach him? "Was it necessary that it should arrive to excite your interest? I cannot believe it! But I confess that your silence and the abandonment of Monseiur de Lafayette and his family for the last six months are, of all our evils, the most inexplicable to me. . . . I will only add that my confidence in General Washington, though severely tried, still remains firm."

Often many weeks went by without Adrienne's hearing what was going on in the great world except as reported in the press. Then Beauchet would appear with first-hand news of her family and of what was going on in Paris. At the time of his January visit, he described in sorrowful detail the trial for treason of King Louis, then in progress. After Beauchet had gone, the Paris papers reported the King's execution on January 23rd.

A few days later, Adrienne read of the removal of Monsieur Roland from the ministry. His fate, like her husband's, had been bound up with that of the King. Roland had always been at odds with the radical Commune of Paris and wanted Louis' penalty to be decided by a national plebiscite. Adrienne no longer had a potent friend in office.

The Girondins were now on the defensive. They were faced in the Convention by the Paris Jacobins, a grimly determined group who were bent on establishing a strong centralized government and even, if necessary, a dictatorship to meet the dangers, internal and external, that had mushroomed in the early months of 1793.

On the 1st of February, war was declared between France and England. An even mightier anti-French coalition was formed, including not only Great Britain but all of Europe except Russia. At the same time, a serious revolt against military conscription broke out in La Vendée. The *élan* which had carried the French to victory in the first few

months after the fall of the monarchy faltered. There were
reverses on every front, though political agents were sent to
the armies to see that their leaders were making every effort,
and the threat of the guillotine hung over those who failed.
In March, General Dumouriez, the most competent French
commander, was defeated and promptly deserted to the
enemy.

This had a direct effect upon Adrienne. Officials came again
from Le Puy to go through the papers in her desk, for
Dumouriez had once been her husband's colleague. A representative of the Committee of General Safety, Lacoste, was
traveling through the Haute Loire in April making investi-
gations and Adrienne heard that he was saying that she, the
wife of another general who had left his troops and gone
across the border, should be arrested. She resented the com-
parison between Dumouriez, who had sold out completely
to the Austrians, and Lafayette, who had flatly refused to
give them any military information. She thought she would
forestall any move the Paris emissary might make against her
by paying him a personal visit. Again she went to Brioude;
she found Lacoste in the city hall.

"I have come to tell you, Monsieur," she said, "that though
I am always glad to be a hostage for Monsieur de Lafayette
I am not willing to be a hostage for one of his enemies. Besides, it would make no difference to Monsieur Dumouriez
if I lived or died . . . All I ask is that I should be left with
my children in the only place that is bearable to me while
their father is a prisoner of the enemies of France."

The commissioner was surprisingly gentle spoken. "Citi-
zeness," he said, using the new form of address which had
been instituted in Paris, "your sentiments are a credit to
you."

"I don't care particularly about their being a credit to
me," Adrienne replied. "I only want them to be worthy of
him—my husband."

She was told that for the present no action would be taken against her.

Other crises, however, could not be dealt with so easily. In Paris a debate was underway to decide whether atheism or the worship of Rousseau's Supreme Being should be declared the state religion and in consequence, persecution of priests became common in the provinces. Several were mobbed to death at Le Puy and one at Brioude. One day Father Durif, the jolly curé who liked to play shuttlecock with the children, was arrested on the village street of Chavaniac.

Adrienne hurried off to Le Puy to see her friend, de Mountfleury of the department Council. He had told her that he would rescue any unfortunate person she recommended to him, but his position in the department was becoming precarious and in this case he could only give advice.

The charge brought against the curé was the old one that in the past had been overlooked; he had refused, as so many others had refused, to take the civil oath. He was to be tried at Aurat before a jury made up of peasants. The Mayor of the Commune, who would preside at the trial, was Monsieur Guitandry, the doctor whom Lafayette had set up in practice at Chavaniac. It was to be expected, therefore, that the prisoner would be acquitted. The rub would come when the decision was submitted to the district court in Brioude for approval.

After the trial, which smoothly ran its predicted course, Adrienne went to Brioude and found that the outlook there for the case was very bad. Power was pyramiding in France. The court was afraid that the judgment was too favorable and might be questioned at Le Puy. This would be a black mark against the Brioude judges, and for the defendant, as Adrienne knew, it would be fatal.

She took it on herself to delay the referral to Le Puy for a few days, using her formidable powers of persuasion on each of the judges in turn to accept the Commune's decision. She succeeded, at least she won over the majority, and Father Durif was sent back to Chavaniac. She realized, however, that in the process she had made some enemies and that some day what she had done might be held against her. She couldn't be accused of aristocratic sympathies, but it could be said that she was a religious fanatic.

This was a consideration to be borne in mind if she were to ask for special favors and only by means of special favor could she gain her end, the end, which she had always kept in sight, of reaching her husband. She clung to it desperately while the Paris papers reported one military disaster after another and all the confusing attack and counter attack that was going on in the National Convention.

The Girondins could control the votes, but it became increasingly plain that they could neither keep order in the country nor, what was even more important, wage a foreign war and win. Only force could oust them; this the Paris Commune was eager to supply.

On Sunday, June 2nd—how many violent Sundays had Paris known in the last few years!—the Convention hall was surrounded by armed roughs, hired by the Commune for forty *sous* a day. There was no blood letting, but the Girondins were turned out into the street. From now on the Commune and a new Committee of Public Safety, which had been formed in April, would govern France—and govern it by the systematic use of fear and repression. A Reign of Terror was about to begin.

For some time Adrienne did not feel the weight of the heavy hand that lay over her. There was no appreciable change in her situation. Moreover, she was completely absorbed by a letter that had come into her possession, a letter

written in Gilbert's familiar pointed script. The old longing
to be with him flared up again and seared her.

*   *   *

That she should hear from her husband at all after
eight months of silence was due to the efforts of Gouverneur
Morris. The American minister had at last bestirred himself.
He was visited in Paris by Madame d'Ayen and later by
Louise de Noailles, who told him she had heard that Lafayette and his companions were being all but starved in the
fortress of Madgebourg near Berlin, where they were transferred from Wesel soon after Pauline de Montagu viewed
the fortress on her way to Holland.

Morris did not believe this rumor any more than Short
believed that Lafayette was dead or had gone mad, but he
sent the equivalent of 10,000 *florins* in United States money
to Germany that Lafayette could draw upon for food and
doctor's bills. In making these arrangements, Morris asked
permission from the Prussian War Ministry for Lafayette to
write and receive a few letters, under the supervision of the
commandant of the fortress. In February, Adrienne wrote
via Morris, taking care in this first attempt to communicate
to say nothing that might be censored and to give as rosy a
picture as possible of affairs at Chavaniac.

The news she read so eagerly in June was two months old.
Lafayette, writing like a schoolboy under the coldly critical
eye of a Prussian officer, could not tell her what life was like
in a Prussian prison—and, besides, he did not want to worry
her unnecessarily.

He and his fellow prisoners had been kept, both at Wesel
and Magdebourg, in dark little underground cells infested
with rats and vermin. They had been badly fed and deprived
of sunlight, air, and exercise. All had fallen ill and Lafayette
had had a return of an old pulmonary complaint that twice
before, in happier days, had put him to bed for months at a

time. He admitted to Adrienne that he had not been well but told her that he was taking as good care of himself as possible.

He had been much alone. The only familiar face that Lafayette had seen, except on rare occasions, had been that of his valet, Chavaniac. For an hour each day, Chavaniac was allowed to visit the cell and for an hour the two men from Auvergne would forget their troubles and gossip of their home town and its inhabitants. Lafayette asked Adrienne to go to see Chavaniac's father, the village tailor, and to give him six *louis* that was due him.

She must also tell the parents of Félix Pontonnier, his other employee, that their boy was well. Félix, who was only sixteen, might easily have escaped when the others were taken in Belgium but he had not been willing to desert his patron. When the Prussians learned that Félix had been Lafayette's secretary and could read and write, he, too, was kept in solitary confinement.

Yet another matter that weighed on Lafayette's mind was *La Belle Gabrielle* Plantation and the Negro emancipation scheme for which Adrienne had done so much when they were living in the Rue de Bourbon. He hoped that the workers at *La Belle Gabrielle* had not suffered because of the change of government in France and that Adrienne had been able to do something for them.

He was sorry, he said, that he could write so little and so insipidly. She must know how great a faith he had in her courage and capability and how constantly he thought of her and all at Chavaniac. The very thought that what he wrote might be read in his home gave a lift to his spirit.

"Adieu, dear heart—adieu again. Here is an end to my paper and, Monsieur le Commandant who is watching me write, must find the time long. I embrace you as tenderly as I love you."

There was consolation in those final words, but on Adrienne the total effect of the letter was depressing. It pointed up how little she had been able to accomplish in spite of all her strivings.

The only replies to the many letters she had written was one from the Princesse of Orange—that said nothing—and one from President Washington, telling her as gently as possible that he could do nothing for Lafayette officially though he had sent, through a bank in Holland, a personal gift of money to the prisoner.

As for Adrienne's business affairs at Le Puy, they were still unsatisfactory. Lafayette could not realize how impossible it was for his wife to do anything about their responsibilities at Cayenne or even how difficult it was to set aside six *louis* for the village tailor. Adrienne's resources were almost at an end; all income from Auvergne and Brittany had ceased.

Spurred to a final effort, she sent Monsieur Beauchet, her faithful mail runner, to Gouverneur Morris with a request for a loan of 100,000 *livres,* giving as security all her dower rights in Lafayette's estate for which she had registered a claim at Le Puy. Morris granted her the loan, saying graciously that he was sure the American government would reimburse him if she could not; he began to send her the money a little at a time, with Beauchet as purveyor. Adrienne used what she received to settle her most pressing debts and reserved part to pay the running expenses of the chateau, which had been put on an austerity program.

In the course of her financial negotiations she had to sign many legal documents. It was becoming a common practice for the wives of emigrant Frenchmen to get a civil divorce from their husbands for reasons of business or security, often with the hope of remarriage in the future. The idea was suggested to Adrienne, but she recoiled from it in horror. Even if she had not been the faithful daughter of a church that banned divorce, she would not have stooped to such a subterfuge if the benefit to herself and her children had been ten thousand times greater than it was. Each petition, each statement to which she put her hand began or ended with the proud words—the Wife of Lafayette.

As the summer ran its course, Adrienne scanned the horizon for a way to open, a way out. Several of the Girondin leaders had left Paris to head up revolt in provincial cities —at Toulon, Bordeaux, Lyons, Caen. It seemed for a time as if the rebellion at Lyons might succeed and Adrienne thought that she might be able to get there. But the Committee of Public Safety was waging war as vigorously at home as abroad—and even more ferociously. When the Girondin defense of Lyons failed and the city had fallen, hundreds of its citizens were lined up against its walls to be shot. The Convention decreed that the town itself should be razed and the name of its site changed to Commune-Affranchie.

But somehow, in spite of the dreadful news that filtered into Chavaniac—and none of it was as dreadful as the reality —life went on much as usual in Adrienne's home. She spent much time with her children. She saw that they did their lessons. She read aloud to them as her mother had once read aloud to her and her sisters in a room looking out on the peaceful garden of the Hotel de Noailles.

With Anastasie, Virginie, and George, Adrienne took long walks through the woods and fields surrounding the chateau. Sometimes they would set off with a book and would sit down to read in a spot by a rushing stream where there was a particularly spacious view of what Virginie called "our charming mountains." On Sundays, Adrienne and her children met with the women of the village to recite the rosary and to read the prayers of the Mass that could no longer be celebrated in the Chavaniac church after Father Durif's arrest.

On September 17th, a Law of Suspects was passed, under which all *ci-devant* nobles and relatives of émigrés could be confined in "Houses of Detention" to be set up in the principal town of each district. Adrienne was alarmed at first not so much for herself as for those of her family who were still in Paris.

The previous autumn, Rosalie de Grammont and her husband had gone to an estate they owned at Villersexel in Franche Comté; and in the spring the Duc d'Ayen returned to Switzerland. The Duchess and Louise had stayed on at St. Germain, though Louise's husband, Louis de Noailles, who had escaped from the country and was in England, urged his wife to join him there. But Louise did not want to leave her mother alone. For a time they both thought of coming to Chavaniac and had even gotten their passports when the Duc Maréchal de Noailles, Adrienne's grandfather, fell seriously ill and they felt that they must stay to be near him. When he died in August, there was his widow, the old Maréchale, to be nursed. Only a few days before the decree of September 17th, they all returned to Paris, were visited by the police, and were put under house arrest in the Rue St. Honoré.

Adrienne learned that the only possible protection from being declared a suspect herself was to get a new card of citizenship, which would have to be examined and countersigned by a special committee in each district. At Aurat, she procured cards for herself and for everyone at the chateau. The Commune offered to write her a special recommendation for civic virtue, but she felt it would be unwise to make any difference between her card and that of Madame de Chavaniac, who had said, with her usual emphasis, that she didn't want to be represented as a loyalist to a government of brigands.

Adrienne took the cards to Brioude and after some difficulty got a visa for all of her servants. There was so much hostility shown, however, so great a reluctance to certify any hireling of the traitor Lafayette, that Adrienne did not even try to present her own card or Madame de Chavaniac's.

A few days later, a member of the Revolutionary Committee arrived to examine all papers at the chateau and to destroy all, as he put it, that were "tainted" to the smallest degree by "feudalism." He was rather surprised to find how indifferent Adrienne was to this procedure and how readily she handed over her keys. He was still at work when, on November 12th, 1793, Adrienne received a notice saying that she would be arrested as a suspect the following day.

She said nothing to her family until the morning came. She softened the announcement by saying that she was sure that she wouldn't be detained very long. All, even the children, realized the seriousness of the situation. The excitement, the high spirits which preceded Adrienne's first arrest had long since evaporated. There were no woods now to which one could fly, no friends to whom one could appeal.

That afternoon the examination of the papers was brought to an end. The commissioner had collected a large pile of yellowed deeds to property and family records. These he loaded into a cart, along with a bust of the late King. He had announced that there would be a Revolutionary fête held in the town that evening and that all its inhabitants should come to dance about the bonfire.

Towards evening the officer who would make the arrest—his name was Granchier—appeared. All the family were gathered, as they had often gathered before, in Adrienne's sitting room. The order was read aloud. Adrienne produced an old card of citizenship. Granchier handed it back to her, saying that it was out-of-date and that it had not been signed by the Brioude committee.

In the silence that followed, Anastasie spoke up, "Citizen, are daughters prevented from going to prison with their mother?"

"Yes, Mademoiselle."

Anastasie, cheeks flaming, tears brimming her eyes, insisted that though she was not to be sixteen until next July, she was in her sixteenth year. She was therefore an adult and a suspect. She should be included under the law that affected Adrienne.

Granchier seemed embarrassed. Perhaps his embarrassment was ideological; one of the declared aims of the revolution was to restore private virtue and the sanctity of the home, yet here he was separating a mother from her children. Or perhaps, being a family man himself, Anastasie's agonized insistence had caught him off his guard. Ignoring the girl, Granchier changed the subject to some other arrests he had already made in the district. The women were all to be taken to Brioude, he said. They had been rounded up from far and wide and some of them were to sleep tonight in the church at Aurat. He would spare Adrienne that discomfort. She could spend her last night at home if she would promise to come to Aurat in the morning.

When darkness had fallen, those who looked out of the high windows of the chateau saw no bonfire light and heard no throb of music in the village. The Revolutionary revel was a complete failure. Adrienne's neighbors had heard of her arrest and out of sympathy stayed at home with their doors closed. Lacking an audience, the cart and its contents was moved on to another, more receptive, village.

The next morning at nine o'clock, Adrienne drove with her children to the church at Aurat. There she said goodbye to them.

CHAPTER XII

Detained

S HE WAS GONE and without her, the chateau was desolate. George and Virginie, with the India-rubber resilience of the very young, went back to their ordinary occupations, but Anastasie grieved and Aunt Chavaniac was sunk deep in sorrow. She and Adrienne might have had differences of opinion, but in all fundamentals they were one and the older woman had come to lean heavily on the younger. There had never been any question as to which of the two was the leader. Too late, Madame de Chavaniac realized the importance to Adrienne of a testimonial from the Commune and asked Dr. Guitandry, the Mayor, to write one for her niece on official Commune paper. All else in Adrienne's behalf she left to Félix Frestel, who was now the active head of the household. "I embrace you all," Lafayette had written, "and Monsieur Frestel too, for he is really one of the family."

After November 13th, George's school work was frequently interrupted because his tutor was often on the road. Frestel went every week on horseback to Brioude with a bundle of clean clothes for Adrienne. A laundry list was neatly sewed to the bundle and on the back of the paper a brief message from home was written. In the same way, Adrienne could send a few words in reply.

In the town, Frestel was able to pick up a little news at second hand. Adrienne was lodged in what had once been a large private dwelling. Meals—for which the inmates were expected to pay—were sent from a tavern across the street and the innkeeper, Madame Pelatan, was a friend of the Lafayettes. Her young daughter, aged thirteen, went in and out of the House of Detention constantly, carrying baskets and kettles of food. She always managed to speak with Adrienne, though sometimes she was shouted at and slapped by the guards for fraternizing with a prisoner.

With the help of Madame Pelatan, Frestel arranged for the Lafayette children to visit their mother more than once —Anastasie first, and later George, then Virginie. They would leave the chateau at night and ride along the dark mountain roads, arriving at Brioude before it was light. The day was spent in hiding at the inn. When it was again dark and all the town was quiet, they were let into the prison by a jailer whom Frestel had bribed. Sometimes they could stay for several hours, but often there was only time for a quick embrace in the dark and a few whispered words, for Adrienne did not have a room to herself. The prison was overcrowded and she and four or five others slept in an alcove, only separated from the corridor by a screen.

Many of the detained persons at Brioude were of the unreconstructed royalist persuasion, people whom Adrienne might have met on her early visits to Chavaniac, but of whom she had seen nothing recently. At first they refused to speak to the wife of Lafayette. She was better received by the less blue-blooded inmates and became particularly friendly with the wife of a Brioude baker, a very religious woman.

Eventually the hostility of the aristocrats disappeared

when they discovered that Adrienne refused to let differences in politics be a bar between them. They were all companions in misfortune here—and there was so much that they could do for one another! Many of the women were old; some were ill. Adrienne acted as nurse and learned to cook for invalids. She arranged to have her meals with a little group of her patients, one of whom was a nun who was almost blind; without their realizing it, she bore the greater part of the expense. With the jailers she got on so well, that she became a spokesman for the prison community and was deputed to ask for favors. In this way, but not without being abused for her pains, she managed to get one of the most seriously sick women moved out of a room where she was sleeping with eleven others.

For a short time, a day in January of 1794, it seemed as if the Brioude prison, full to overflowing though it was, might have another guest. A commissioner came to the chateau to arrest Madame de Chavaniac. She received him with her usual intrepidity but when he read out the order of arrest she suddenly burst into tears. She had been listed as the parent of an émigré, but her only child, her daughter, the little girl who had been almost a sister to Lafayette, had been dead for more than sixteen years.

"Citizen," she sobbed, "I no longer have the happiness of being a mother."

The commissioner withdrew, overawed by her grief and said that, since a mistake had been made and since she was so well along in years, she could stay where she was.

Through her midnight meetings with Frestel and her children, Adrienne was able to get news of her mother and sister in Paris and to keep in touch with her business affairs, which still needed much personal attention. She asked Frestel to do her a favor. Last spring the first parcel of Lafayette real estate, a mill at Langeac, had been put up for auction. Adrienne, who was present, had lodged a protest against the confiscation, and Madame de Chavaniac was able to buy the mill with the claim that Adrienne had registered for her as one of those to whom Lafayette owed a debt. Now other, larger, holdings were to be sold and Adrienne wanted to go— on parole, or guarded, if necessary—to the sale.

Frestel journeyed to Le Puy to beg permission from the authorities. He was given a bad half hour at the municipal building by President Reynaud of the Department Council, a successor to Adrienne's friend de Montfleury, who was now himself under arrest. The request was angrily rejected. Reynaud raged against the Lafayettes. He would like to tear out Lafayette's bowels with his own hands, he said. Adrienne was "the arrogance of the Noailles family personified," and her children were "little serpents that the Republic had nurtured in its bosom."

Frestel came home much shaken and full of gloomy forebodings for the future. He was glad to hear later that Reynaud had been recalled to Paris but that only meant that the man's venom had been shifted to the place where it could do the greater harm.

As long as she was at Brioude, Adrienne might be irked by restraint and lack of privacy but she was in no immediate danger. The threat that hung over her and all others in similar plight was of being taken to Paris and of being called before the Tribunal of the Committee of Public Safety. The fact that she was a woman would be no protection; since the execution of the Queen in October, women were being included in the national blood purge.

The winter dragged to its end and it seemed as if she might have been forgotten. It was lambing time in Auvergne; it would soon be time to take the cattle to the high pastures. Spring was far advanced when, early on a morning at the very end of May, a messenger arrived at Chavaniac to say

that the order had come from Paris. Adrienne—after six
months of detention—was to leave that very day at noon.

Frestel hurriedly collected all the jewelry in the chateau
that had not been sold, the servants contributing their share,
and galloped with it to Brioude. The children were to follow as quickly as they could in a carriage. He found that
Adrienne had been removed from the House of Detention
and was in the common jail. It was a shock to see her in a
cell in which there was nothing but the cot on which she
was lying and some chains stretched out on the floor.

As usual, however, she was in command of herself and of
the situation. She had seen a priest, none other than Father
Durif, who had been arrested again and who was so overcome by grief that he could hardly listen to her confession.
She had likewise seen de Montfleury, another prisoner, and
had asked his advice. Her friends in the House of Detention
were dismayed to hear that she was leaving them, but she
refused to be completely downhearted.

"I am not called before the Revolutionary Tribunal," she
said stoutly. "I am only being transferred."

Oddly enough, the officer who was to take her to Paris, a
Captain of Gendarmerie, was a brother of de Montfleury.
He was so disposed in Adrienne's favor, even before he had
seen her, that he refrained from reading aloud the order of
arrest and merely handed it to her in silence. They should
have left for Paris yesterday, but he had consented to a
twenty-four hour delay so that she could see her family. In
addition to all of this, he had offered to take her in a postchaise instead of an open cart, which was the transportation
that the government provided in such cases. It was to pay
for this journey that Frestel had brought the jewelry with
him from Chavaniac.

He and Adrienne discussed what was the best thing for
him to do and decided that he should follow her as far as
Melun, near Fontainebleau, where Gouverneur Morris had

a summer home. The American Minister would, of course, help them if he could.

Soon the children trooped into the cell—George and Virginie, solemn, frightened, Anastasie crying hysterically. She flung herself on her mother. She would not be left behind, she cried. When Anastasie heard that Frestel was going to Melun she begged so passionately to go with him that Adrienne, seeing how overwrought the girl was, consented. In an instant Anastasie was wild with delight. It was almost as if her mother was not being taken to Paris if she could follow her. She drove off at once to Le Puy to get a traveling permit.

Frestel left also to prepare for his journey. He already had his passport which only needed to be visaed at Aurat. George and Virginie remained alone with their mother. Hitherto she had shielded them as much as possible. Her own childhood had been so sheltered that it had been a surprise to her and her sisters to discover that there was any wickedness, any man-made sorrow, in the world. But her children had been born to be wise before their time.

She knelt down and prayed with them. It was Ascensiontide and she repeated with them the *Veni Sancte Spiritus—Come, Holy Spirit*. She talked very seriously with George about his responsibilities. He was now the man of the family. He must take care of his sisters; he must comfort his Aunt Chavaniac.

At noon, the postchaise and the Captain arrived at the prison. It was time to say goodbye. Adrienne gave the children some last instructions—and then the final instruction, the one that she had saved to the end so that it would make the deepest impression—if she should die, she said, George and his sisters must make every effort to find their father in Germany and to set him free.

When the postchaise had disappeared, George and Virginie went back alone to Chavaniac. Late that night they were joined there by Anastasie. She had had a harrowing experience at Le Puy. At first the door to the municipal building was barred to her. The official whom she finally reached was not the one who had stormed at Frestel, but he was even more vindictive.

He had been writing at his desk when Anastasie came in and did not even look up at her while she poured out her story and begged for the traveling permit. He brushed away a letter that Adrienne had written him and refused to read it; he couldn't be bothered, he said, to lift so much as his little finger for a prisoner who had been summoned to Paris. Looking up at last, seeing that Anastasie was a grown girl, he made an unpleasant comment on her motives in wanting to go to Melun with Frestel and laughed at his own joke.

Anastasie left the room trembling with rage and disgust. She drove back to Aurat where the tutor was waiting for her. The officials there were sympathetic, but they did not dare to give her the permit. Anastasie, in despair, saw Frestel ride away without her, for he couldn't wait a moment longer if he was to catch up with the postchaise before it reached Melun.

When Frestel was having his passport signed, one of the clerks said sourly, "There goes an officious fellow! He wants to defend people who are not worth defending."

"I only hope that I am clever enough to succeed," Frestel shot back at the man who had taunted him. "If I do, I know there are plenty of people—even in this room—who will envy me."

*   *   *

Meanwhile Adrienne and the Captain were on their way to Paris, traveling the same roads, passing through the same towns where two years earlier there had been triumphal arches put up to welcome Lafayette. By the time they drove into Melun, Frestel was riding beside them.

Adrienne was given a day of rest and the opportunity to

write a letter to each of her children which the tutor would take back to Chavaniac after he had seen Gouverneur Morris. Frestel told Adrienne of Anastasie's state of mind when she returned from Le Puy. In the letter to her elder daughter —it was the longest of the three—Adrienne begged Anastasie to stand up to persecution as a Christian should. She should try to forgive her enemies, even the man who had treated her so cruelly and refused her the permit.

The travelers noticed no signs of hostility until they neared the capital. When they passed through Fontainebleau, a mob seemed to rise from the cobblestones and surrounded the postchaise, drumming against its sides with fist and stick and shouting threats. This was a frightening foretaste of what might lie ahead.

Throughout the journey, Adrienne had refrained from saying too much about her misfortunes. She knew that the Captain was sorry for her and did not want to play upon his feelings. Before leaving, she had asked him if there would be any chance of escape during the trip and he had said that there would be none. Now she asked herself what she would do if he should offer to save her. It was not impossible; and he might save himself as well. But there was his brother, de Montfleury, in prison, who would certainly pay the penalty. Would I have the strength to say no, Adrienne wondered.

In the opposite corner of the chaise, the Captain was thinking the same thoughts, but in reverse. He was asking himself what he would do if Adrienne should break down and beg him pitifully to rescue her. He had seen the two pale, frightened children she had whispered to so earnestly at the prison door. Would he risk his brother's life? Or would he refuse?

When they were driving through the suburbs of Paris, they turned to one another and, as if they had read one another's minds, they made a joint confession. Now that it was too late for action, they could speak out.

In the press of city traffic the postchaise passed unnoticed. It headed towards the Rue Pavée and drew up before the gate of a building still under construction that adjoined an even larger one. This was La Petite Force Prison. The Captain, still suffering from a sense of guilt, asked Adrienne if there was anything he could do for her, short of setting her free. She gave him the address of Monsieur Beauchet, who had traveled back and forth so faithfully between Paris and Chavaniac and done so much important business for her. She wanted the Beauchets, man and wife, to know that she was here and if possible to let her mother know.

Before she left Brioude, Adrienne had learned, to her sorrow and consternation, that her mother, her grandmother, and Louise had been taken to the Luxembourg Palace, which was now used as a House of Detention. They, too, were prisoners in all but name.

PART FOUR

June, 1794—January, 1795

CHAPTER XIII

Le Plessis Prison

THE DAY THAT Adrienne arrived in Paris was June 7th, 1794, the 19th of Prairial, Year II of the new Revolutionary calendar. On the 20th of Prairial, the Fête of the Supreme Being would be celebrated in the garden of the Tuileries— the Jardin National, as it was now called.

A large amphitheater, designed by the painter David, had been constructed. There would be music; there would be a procession of girls, dressed in white, carrying armfuls of roses. At the climax of the day's program, the members of the Paris Convention would appear on the palace steps and Robespierre, its President, the dictator now of France, daintily dressed in sky blue coat, silver waistcoat, and golden shoe buckles, would make a speech and set fire to dummy figures of Atheism, Discord, and Selfishness, while the crowd chanted a newly-composed anthem:

> "Thy temple is on the mountains, in
> the winds and on the waves.
> Thou hast no past, no future . . ."

In preparation for the Fête, the streets through which Adrienne rode were decorated with green boughs and in prison
coutryards throughout the city, wreaths of laurel were being
manufactured.

In Le Plessis Prison in the Rue St. Jacques, across the river
from La Force, a white-haired, aristocratic lady, who thought
that all this fanfare for a new religion was foolishness and
wicked impiety, slipped quietly away from the wreath-
making and went upstairs to her room. She was the Duchesse
de Duras, a daughter of the Duc de Mouchy, Adrienne's
great-uncle. She was also a sister of Louis de Noailles, who
had married Adrienne's sister, Louise. According to the complicated relationships that existed within the Noailles clan,
she was a relative of Adrienne by marriage as well as by birth.

Madame de Duras, who was separated from her husband
and whose only son had escaped to England, had been living
quietly in the country with her father and mother when she
was arrested in August of 1793. She had spent several months
at Beauvais and Chantilly before being brought, in April,
to Le Plessis, which housed seventeen hundred "detained
persons" and which had been a boys boarding school, the
same school where Lafayette was a pupil when his guardians
were arranging his marriage with the daughter of the Duc
d'Ayen. Madame de Duras recognized familiar names—names
of men whom she knew well—scribbled up, schoolboy fashion, on the walls of her new home.

By this time, she was a seasoned prisoner. Only occasionally did she allow herself to think how splendid and luxuri-
ous life had been in the past, though she was sometimes close
to tears when she looked out of the window and saw the
roofs of the great houses in which she had been a guest and
the spires of churches in which she had worshipped. Most
of the time now, she thought of food, of the small amount of
money she had managed to conceal, of the little comforts
she might buy from her greedy jailers. Each day had its prob-

lems and to her, the future was a blank. She had a stoic conviction, not untinged with pride, that all of her caste were
doomed to destruction. A law had just been passed that
"enemies of the people," a term that could be loosely inter-
preted, were liable for the death penalty and could be tried
without counsel. Each night when she said her prayers, Madame de Duras included her own name in the prayers for the
dying; she had said them so often that she knew them by
heart.

Life in Le Plessis was disgusting and chaotic. The company was mixed; not all here were political suspects. Street-
walkers and nuns, pickpockets and duchesses shared the
same bedrooms and scrambled for food at the bare board
tables in the refectory which were never scrubbed and smelt
horribly of grease and stale wine. There was squalor in Le
Plessis, but, though there was much brutality, it was haphazard and unsystematic. The prisoners were locked in at
night; they sometimes had to stand at attention for hours at
the doors of their cells while they were being counted and
they were forced out into the courtyard daily, rain or shine,
for exercise. Except for these inconveniences they could do
very much as they pleased during the daylight hours.

There was much visiting back and forth. Games of picquet
and chess were played, musical groups were formed. Madame
de Duras, who was not sociably inclined, regretted that she
had so little uninterrupted time for reading. Before leaving
Chantilly, she had stuffed the pockets of her voluminous
skirts with books.

Some were books of devotion—well-worn and well-
thumbed. Madame de Duras, for one, could never forget that
this horrible place might be the anti-chamber to sudden
death. A dozen times a day, when a guard appeared—and
they were constantly in and out of the cells on one pretext or
another—she thought that her last hour had come. She was
determined to meet her hour as a Noailles should. She was

so impassive, so unemotional, that one of the jailers paid her a sincere compliment. "You would make a fine appearance on the scaffold," he said.

"I certainly hope so," she answered proudly.

She had decided that if she were brought before the Tribunal she would answer no questions. If she were condemned, she would say, "You have sentenced to death an innocent woman. As a Christian, I forgive you—but you in turn will be judged by a God of Vengeance!"

Though in the old days Madame de Duras would have gone a long way round to avoid meeting a condemned man on his way to the gallows, she now ran to the window whenever she heard the creaking of wheels in the street and the opening of the outer gate of the prison, which announced the arrival or departure of a fresh batch of prisoners. One day, a fortnight after the Fête of the Supreme Being, a convoy arrived from La Petite Force. Madame de Duras, looking down, recognized a familiar face in the crowd that was being hustled into the courtyard of the prison. It was the face of her cousin, Adrienne de Lafayette, the sister of her sister-in-law, Louise. They had not met for several years. Madame de Duras, whose mother had been chief lady in waiting to Marie Antoinette, was of the court party and had firmly turned her back on the radical Lafayettes.

As soon as the newcomers were enrolled at the office and were allowed to mingle with the other inmates, Madame de Duras hurried to find her cousin, to embrace and kiss her as affectionately as if they had parted only yesterday after a harmonious family dinner party.

The older woman—and the senior captive—took the younger under her wing and inducted her into the ways of Le Plessis. Madame de Duras felt that Adrienne, who had led so pure a life in a society where there was much philandering, needed her protection. She herself had gone to great pains and some expense to get a tiny single room on the fifth

floor of the building where she would not have to listen to
the loud-mouthed quarrels, the moans and nightmare mut-
terings of fellow sleepers. She did the same for Adrienne,
though the room was a mere cubbyhole, just large enough
for a cot and nothing else.

During the day the cousins were often together. Unlike
though they were in temperament—there was little warmth
and little magnetism in Madame de Duras' make-up—they
shared a common background and a common anxiety for
their relatives in the Luxembourg, only a few blocks from
Le Plessis.

Adrienne's mother, sister, and grandmother had only been
there since the end of April, but her cousin's parents had
been there all the winter. The Duc and Duchesse de Mouchy
were arrested in October and Madame de Duras had asked
to be brought to Paris from Chantilly, thinking that she
might be with them. During the past months much of her
little hoard of money had been spent in corresponding with
the Luxembourg. Letters could be despatched and received
through the prison office—but at a price.

On the whole, the news from day to day had been better
than one could expect. The Duke and Duchess were old and
ailing and had never completely recovered from the shock
of being separated from their child, but they were not too
uncomfortable in their present quarters. They were familiar
with the Luxembourg. The Duchess had, in fact, been born
there, her mother having been lady in waiting to a royal
princess in the days of Louis XIV.

A devoted servant, Madame Latour, had followed her
master and mistress to the prison, served their meals, which
were sent in from the Hotel de Mouchy, and helped them to
dress in the morning—something they had never learned to
do for themselves. A daily programme was followed, similar
to the routine to which they were accustomed. In the morn-

ing the Duke and his wife took a slow-paced walk in the courtyard or the corridors while their room was being tidied; after dinner they played cards and "received" their friends; in the evenings they read the newspaper, though Madame Latour would sometimes hide it if she saw that there was anything in it that might distress them.

They had been disturbed when their Noailles relatives arrived in April and were given the room above them, for the old Duchesse Maréchale de Noailles, the de Mouchys' sister-in-law, was eccentric, to say the least. She had once stolen a holy relic from a church and had corresponded, so she thought, with the Blessed Virgin, whom she called "that little *bourgeoise* of Nazareth." The Duke feared that the Maréchale might commit some fatal indiscretion.

Shortly before Adrienne came to Le Plessis, Madame de Duras learned that a great calamity had befallen her parents; their beloved Latour, who was so indispensable to them, had been ordered to pack her belongings and to leave the prison. Madame de Duras saw in this a very evil omen.

There was still more disturbing news on June 26th, two days after Adrienne's arrival. Madame de Duras received a note from her father, saying that her mother had had a violent attack of indigestion in the night. He had done what he could for her, neighbors had helped, and one of them, a doctor, had prescribed a few grains of emetic with good result, but the patient was still very weak. He would certainly write to his daughter again the following day. He ended, as always, "We embrace you and love you, my dear child, very tenderly."

On the following day, Madame de Duras repeatedly went down the five long flights of stairs from her room to the office on the ground floor to ask for a letter, but always in vain. It grew late. She was told that no more mail would come that day. She sought out some women who had husbands at the Luxembourg and who heard from them regularly. She asked

them if they could tell her anything about her father and
mother, the Duc and Duchesse de Mouchy. Some said no.
Some seemed embarrassed and evasive.

All evening she could talk of nothing else to her companions and noticed how they withdrew from her, almost as if
they were frightened. "They are hiding something from me,"
she said to Adrienne. "I can guess what all of you are trying
to keep secret. Cousin, you will have some dreadful news to
tell me tomorrow."

Early next morning, as soon as she was let out of her room,
Adrienne went to Madame de Duras' door. She had been
selected as the one to tell her cousin that there had been no
letter yesterday because the old people had been taken to
the Conciergerie before the Duke had had a chance to write.
At the Conciergerie, prisoners spent but a single night before appearing at the bar of the Tribunal in the Hotel de
Ville.

The de Mouchys had been accused, among many other
crimes against the state, of having caused the massacre in
the Champ de Mars on July 17th, 1791. After three years of
uncounted, immeasurable bloodshed, the memory of the
day when Lafayette had ordered his men to fire on the crowd
about the Altar of Liberty still rankled and could be used
to deadly effect. No defense being allowed to the accused,
Madame de Duras' parents were executed within a few
hours.

Adrienne, who knew only that they were gone, did not
need to speak. One look at her sorrowful face was enough.
Madame de Duras' iron composure was broken. She asked
in a voice strangled by sobs to be left alone. For several days
she did not leave her room and only came out at last to pay
a visit of condolence on one of her neighbors, who, she
learned, had just lost her husband and her sixteen-year-old
son.

*   *   *

For the tempo of executions was quickening now. The Terror, which had been adopted as a policy to enforce obedience to the state, had become an end in itself, while the state had dwindled to the will of a single individual. Sixty persons were being put to death daily at the Barrière de Trône outside the city walls. Daily, prisoners disappeared from Le Plessis. No sooner had they gone than their beds in the dormitories were filled by fresh arrivals and the jailers, who always snatched up the few belongings that were left behind, did a brisk business in selling to newcomers.

Under pressure of despair, a few took what seemed to them the easiest, the least painful exit. In the portion of the prison where the men were kept segregated from the women, a man summoned to the Conciergerie stabbed himself and was carried out, still living, on a litter. One day when Adrienne and Madame de Duras were in the refectory, a young woman leaped out of an unbarred window to her death in the courtyard. But these were isolated cases. There was a tendency among the survivors—Madame de Duras, the fatalist, had noticed it—to discover reasons why one should escape and another be taken.

It was in this way that Adrienne tried to persuade herself that her mother, sister, and grandmother would be overlooked. Her great-uncle, the Duc de Mouchy, had been a Marshal of France and had held many important offices; the Duchess also had been closely identified with the Queen. None of the three Noailles women now left in the Luxembourg had been in any way prominent. The Maréchale was old and senile. Madame d'Ayen had always led a very retired life, seldom going to Versailles, devoting herself entirely to her children and her grandchildren. And Louise—how could anyone think that Louise, with her angelic face and gentle ways, was capable of the sinister political plotting that was now being used as the most common accusation?

Though she had always been able to face up to reality, as

far as it affected herself, without flinching, Adrienne continued to hope, though Madame de Duras gave her no encouragement. Several weeks passed. On July 22nd a rumor—one never knew where these rumors originated—began to circulate in the prison that some members of the Noailles family had been guillotined. Madame de Duras heard it first and kept it to herself. She questioned the jailers, but they were unusually reticent. Newspapers seldom penetrated to Le Plessis, but one came her way; in it was a brief notice saying the Duchesse Maréchale de Noailles and the Duchesse d'Ayen had been executed.

It might not be true, however; one couldn't believe everything that was printed nowadays. Madame de Duras used some of her little supply of *assignats* to bribe a jailer to go to the Luxembourg to make inquiries. He brought back word that confirmed the newspaper item. Louise, of whom no mention had been made, was also dead.

Still Madame de Duras hesitated to say anything to Adrienne. Her cousin had been so kind to her in her own bereavement, and so kind to others, that she shrank from telling her. She, too, had been deeply attached to Louise, who, being so much younger than she, she had looked upon almost as a daughter.

Again it was the embarrassment and silence of others that forewarned the victim. Adrienne, alarmed at last, finding that people looked away when she spoke to them, came running to Madame de Duras with a direct question—"they are dead?" Again Madame de Duras could not speak for her tears.

CHAPTER XIV

Outside the Walls of the City

IT WAS NOT UNTIL many weeks, and even months, later that Adrienne learned the pitiful details from two persons who were close to her mother and sister during their last hours.

When in April the three women were told that they must go to the Luxembourg they were not very much alarmed. During their house arrest in the Hotel de Noailles they had become used to never going out, to being visited only by a few intimate friends, among whom was a priest, Father Carrichon, who came regularly to see the old Duchess and sometimes stayed to dinner. Their chief concern was leaving behind them Louise's three children, Alexis, Alfred, and Euphémie. Euphémie, who was only four-years-old, was sent to board with a Madame Thibaut who lived at Saint Mandé on the edge of the Bois de Vincennes. The boys would go back to the house of their grandfather, the Duc de Mouchy, in the Rue de l'Université and live in the suite of rooms formerly occupied by their father. They would be cared for by their tutor, Monsieur Grelet.

Monsieur Grelet was only twenty-three-years-old, a lay brother of a monastic order. He had been teacher of the youngest class in the Oratory School that the boys had attended. Grelet had shared what little money he had with the family, which had been living for some time past on what could be realized by selling jewelry and knickknacks. Louise was so grateful to this generous and devoted young man that she had adopted him spiritually—if not legally—as her eldest son, and the many letters she wrote to him after leaving home began with the words, "my dear child."

Twice a day a basket of food was brought from the Hotel de Mouchy to the Luxembourg and this was the means of carrying on the correspondence. Louise was busy from morning to night with house cleaning, making beds, washing dishes, and caring for her two elderly companions. She asked for brooms, cooking utensils, and screens to be sent from home to make their room more livable. One of her commissions for Grelet was for two ear trumpets; both her mother and grandmother were deaf and she had to shout so loudly to make them hear that she was afraid she was annoying her next door neighbors. The old Maréchale, always notional and flighty, was a difficult patient. At night Louise tied one end of a string to her own arm, the other to her grandmother's bed so that she would be sure to wake if the old lady was restless and needed attention.

When the food basket arrived, Louise would hastily scribble a note for Grelet or Alexis. She told the boys to be sure to speak of her to Euphémie when they went, as they often did, to Saint Mandé; Euphémie was so young that she might forget her mother.

Louise was anxious, she begged for news, when Alfred was sick for several days in May. The boys must work hard at their lessons, she wrote, but they must also be out-of-doors often in the fresh air. They came sometimes to play in the Luxembourg gardens and she told them that she would be looking out of a friend's window to see them. If they caught sight of her, they must be careful not to wave or to show any sign of excitement, for someone—a guard—might be watching.

After the death of the Duc and Duchesse de Mouchy, Louise asked for a white dress, the only mourning she could wear for her husband's parents. Her own death, she realized, might be near and she confided to Grelet how earnestly she struggled to accept the will of God. Sometimes she was frozen with terror of what might lie ahead and was humiliated to find how tenaciously she clung "to this unhappy earth," in spite of all its sorrows. She wrote a will and a letter to her husband telling him that it was her last wish that the boys and also Euphémie should remain under Grelet's care. She wrote also to Alexis, telling him that some day he must tell his father how much they owed to the tutor. To Grelet himself she wrote, "You are my only, but my abundant, consolation on this earth."

On the evening of July 21st, Grelet was walking towards the Luxembourg, carrying a bundle of things that Louise had asked him to bring her. When he came in sight of the prison, he saw from far off that a large crowd was gathered around the gate. He left his package in a shop in the Rue Tournon so as not to be too conspicuous. As he drew nearer, he saw that there was a big open wagon with seats down the two sides, standing in front of the prison. The crowd had gathered to see some prisoners taken to the Conciergerie. Grelet had seen such sights before unmoved, but this time he felt a dreadful premonition.

He pushed through the crowd to get as close to the gate as possible. A wicket swung open and the doorman, who knew him by sight and knew his errand, looked out and waved him away. "Be off with you," he said. "They're in for it."

Grelet ducked back into the crowd and waited until the

doorman had disappeared before trying to edge closer. In a few moments, the gate itself was opened and the prisoners began to file out, preceded by two guards. Louise de Noailles was the first woman to appear. She passed so close to Grelet that she was able to take his hand and squeeze it affectionately. Grelet was aware that a guard was watching them. Louise was helped into the wagon; her mother and grandmother came next, followed by a dozen or more men and women.

For some time the wagon stood still and Louise, looking at the tutor, clasped her hands and bowed her head, her lips moving in prayer. She gestured a benediction—and then three more for Alexis, Alfred, and Euphémie. Her mother also saw Grelet and raised her hand several times to her lips to symbolize a kiss. All this pantomime was not lost upon the crowd. People began to look about them to see who was being signaled. Grelet stared stolidly ahead of him. When at last the procession began to move, he plodded close beside the wagon.

They were crossing the Pont Neuf when Grelet, still close to Louise, heard a shout behind him: "I arrest you! You there—I know you!" It was the guard who had seen Louise clasp his hand.

Grelet took to his heels and raced down the Quai des Lunettes, the gendarme in pursuit and shouting, "Stop him—stop!"

Grelet turned the corner into the Rue de Harlay and would have won the race if a crowd of workmen had not just then begun to pour out into the street from a factory. Several tried to stop the fugitive but Grelet slashed at them with his cane. He was almost out of the crowd and could see ahead an empty street where the going would be good when he stumbled and went down with two men on top of him.

The gendarme pounded up. "He was communicating with a prisoner," he panted.

A few minutes later, Grelet found himself walking into a police station near the Conciergerie. Just before the door closed on him, he saw the van from the Luxembourg discharging its freight at the prison door.

Grelet was pushed into a dark little cell and for several precious moments was alone. He had time to get some papers out of his pocket, tear them to pieces, chew them to a pulp and swallow what he could of the sticky lump. When the jailer returned, the prisoner was asked for the card of identity that all citizens of Paris were supposed to carry, giving name, address, and occupation.

Grelet handed over his card. "Let me tell you how it happened," he said.

He told the guard what was almost, but not quite, the truth; he had been near the Luxembourg by chance when the prisoners were coming out, and one of them recognized him and took his hand—that was all, not a single word had passed between them.

The man listened impassively and went away with the card. He was gone for a very long time, so long that Grelet could picture—with anguish—a squad of police knocking at the door of the Hotel de Mouchy and ransacking it from top to bottom. There were letters, including all the correspondence with Louise, hidden in the rooms that Grelet occupied with the children. He had told Alexis where they were and to destroy them if any strange men came to the house while he was away. But Alexis might not have had time; the child ought to be in bed and asleep at this hour. Grelet realized that his very life might depend on the quick thinking and prompt action of a boy who was only eleven-years-old.

After what seemed an endless wait—it had been several hours—the guard returned. "Here's your card," he said gruffly. "Now get out. And the next time don't stand so close to a prisoner."

Grelet took his card and cane and, as he went out into the

night, felt a brief moment of absolute happiness. Then he remembered the three women whom he had last seen vanishing into the Conciergerie. They must have seen him dash away with the gendarme running after him. He hoped that it would be some comfort to them to know that he had escaped and that the children were not left unprotected.

It was eleven o'clock when Grelet reached the Hotel de Mouchy. All was peaceful there, though the two little boys were still wide awake. They were full of questions. They told him how frightened they were when he didn't come home at his usual time.

Grelet said that he had had a lot of business to attend to and had been detained. He couldn't tell them about it now because it was so late, but tomorrow he would surely tell them. This seemed to satisfy the boys. After the tutor had heard them say their prayers, he put them to bed.

Very early the next morning, at six o'clock, Grelet woke the children and said that they were going to spend the day in the country. They would go to Saint Mandé to see their sister Euphémie. On the way they would call on Father Carrichon.

*   *   *

Father Carrichon, the priest who had visited Louise and her mother while they were still under house arrest, had made a promise that he hoped—and at the time believed—he would never have to fulfill. He was talking with them of the executions that were becoming more and more frequent, of the need to be prepared for death, since no one, apparently, was safe. "If you should ever go to the guillotine," Father Carrichon said, "I—God helping me—would go with you."

They took him at his word and several times thereafter reminded him that he had agreed to be with them at the end and to give them Absolution.

On the morning of July 22nd, the priest was just about to

go out on an errand when there came a knock at his door. He opened to find Madame de Noailles' two sons and their tutor. The boys seemed to be in high spirits, but the tutor was pale and haggard.

"Let's go into your bedroom," Grelet whispered. "We will leave the children here in the study."

When the door was closed, the tutor sank down in an armchair and covered his face with his hands. "It is all over, Father," he groaned. "The three Noailles ladies are to appear before the Revolutionary Tribunal today. I have come to remind you again of your promise. The boys are going with me to Vincennes to see their sister. When we are in the woods, I will try to prepare their minds a little for this terrible tragedy."

Father Carrichon was horrified. Priest though he was and used to minister to the dying, he shrank from the sight of death—and such a death as this! He thought of the boys in the next room who were looking forward to a day in the country, who could hardly wait to reach the woods; he thought of the baby sister who would not be old enough to understand.

"I'll go," he said. "I'll change my clothes—but what an errand! Please God to give me strength to see it through!"

The boys were skylarking when the priest and Grelet returned to the study. Father Carrichon saw them go off gaily. God have pity on them and on me, he groaned as he took off his cassock and put on a blue coat and a red waistcoat. Nowadays it was unsafe to wear canonicals in the street; he had told the Noailles women when he made them his promise that he would wear a red waistcoat so that they would be sure to recognize him in a crowd.

At two o'clock, very heavy hearted, his head aching violently, Father Carrichon went to the Palais de Justice. The great gate into the courtyard was closed. He questioned a man who was coming out and learned that the Tribunal had only just begun and would be in session for several hours. He went away, did some trivial errands, and drank a cup of coffee at a friend's house to clear his head. At five, he was back at the Palace.

There was still no sign of the court having risen. Father Carrichon wandered restlessly about the building, climbed the steps to the Sainte Chapelle, sat down there a moment, returned to the great hall, and frequently went to listen for any signs of life in the courtyard. He wanted this hour to pass quickly, yet dreaded its end.

At six there was a sound of movement, the opening of heavy doors, the creaking of wagon wheels. The tumbrils were being loaded inside the court and were coming out. In the first were seven women, one of whom was the Maréchale de Noailles. She was dressed in black, her hands were tied behind her. For a moment Father Carrichon thought that the other two, her daughter-in-law and granddaughter, might have been acquitted, but in the last cart to emerge were Louise and her mother.

Louise was dressed in white and looked incredibly young. Instead of being a woman in her middle thirties, she might have been a girl. She was talking to her mother and was looking about her eagerly. Someone close at hand in the crowd said "Look at that young one—how lively she is! See how she is talking to the woman next to her."

Father Carrichon, who knew that Louise was looking for him, could imagine what the two women were saying: *"Maman,* he isn't here!"

"Look again."

"I am looking as hard as I can, *maman*—but he isn't here!"

The carts passed slowly by without Louise once looking in Father Carrichon's direction.

The priest went back into the Palace, hurried through it to a farther door and took a short cut to stand in a conspicuous spot by the entrance to the bridge which led to the right bank of the Seine. The crowd was denser now. Again the procession lumbered by without the priest's being seen, though still Louise was searching for him and on her mother's face was an expression of strained anxiety.

Father Carrichon felt infinitely weary. It was hopeless, he said to himself. She would never see him. The crowd was too great. He longed to give up, to go home—but not without making one last attempt.

Again he took a short cut and reached a spot in the Rue St. Antoine, almost opposite La Force Prison. As he hurried along, the sky began to darken, thunder grumbled in the distance. Just when he had reached his station, the storm broke in a wild gust of wind—flashes of lightning, thunder claps. The rain poured down, and in an instant, the street was swept clean of people except for those who, like the priest, had taken shelter in a doorway.

Now the carts were coming up at a quickened pace. The women in them were buffeted about by the storm; with their hands tied behind them they couldn't protect themselves. The old Maréchale's bonnet was swept back from her face; a lock of her white hair was tossed by the wind.

Just as the last cart drew abreast of him, Father Carrichon stepped out from the doorway and stood, a solitary figure in the downpour. Nobody could miss seeing him now. Louise smiled, as if to say, "At last you are here! We have waited so long." She spoke to her mother and Madame d'Ayen's sad, anxious face brightened.

Marching boldly beside the cart and sometimes hurrying on ahead of it, Father Carrichon looked for a good place in which to carry out the really important part of his promise. As the procession entered the Faubourg Saint Antoine, it slowed at the crossing of two streets. Father Carrichon turned and made a sign to Louise. She and her mother bowed their heads as he pronounced very slowly and distinctly, and with what seemed to him divinely inspired conviction, the entire formula of Absolution.

Almost immediately the storm was over, as though it's work was done, the rain died down to drizzle and then ceased altogether. As they moved through the Faubourg Saint Antoine, one of the most wretched, overpopulated slums of Paris, a crowd again collected and insults were shouted at the rain-soaked, bedraggled women in the carts. The Maréchale was the chief target; her identity was known. "Look at her," someone shouted. "Look at that Maréchale, who used to be so grand, who used to ride in a fine coach! Now she's in the cart like all the rest!"

The last cart, for some reason, passed unnoticed and in it, the two women whom Father Carrichon had soothed and served, rode serenely, a look of peace and contentment on their uplifted faces.

They were nearing the end of their journey. The big open space outside the city wall, which is now the Place de La Nation, was crowded. In its center, the guillotine stood on a raised platform. The executioner and his two assistants were waiting. One of them was a tall, handsome young man, who held between his teeth the stem of a full blown rose.

The carts were unloaded, the prisoners drawn up in two long lines facing the city, with their backs to the scaffold so they could not see it. Again Louise searched for Father Carrichon in the crowd and found him. A man at his elbow said, "That young girl seems happy; she's looking up to heaven, she's praying—but what good will it do her?" As if on afterthought, he muttered something about "rascals" and "bigots." Madame d'Ayen stood with her eyes closed, as if she were praying at the altar and offering a final act of contrition.

The priest longed to go away now. He shifted his position and saw the old grandmother sitting on a block of stone near the steps that led to the scaffold; she was staring ahead of her with vacant eyes. The first to climb the steps was a big, burly, white-haired man who was said to have been a tax collector. The Maréchale was the third victim. When it came her turn it was necessary to cut away the upper part of her dress to bare her throat. The executioner and his men worked quickly and quietly, without exchanging a single word. Each time, after the knife had fallen, the severed head and headless body were thrown down into a cart.

Madame d'Ayen was the tenth to die. The executioner tried to pull her cap off without drawing out the pin that fastened it to her hair and for a moment a grimace of pain distorted her features. Louise came next and suffered the same minor brutality. As she stood there in her white dress, looking so youthful and so innocent, Father Carrichon thought of the virgin martyrs of the early church as pictured by the master painters. She is in Heaven, she is happy now, he said piously to himself, as the abundant stream of blood gushed out and her body went down into the cart.

CHAPTER XV

In the Shadows

ADRIENNE DID NOT KNOW; she could only imagine. She could grasp the fact that her mother and grandmother were dead, but it seemed impossible that she would never see Louise again. For a long time she was absorbed by her grief; it seemed to put a barrier around her. Her faith in God stood firm, but she wondered sometimes if she were not going mad, for strange thoughts crossed her mind. She was glad that her husband and her children were not with her; she felt that in this deeply shadowed hour, even the semblance of human comfort would be more than she could bear.

Like Louise, Adrienne had prepared herself to die. When she felt her strength ebbing she would recite the beginning words of the Credo, "I believe in God, the Father Almighty." The only book to her hand in Le Plessis was a Latin psalter and, although she had never studied Latin, she was so familiar with the liturgy of the church that she could read it without too much difficulty. The psalms, with their somber beauty, their universal expression of man's sense of the divine, she had known intimately since childhood; many of them she could repeat by heart. Coming on them now in a new medium, she found that they had a new poignancy. They spoke to her of virtues she had most admired in her mother and sister, virtues that she coveted for herself and had prayed God to give her.

Like Louise, Adrienne had set down in writing a testament to her religious faith. "I have always lived and I hope with the grace of God to die in the bosom of the Catholic Apostolic and Roman Church," she wrote. "I declare that in the principles of that holy religion I have found my support, in its practices my consolation. I am confident that it will bear me up at the moment of my death. I believe in You, oh my God. I hope for all that You have promised. I put all my trust in the merits of Jesus Christ and in the price of His blood; I wish to liken my life to His, and I unite my suffering to His suffering, my death to His death. . . ."

"With all my heart," she continued, "I pardon my enemies—if I have any—and my persecutors, whoever they may be, and even the persecutors of the one I love. I pray God to heap His bounty upon them and to pardon them, as I have pardoned them. Lord, in praying for my persecutors as sincerely as Your grace inspires me, You will surely not reject my prayers for the one who is so dear to me and You will deal with us according to the magnitude of Your mercies."

To her children, Adrienne gave her most tender blessing, but not to her husband—not openly, at least. Even in this most intimate outpouring, she felt that she should protect him, that she should refer to him only as "the one I love," or "the one who is most dear to me." Since she had been in Paris, his name had never crossed her lips and she could not be sure who might read what she had written after she was gone. That God would deal with Gilbert according to the magnitude of His mercies she could not doubt, for she had never been able to believe in a hell for nonconformists. Those who were doing the Lord's work on this earth would be saved. Surely at the moment of their death God would enlighten them!

In order that nothing should be lacking, however, she incorporated into her testament yet another paragraph in which she spoke of her love for her country, her loyalty to it, that "no persecution, from whatever quarter it may come," could shake. Again she obliquely mentioned Lafayette. In her feelings of patriotism, she said, she had found a model in "someone who is very precious to my heart."

"Oh God, in You have I put my trust," she concluded, "You are all powerful and in the great day of eternity, You will bring us all together to praise You for evermore. In You, in You alone is my hope. Have pity on me, oh my God!"

There was nothing that she could add to these words after Madame de Duras' shattering announcement, except perhaps the thought that following in the footsteps of those she loved might make the end less bitter. Preoccupied, withdrawn into herself, Adrienne paid little attention to what went on around her, though, in the days immediately following her mother's and sister's death, her own fate and the fate of all in Le Plessis was being decided.

Louise, Madame d'Ayen, and the Maréchale had died on July 22nd. On the 27th, the 8th of Thermidor by the new calendar, a fearful sense of uneasiness spread throughout the prison. Something unusual had happened outside there in the city—no one knew exactly what. The prisoners were not allowed to go down to the courtyard. All the wickets that at intervals were set in the passages and on the stairs were closed. Was there to be an indiscriminate massacre, as there had been in the early days of the Revolution? Would the prisoners be lined up against the walls to be shot like the people of Lyons after the city had fallen to the Convention?

On the 9th of Thermidor, cannon roared in the distance. The guards seemed frightened; they whispered excitedly to one another; they looked suspiciously at the prisoners and refused to answer questions. On the following day, the 10th, they returned to normal and were more talkative. The news spread rapidly that there had been another revolution—minor in scope—which had overthrown the dictatorship. Robespierre and twenty-one of his stalwart supporters had been executed as outlaws, without trial. The Terror was at an end!

The change in atmosphere was immediate. People leaned out of the windows of the houses that surrounded Le Plessis and waved joyously to the inmates. Down in the courtyard, there were cheers and hand clapping because a prisoner who had been kept in solitary, whose very existence was unknown to the rest, had come out into the daylight. The same afternoon, a woman was set free. As she went out the gate a great shout of "liberty—liberty" went up and was echoed from room to room, from floor to floor.

During the next few weeks discipline was relaxed, visitors were admitted, and male prisoners, till now severely segregated, were allowed to walk in the courtyard with the women. Madame de Duras was shocked by the talk, the amorous doings, that went on there and offered her room as a refuge to some youthful Carmelite nuns, who were afraid to go down for their daily exercise. She felt that the doom that hung over her and her ilk had not been lifted. Every day people were going out of the prison, but as yet no nobles had been released.

One day, however, as Madame de Duras was reading in her cell, she was surprised by a call from a lawyer who worked for a Paris Deputy, Citizen Legendre, a member of the Committee of Public Safety. He questioned her carefully and said that he might be able to do something for her. Legendre and another deputy would soon come to the prison to review the cases of the prisoners and to set free the ones whom they thought had been falsely charged.

On October 16th, the great gate of the courtyard was thrown wide and the carriage of the two deputies rolled in. It was the first time that any vehicle had been admitted except the carts that had brought and taken away fodder for the guillotine. Two days later, Madame de Duras and Adrienne were summoned to the office.

Just as they were going in one of the deputies looked up from his desk and said severely to the guard, "Take the ex-nobles out of here! It isn't proper that they should be questioned before the worthy *sans culottes*."

It was a bad beginning. When, after a three hour wait, Madame de Duras was called into the room and gave her maiden and married names in answer to the first question, the deputy bounced up and down in his chair with rage.

"Those are terrible names!" he cried. "We can't free this woman! Her case must be referred to the Committee."

The other official—he was the Citizen Legendre of whom Madame de Duras had heard—was less menacing but the prisoner went away feeling that no good would come of the interview.

The next morning, while she was sweeping out her room, her door was pushed open. She was so attuned to disaster that her heart missed a beat, but it was only one of her fellow prisoners. She shouted cheerfully, "You're free!"

Until the jailer appeared with a written order for her release, Madame de Duras refused to believe that this was anything more than a cruel joke. But there was the order in her hand! She swiftly made up her few belongings into two small bundles and went to say goodbye to Adrienne.

For there had been no mercy shown to Adrienne. Her encounter with the deputies had been even more unsatisfactory than her cousin's. She was last of all to be questioned; Legendre was hostile from the outset.

"I bear a grudge against you," he said, with cold ferocity. "I detest your husband, you, and your name!"

"I will always defend my husband," Adrienne replied wearily, "—and there's no crime in a name."

The other deputy said that Lafayette had betrayed his country. Neither he nor Legendre could take the responsibility of judging her. She must send her papers to the Committee.

"Will you take them for me?" Adrienne asked. "There is no one else here to whom I could give them."

The man shook his head.

"When you were surrounded by your aides-de-camp," Legendre growled, "you sang a different tune. You were more insolent then!"

Adrienne realized with dismay, that this might mean that she was being accused, as her mother and Louise had been accused, of taking part in a conspiracy. That evening she wrote a hurried letter, full of blots and erasures, asking the American Minister to France to take her papers, such as they were, to the Committee of Public Safety.

It was not the first letter she had sent out into the world. Numbed though she was, Adrienne had taken immediate advantage of the opportunities to communicate that developed after the 10th of Thermidor, when each outgoing prisoner was laden with messages to friends and relatives of those who were left behind in Le Plessis. Adrienne had written twice to the Minister and had given the letters to Monsieur Grelet, who had come to see her and Madame de Duras, bringing Alexis and Alfred de Noailles with him. Grelet was about to take the boys and Euphémie to their aunt, Rosalie de Grammont in Franche Comté, but Adrienne had thought to interest the Minister in her sister's motherless children, whose father, Louis de Noailles, had fought for America. Her petitions were addressed not to Gouverneur Morris but to his successor in office, Mr. James Monroe, who, the papers announced, had arrived in Paris shortly after the death of Robespierre.

Morris, unpopular though he was with the Jacobins, had served Adrienne well. When Frestel had gone to see him at Melun in June and told him of her danger, he wrote forcibly to the French Commissioner for Foreign Affairs, saying how badly any action against the wife of Lafayette would be viewed in the United States. This letter, no doubt, had saved Adrienne's life. The French Republic, with all of Europe against it, did not want to offend its only ally, feeble and distant though that ally was. During the weeks that she had been in La Petite Force and Le Plessis, Adrienne's dossier may have come often to the top of the pile on the public prosecutor's desk, but if so, it had always been put back again at the bottom.

This she did not know, however, nor did she know that Monroe had been enthusiastically and fraternally received by the Convention and was in a far better position to help her than Morris. Being so newly arrived, he felt that he must move delicately, but through Grelet, he had assured her that he would work unofficially for her freedom and that he was ready to go much farther than that if any serious move was meditated.

Adrienne did not have to wait long for a reply to her latest appeal. A secretary came to take her papers to the Committee and, a few weeks later, on October 27th, 1794, she was removed from Le Plessis to a prison infirmary in the Rue des Amandiers.

*　　　　*　　　　*

Her new place of enforced residence was a small one where the inmates were somewhat better fed and lodged than in Le Plessis. Adrienne found herself the only woman among twenty men, all of whom were French creoles from the West Indies. They had heard of *La Belle Gabrielle* Plantation at

Cayenne and at first, like the aristocrats at Brioude, they showed her great ill will because of the stand she and Lafayette had taken against Negro slavery.

Again, as with the aristocrats, Adrienne won them over by refusing to take offense and by meeting them on the ground of their common humanity and their common misfortune. All of these slave holders came to respect and admire her, as did also the inmates of another House of Detention—the Maison Delmas, in the Rue Notre Dame des Champs—to which she was transferred eight days later. There, her companions were members of the group which was responsible for the terrorist regime. Even with them she was able to live at peace.

One day the jailer told her that there were two people, a man and woman, asking for her at the outer gate of the prison. She hurried downstairs and, in her eagerness, ran across the courtyard to the gate. Beyond it stood a short, erect, slender man who was James Monroe; with him was a dark-haired, beautiful young woman, his wife Elizabeth. In the background, a crowd had collected about a handsome carriage. Carriages were very rare now in Paris. Only officials were able to use them and the fact that the American Minister had come to call on a prisoner in such state was causing just the sensation that Monroe had planned.

Adrienne had not seen an American since the days when there were weekly American dinners at the house in the Rue de Bourbon. She had never met Monroe, but she knew that he had been her husband's friend and comrade-in-arms at the Battle of Brandywine. Her English, never as fluent as her husband's, was in bad repair but she was able to exchange a few words with these friendly people who, with their well-kept clothes and smart equipage, seemed to have stepped out of a remote, an almost forgotten past.

Monroe gave her to understand that her release was certain—and not far off, he hoped. When she was free, she and her family would need help and he suggested that she should draw up a list of the things that her American friends might do for her.

"If I should obtain my liberty," Adrienne wrote—it was still an "if;" she was still a prisoner and could not take it for granted that she would survive—"I make with confidence the following requests . . ." First, she would ask America to care for the future of her son, George Washington Lafayette, who, as his father's heir, shared his father's American citizenship. George, she hoped, might go to America and finish his education in the United States. She would like him to have some sort of business training, or she would like him to enter the American navy. Secondly, she asked her American friends to take charge of her will and a letter to be given to George in case of her death.

Since she was penniless now, there were certain financial obligations that she was unable to meet and that she hoped might be taken care of by the American government. Adrienne had learned how wretchedly things had been going at Chavaniac. The family had at times been dependent for food and fuel on what their neighbors in the village had brought. They were living now on sufferance in the chateau, which had been sold over their heads. At the sale of the house furnishings, Madame de Chavaniac was able to buy her bed and a few necessities, but had had to part with everything else, including the picture of her beloved brother, Lafayette's father.

Adrienne, therefore, asked that the interest on the promissory note that Lafayette had given to his aunt in 1785 and which had caused Adrienne so much concern, so many weary journeys to Le Puy, should be paid. There were also pensions she wished to give various dependents: to her mother's elderly governess, who was here in Paris; to Mademoiselle Marin, her daughters' governess, who had shared all their hardships at Chavaniac.

There were others to whom Adrienne felt that she owed an infinite debt—the Beauchets; her personal maid, Mademoiselle Benjamin, who had insisted on lending her her savings; Mercier, the butler, who had found another place, but who some day might come to want. And there was Félix Frestel; Frestel had left a little library behind him in Paris that had been impounded with the Lafayette belongings in the Hotel de Lafayette. If the books could not be returned to him, Adrienne felt that he should be reimbursed. She also remembered two other of the men servants at Chavaniac and the coachman, Pontonnier, whose son, Félix, had chosen to share Lafayette's prison in Germany.

As the list lengthened, Adrienne's fingers grew numb, for the weather had become very cold. The winter of 1794-1795 was to be remembered as one of the worst that Paris had ever known, only to be compared with the winter of 1788 just before the Revolution. Adrienne had always craved warmth and suffered severely. The water in her room was always frozen. The dining room in which she and her housemates ate was without heat of any sort.

She found unexpected comfort, however, in talking to a carpenter who came to make repairs to the Maison Delmas. The carpenter was Father Carrichon. He had exchanged his disguise of a red waistcoat and a blue coat for a workman's apron and in this way was earning his living. Adrienne could speak to him of her mother and sister and hear what he had to tell—with horror, it was true, but with a welcome release of emotion. She made to Father Carrichon a general Confession, one that covered her entire life and this return to the past drew her mind away from the dreary present.

Meanwhile not only Monroe but other friends were trying to break the deadlock that held her a prisoner. Madame Beauchet, who had come daily to the prison to ask for Adrienne, even when this meant personal risk, was working on the sympathies of a clerk she knew in the Committee of General Safety. He always put her off by vague promises, but at least she learned from him that all the members of the Committee had come around to a favorable view of Adrienne's case—all except her declared enemy, Citizen Legendre.

One day in January, Madame de Duras, who had also been tormented by the cold and was living in an unheated attic, went to see Legendre very early in the morning before he had finished dressing to go to his office. She reminded him that, though she was an aristocrat, he had let her go, saying that she had suffered more than she deserved. Surely her cousin, Madame Lafayette, could make the same claim.

Whether it was this argument, or the early hour, or the sheer weight of Madame de Duras' impressive personality, Legendre promised to do what she asked, and on the 22nd of January, 1795, put his signature to Adrienne's release.

PART FIVE

January, 1795—November, 1795

CHAPTER XVI

Mrs. Motier

PARIS WAS ICEBOUND, the Seine was frozen over, and in all the city there was no place that Adrienne could call home. The two great houses where she had lived, the Hotel de Noailles and the Hotel de Lafayette, stood vacant, their doors and courtyards sealed, their windows shuttered. To neither had she any legal claim, and except for Madame de Duras, shivering in her garret, none of her large family connection was in Paris. Those who were not dead were widely scattered. But an aunt—a very youthful aunt, a half sister of Adrienne's mother—who had married a friend of Lafayette, the Vicomte de Ségur, was living with her husband and children at Chatenay, on the city's outskirts. To Chatenay Adrienne went directly from the house in the Rue Notre Dame des Champs.

She was tenderly welcomed by her relatives and, after months of sorrow, loneliness, and discomfort, she was warmed in body and spirit. The feeling of deadness, of futility, that had oppressed her gradually receded.

The Ségur household was a busy one. The children worked

indoors and, weather permitting, worked in the garden. The Vicomte, a clever man who could turn his hand to anything, was earning a small income by writing skits for the Paris theaters. Adrienne's aunt, only a few years older than she, was gentle and beautiful. She had the same soothing quality that had made Louise de Noailles so universally beloved.

Her oldest daughter, Laure, was the same age as Adrienne's Anastasie and the two girls had been prepared for their First Communion together. Sixteen-year-old Laure was now going through a period of great religious excitement and uncertainty that reminded Adrienne of her own adolescent sufferings in the early days of her marriage. She talked with Laure about her troubles and gave her advice drawn from her own experience, the substance being that faith was a gift from God and that in God's good time the gift would come. The feeling that she was being useful to someone—for Laure responded to her spiritual therapy—gave Adrienne the energy she needed to attack her own difficult practical problems.

There was only one problem really, but it had many contingencies. It was the same problem that she had been unable to solve, that she had had to lay aside when death hung over her—the problem of how to reach her husband. While Adrienne was in Brioude and in Paris, a whole new chapter— she knew it only in outline—had been added to the saga of Lafayette's imprisonment.

The last letter she had received from Gilbert was written in October of the preceding year and reached her while she was in the Brioude House of Detention. It gave an account of improved health and its tone was cheerful. For this there was a reason that could not be given openly in a letter to be scanned and passed upon by the Commandant of Magdebourg.

Lafayette had at last been able to get in touch with the outside world. The American money that Gouverneur Morris had deposited to Lafayette's account was used not only

for food but for financing a secret, uncensored correspondence with friends in Hamburg and London, where many
French Constitutionalists had fled after the Jacobins took
over in August of 1792. The letters were written—with a
toothpick for a pen and with soot mixed with vinegar for
ink—on blank pages torn from books. Lafayette's valet, Chavaniac, who was allowed to spend an hour each day in the
prisoner's cell, bribed one of the garrison soldiers to take the
letters into the town where a resident American sent them
on their way.

In London, the leader of the movement to free Lafayette
was his cousin, the Princesse d'Hénin. She was one of the
intellectual ladies who had fluttered about Lafayette in the
early, pre-Revolutionary phase of his career; some had even
said that she was a rival to Madame de Simiane.

Madame d'Hénin worked for Lafayette with Thomas
Pinckney and others of the Franco-American community in
Britain. Conferences were held with the Prussian and Austrian Ministers, appeals were made to the Prussian King,
and Lafayette's letters, as they now came through, were copied and sent far and wide, some to America. The Whig op-
position in Parliament was inspired to make speeches in
Lafayette's behalf in the House of Commons and motions
were brought, all of which were defeated by the Tories, for
the English to intervene.

On the other hand, much of Lafayette's correspondence
with Hamburg was concerned with an escape plot that for
months kept his hopes and spirits at a high level. They fell
to zero when the plot collapsed and he was transferred to
another Prussian prison at Neisse in Silesia. Lafayette was
again very ill and thought he might be dying. He wrote a
letter of farewell to the Princesse d'Hénin and asked her to
communicate with Adrienne, his children, and his aunt.

Before long he faced a new removal that swept him still
deeper into enemy territory. After four months at Neisse,

from January to May of 1794, Lafayette and the two friends
who had been with him at Magdebourg, César de la Tour
Maubourg and Xavier Bureau de Pusy, were handed over
by the Prussians to Austria and were carried across the frontier. Nothing more was heard from them; for months even
their whereabouts were unknown.

Then, in November, two young men—a German, Dr. Justus Erich Bollmann and an American, Francis Huger of
South Carolina—had made a daring attempt to rescue Lafayette from his prison and came within an ace of succeeding.
Failure though it was, this exploit advertised the fact that
Lafayette, de Maubourg, and de Pusy were at Olmütz in
Moravia, a three days' journey to the east of Vienna, near the
foothills of the Carpathian Mountains. A much longer faring
lay ahead of Adrienne than she had imagined and tried to
encompass two years ago.

Adrienne's first move was to go to call on the Monroes and
to thank them for their services. She told Monroe what she
intended; to go to Vienna and beg the Austrian Emperor for
permission to live with Lafayette in the prison of Olmütz.
She would take her daughters with her, but she felt she could
neither take George into Austria nor leave him behind in
France. She wanted him to go with Frestel to America to
live under the protection of his namesake, President Washington.

Monroe promised to cooperate in getting her passports
and told her that the United States would stand behind her
financially. A year ago, in March, 1794, Congress had appro-
priated $24,000 dollars in back pay for Lafayette, who in
the past had refused to accept any return for his services as
a Major General in the American army. There was also some
money, untouched as yet, that Washington had sent as a personal gift. That alone would more than cover traveling expenses.

Before she left prison, Adrienne had written to George and Frestel to come to Paris. They arrived within a week after she had gone to stay with the de Ségurs. She did not want to meet them there, for she was afraid that that might bring trouble to the family that sheltered her. She made a rendezvous with them at the house of two elderly spinsters nearby at Chilly, where an old friend, a Dominican priest, had been hiding all during the Terror.

Her meeting with George was ecstatic. "I never thought I could feel such happiness again," she cried as she kissed him and held him close. Other joys might come, but this, the first, had proved that she could meet them more than halfway.

George had changed very much in the months since she had said goodbye to him in the jail at Brioude at the moment of her departure for Paris. He was fifteen now; he was as tall as she was. He had become just the sort of boy that she had always wanted him to be. He didn't want to go to America—there was none of the spark of adventure in the undertaking that had lured his father across the ocean—but he was willing to shoulder his share of the family burdens.

Frestel also offered to fall in with Adrienne's plans, though she knew he would have much preferred to go back to his family in Normandy. She made it plain that it was not George's safety of which she was primarily thinking. In the United States they would have a mission. Just as she once had tried to send them to Thomas Pinckney in London, she was sending them now to persuade George's godfather to take a definite step towards freeing Lafayette.

For the passports, Adrienne could not rely entirely on her American friends. The Vicomte de Ségur introduced her to an influential member of the new Committee of Public Safety, Boissy d'Anglas, who had led the movement to overthrow Robespierre and was anxious to set right all that Robespierre had set wrong. Boissy d'Anglas made out a passport for George under the family name of Motier, which was little known in France, and got his colleagues to sign it without telling them for whom it was intended.

An American businessman in Paris, James Russell, offered to take George with him to Le Havre and put him on board a little vessel bound for Boston. No one on the ship would know the passenger's true name. In Boston, George would go to stay with Mr. Russell's father until Frestel arrived by another ship. When Frestel was there, they would communicate with President Washington, go to Philadelphia, and deliver a letter from Adrienne.

"Monsieur, I send you my son," she wrote. "Although I have not had the consolation of being listened to, nor getting from you the help that I thought most likely to deliver his father from the hands of our enemies . . . still, it is with deep, sincere and undimished confidence that I put my dear child under the protection of the United States. He has long looked upon it as his second country. . . ."

Her wish for George, she said, was that he should lead a very secluded life in America, that he should resume his education, so interrupted during the past three years, and fit himself to become a good American citizen.

Adrienne was moved to speak feelingly of Frestel. "The one who will give you this letter, Monsieur, has been our support, our protector, our comfort, and my son's guide since our misfortunes. I hope that . . . they will never be separated and that some day we will all be reunited in the land of liberty. It is to this generous friend that my children owe the saving of their mother's life. . . . He will tell you that I have given no cause for accusation, no reason for reproach from my country. . . . The supreme sacrifice that this friend has made is leaving a family of his own that he dearly loves. I ardently wish Monsieur Washington to know what he is and how much we are indebted to him. . . .

"I will say nothing now of my own situation, nor of that

of the one that interests me even more than my own. I rely upon the bearer of this letter to interpret the feelings of my heart. . . ."

After the letter had been written and the passports were in order, Adrienne said goodbye to George—an ordeal for her, an even greater ordeal for the boy who had to go so far away among strangers and whose exile would begin with a long sea voyage without even the comfort of Frestel's company.

Adrienne was so afraid that at the last moment she might not be able to part with her son that before George's ship had left Le Havre she had taken the second step towards her goal of Olmütz—she was on her way to Auvergne.

The long, hard winter was over and it was again spring-time as she followed the familiar route south. The fields, the forest, even the towns, showed little sign of the guerrilla battles that had been fought, the fearful toll in lives that the last few years had taken. Again, almost at the end of her journey, Adrienne came to Vaire, the posting stop where—was it only four years ago?—she had met Pauline de Montagu. In the same shabby little inn where Pauline had hidden herself, she found Anastasie and Virginie. She had told them that she was coming. They couldn't wait to see her and had rushed to Vaire. They were hysterical with joy and excitement.

Last summer they had expected everyday to hear that their mother was dead and they had never known when they might be separated from one another. They had been told —cruelly—that Aunt Chavaniac and Anastasie might be taken to the House of Detention at Brioude and that George and Virginie would go to an orphan asylum. But now their mother was here, only a little changed, a little pale and worn after her long ordeal. She promised that she would not leave them again. Wherever she went they would go with her.

It was Saturday when Adrienne arrived. In a few remote places church services were being resumed and she heard that Mass would be celebrated the following day in a small village, Montout, three miles up in the hills from Vaire. Adrienne, Anastasie, and Virginie climbed the steep way to the little church. They knelt together to say prayers of thanksgiving and to witness again the solemn mystery of the Mass performed by a robed priest.

Then on to Chavaniac. Adrienne had allotted herself only a week at the chateau, most of which would be devoted to business. With the money that Monroe had given her, she could make payments to her creditors; she could give a substantial sum to Madame de Chavaniac. When the week was up, it took all of Adrienne's resolution to say goodbye to the old woman and to leave her alone in the dismantled house, brooding on the sorrows of the past and present; on Gilbert, who was a prisoner in Austria; on George, who was a wanderer to the uttermost ends of the earth. Adrienne and the girls—Madame de Chavaniac loved them too—were going very far away. Would she live to see any of them return?

On a May morning, depressed by a leave-taking that seemed so final, Adrienne, Anastasie, and Virginie set off for Paris in a rickety postchaise that could be sold for a song or abandoned at the end of their journey. They had only got as far as Brioude when they met two wayfarers coming toward them on foot, a man and a tiny woman, her odd little face, with its slits of eyes, bronzed by the sun. It took a moment to realize that this was Rosalie de Grammont and her husband, Theodule. They had been for weeks on the road, trudging all the way from Franche Comté to Paris to see Adrienne and, not finding her there, farther still to Auvergne.

This youngest of the daughters of the Duchesse d'Ayen had been the most difficult to manage and to settle in life. Rosalie was stubborn and she was not as comely as her sisters.

She was not married until she was an "old maid" of twenty-
one, having herself refused several offers made to her parents.
She only accepted her present husband after prayer and
saying that she didn't believe that true happiness could be
found upon this earth. In spite of this bleak prelude, the
marriage had been amazingly successful and harmonious.

The de Grammonts had walked their long road because
they had no money to spend on traveling post and were
afraid of the company they might meet in public convey-
ances. They were not as indigent, however, as they seemed.
Rosalie, who had urged Pauline to take her diamonds with
her to England, had some of her own marriage jewelry concealed on her meager person. She wanted to give it to Adrienne. She wanted also to lament with her their common loss.

It was impossible to part after a brief roadside talk. The
de Grammonts turned about and the whole party went on
slowly towards Clermont, taking turns walking and riding
in the chaise. At Clermont they read news in the papers that
halted them for three weeks.

There had been new disorders in Paris, a final effort of the
Jacobins to regain control of the government. Again the
Assembly hall was invaded by an armed mob and one of the
deputies was killed. That day, May 20th, Boissy d'Anglas,
the de Ségurs' friend who had got the passport for George,
was presiding. He respectfully saluted the bleeding head of
his colleague that was held up to him and, though pikes were
at his breast, refused to put the motions that the mob demanded. For a few hours the Jacobins were again in control
until the hall was cleared at bayonet point. There followed
a mopping up period when the insurgents were brutally
liquidated and the Faubourg St. Antoine, the cradle of Paris
mobs, was stripped of all arms by government troops.

When word reached Clermont that order had been re-
stored in the capital, the Lafayettes started again for the
north. Adrienne had used her three weeks in Clermont in

preparing her little Virginie, who was now twelve, for her First Communion. The de Grammonts went on, as they had intended, to Chavaniac. Adrienne did not need Rosalie's diamonds for herself, but there was another use to which they could be put. With them and the money Adrienne had given her, Aunt Chavaniac might be able to buy back the chateau or at least to make the first down payment on the purchase. This would give the lonely soul a motive to survive, a look into the future.

When she reached Paris, Adrienne found that Boissy d'Anglas was the hero of the hour and that this would be a help to her in getting a passport. While Monsieur de Ségur conferred with the Deputy, Adrienne was forced to give all her attention to legal and business matters.

It seemed as if she might some day have some property in her own right. A law had been passed which recognized inheritance from those who had been condemned to death during the Terror. The Duchesse d'Ayen had owned several estates, one in the Pas de Calais, two in Brie at Fontenay and La Grange-Bléneau, about thirty miles from Paris. Adrienne registered a claim for herself and her joint heirs and went to Fontenay and La Grange. She and the girls moved into the empty manor house at Fontenay, which was the nearer to the capital of the two estates.

There were many errands that took her to Paris in the ensuing weeks. The Duchess had left a will, with many charitable bequests, and Adrienne had to find—that is, borrow—the money with which to meet them. There was also some work to be done for Aunt Chavaniac, who had gladly accepted the de Grammonts' loan and had bought back the chateau from its recent owners.

To economize, Adrienne made her frequent trips from Fontenay to the city on foot. She was stronger now and felt equal to any exertion. Along the way, doors of churches stood open. She would slip in out of the hot summer sun and sink down to rest. Though worship was no longer forbidden, the churches were, for the most part, empty. There in the dark and quiet, Adrienne said prayers for her dead and sometimes found relief in weeping for her mother and sister.

But however much else she had to do, her chief aim in going to Paris was to find out if her passport was ready. She was prepared to leave on an hour's notice. At last she was told that the Committee of Public Safety could not give her a passport for Germany and Austria but they could for America. Her American friends suggested that she should leave on a vessel that was America bound, but which would be going first to a German port, Hamburg. There the United States Consul would issue a traveling permit—valid for travel to Austria—to "Mrs. Motier of Hartford, Connecticut," one of the states of the union in which Lafayette had been naturalized.

Adrienne was well-satisfied with this arrangement. On September 8th, the future Mrs. Motier and her daughters, Anastasia and Virginia, found themselves on board a tiny ship, *The Little Cherub,* out of Boston, lying in the harbor of Dunkirk. The night preceding, they had slept at the house of the American consul. Adrienne was writing a letter to Gilbert to send on ahead of her to Olmütz:

"So I am free, my dearest, since here I am on the road that brings me closer to you. The excess of my joy is such that I cannot describe it except by saying that I reproach myself for being still capable of having such a strong feeling after our misfortunes. They will poison the rest of my life, but I feel that the One who could snuff out my life has spared me so that I might find you again. This hope revived me, almost at the foot of the scaffold. . . . It has seemed to me—and the experiences of our three years of captivity come to the support of what I think—that the only one to serve you properly is the one who is yours alone . . ."

On September 9th, *The Little Cherub* lifted its anchor
and, beaten and tossed about by unfavorable winds, took
eight days to round the bulging coast of Holland and to come
to Hamburg. There Adrienne's arrival was being eagerly
awaited by Pauline de Montagu.

CHAPTER XVII

A Nest of Exiles

PAULINE DE MONTAGU in the past four years had led a vagrant life. She had had much to contend with. After the death of her child, Noemi, the disastrous Rhineland campaign, and the flight into Holland—during which she had a brief glimpse of Lafayette's prison—Pauline, her husband, Joachim, and her father-in-law, the Vicomte de Beaune, returned to England.

For a time they lived in a cottage at Richmond, where the Vicomte complained continually of the weather—it was forever raining—and insisted on reading frivolous novels aloud, which serious-minded Pauline found hard to bear. The old gentleman was extravagant also and must have his valet, come what may. Pauline struggled to do the housekeeping and marketing, but in the old days she had never entered a shop and she couldn't remember which sold meat and which vegetables. When she asked Joachim, he couldn't help her.

It was lack of money that sent the family, now augmented by a baby boy who had come to replace the dead Noemi, back to the Continent. By that time, August of 1793, all of

Pauline's diamonds had been sold, hither and yon, and always at a loss; even a pair of gold-handled embroidery scissors had disappeared from her sewing basket.

In Brussels, Joachim went briefly into the secondhand clothing business with a rascally partner—and then the money was gone. Pauline's poor little baby died. In their distress, the parents didn't know where to turn. At this moment, a letter arrived from Switzerland, from Pauline's aunt, the Comtesse de Tessé, a sister of the Duc d'Ayen, asking her to come for a visit. Madame de Tessé had also sent her niece a handsome gold snuff box to pay for the journey.

It seemed hard to part—Joachim had not been included in the invitation—but the de Montagus decided that Pauline should go to her aunt at Lowemberg and Joachim and his father would go to Constance, where some relatives of Joachim's mother would welcome them.

At Lowemberg, Pauline was far from happy. The Comtesse de Tessé was one of the eccentrics of the Noailles family. Very pretty as a young woman, she had lost her good looks after an attack of smallpox. This was a good thing, she stoutly declared, because it had forced her to sharpen her wits and develop her mind. Her face was deeply pitted; she had a ridiculous habit, nervous in origin, of making faces as she talked.

And she was a mighty talker. Before the Revolution, only the most advanced ideas had been discussed in her Paris salon. Madame de Tessé had a taste for metaphysics; she was a free thinker and an agnostic, a former friend and disciple of Voltaire. This did not prevent her, however, from making the sign of the cross whenever she took a dose of medicine.

In action, Madame de Tessé had proved to be more canny than the rest of her family. When she emigrated from France, she took with her a considerable sum of money and many portable valuables, such as the gold snuff box. Instead of consuming her hoard, bit by bit, she bought a dairy farm in Switzerland which produced enough food to feed herself and the large number of unfortunates she had taken under her wing.

One of her guests was the Marquis de Mun, an old admirer, a dashing cavalier in his day, whose chief function now was to talk wittily—and sometimes profoundly and philosophically—with his hostess. Pauline was distressed and bewildered by the daring opinions that were tossed back and forth in Madame de Tessé's drawing room. She would sit, quietly sewing in one corner of the salon, and take as little part in the conversation as her elderly uncle, the Comte de Tessé, who long ago had given up trying to compete with his wife on an intellectual plane. Pauline tried to make herself useful, but except for her skill with the needle she was feckless, and when given the task of weeding and watering the vegetable garden raised a fine crop of thistles.

When summer came, Pauline wanted to see her father, the Duke, who was also in Switzerland in the Canton of Vaud, not far from Lauzanne. She set out on July 26th, squired by another of Madame de Tessé's protegés, the son of the Marquis de Mun. This gay young man liked to tease Pauline, whose sense of humor was not robust, but today he tried to amuse her by stopping to pick her a bunch of flowers in the forest and singing her a burlesque ditty which he made up as they drove along. But Pauline, though she tried to show her appreciation, was sad. She had heard recently of the death of the Duc and Duchesse de Mouchy and had a premonition that this meeting with her father would be sorrowful.

Early on the second day of their journey, they saw a two-wheeled trap coming towards them, in it an elderly man holding a large green umbrella over his head to shade him from the sun. Pauline did not recognize her father immediately. The Duke had aged; on his face was a tragic look.

When the carriages were abreast, he called out to ask if she had heard any news.

News—what news? Pauline was so frightened that she leaped impulsively out of the carriage and ran towards her father. He helped her into the trap and told young de Mun to turn around and drive back to the inn where they had spent the night. He and Pauline would follow.

While they were on the road the Duke was silent. He asked Pauline not to question him until they were alone. When they were closeted in a room at the inn, he told her first of her grandmother's death, then of her mother's and her sister's. The news of what had happened only five days earlier at the Barrière du Trône in Paris had traveled fast to Switzerland.

Pauline had begun to tremble even before he began his recital. She flung herself into his arms and wept on his shoulder. She had always stood in awe of him, she and her sisters having realized, with no word spoken, that, though he respected their mother, he did not love her—and there had never been any question of where their loyalty lay.

Never had he been so tender as now. Though he was not a religious man, he wept too as Pauline recited *The Magnificat,* her mother's favorite portion of the liturgy in time of stress and fell on her knees to repeat the prayers for the dead.

When she was a little more calm, she said that she was ready to go with him to Lausanne, but he thought it better to take her back to Lowemberg. There Madame de Tessé, forewarned by de Mun, fell on her knees before her niece, with arms spread wide to enfold her. All the household showed their compassion by treating Pauline as if she were an invalid, her aunt tiptoeing to her door in the morning to see how she had passed the night. Joachim came hurrying from Constance to comfort her. Masses were said for the Noailles martyrs at Fribourg and in the cathedral at Constance, where Joachim took his wife for a long visit with his relatives.

While Pauline was gone, Madame de Tessé was being persecuted by a Swiss banker, who in the past had lent the Maréchale de Noailles some money. Not content to register a claim on the dead woman's estate, he tried to collect it from her daughter. If the debt had been small, Madame de Tessé would have paid it, but the sum was so large that to do so would mean ruin to her and all who lived on her bounty. The banker threatened court action and Madame de Tessé was sure that the canton, which had shown marked hostility to émigrés, would decide against her. Ever practical, she resolved to sell her farm, shake the dust of Switzerland from her feet, and go to Germany.

On the 1st of January, 1795, the farm having been sold and the proceeds safely deposited with a bank in Hamburg, Madame de Tessé left Lowemberg with her flock. Making leisurely stops at Erfurt, Nuremberg, and Ulm, they came to rest at Altona, just across the river from Hamburg. There Madame de Tessé rented a house while she looked about her for a farm in the neighborhood. She would not be hurried in her choice; for one thing, the new property must have a large enough dwelling on it to accommodate all her non-paying guests.

At Altona, the same sort of life was followed as at Lowemberg, a large part of every day being given up to cards, intellectual readings aloud, and endless, scintillant conversation. Pauline registered her usual silent protest and would slip off frequently by herself to Mass in the one small chapel that existed in this Protestant town. She spent much time in visiting émigrés even poorer than she and in making clothes for them. She was at work on a large wool afghan for a needy priest, the exiled Bishop of Clermont, when she heard that Adrienne was coming to Hamburg with her daughters. The news came indirectly via the Princesse d'Hénin, Lafayette's cousin in London.

The day that the letter arrived, Pauline's knitting was laid aside. She was too nervous, too excited, to sit still. She had heard, of course, of Adrienne's imprisonment and release. She herself had written to Adrienne from Erfurt, warning her that if she left France she should be careful in her dealings with French people she might meet, for, since the Terror, the emigrant aristocrats felt still more bitterly towards Lafayette.

Pauline had thought that Adrienne might be planning to come to Switzerland—but here she was on her way to Hamburg. Why? Was she escaping from a fresh wave of horror at home?

The bond that united the daughters of the Duchesse d'Ayen, the bond that had set Rosalie de Grammont tramping from Franche Comté to Auvergne, was strong, and Pauline longed to see her sister whom she looked up to and admired for the qualities she felt lacking in herself; Adrienne was so brave, so capable, so resolute in action.

At the same time Pauline dreaded the encounter. What things they would have to say to one another! Before she left Switzerland, Pauline had had another visit from her father. From something that he said, she suspected that he was staying in Switzerland because he expected to be married again, to a Countess Golovkin, whom Pauline had met in the course of her wanderings, but whom she barely knew. The knowledge that their mother was to be replaced so soon would make the meeting with Adrienne still more heartbreaking.

The next day, September 17th, Pauline forced herself to take up her knitting, but again the afghan dropped from her fingers as she heard the firing of a cannon, the signal that a foreign ship had entered the harbor of Altona. This was not unusual, but Pauline had another of her strong presentiments; she was sure that Adrienne was on board. She was just about to rush out of the house and down to the waterfront when Madame de Tessé stopped her in the hall and tried to persuade her not to wear herself out unnecessarily. They were still arguing when Adrienne, Anastasie, and Virginie walked into the house.

One look at Adrienne told Pauline that, though her sister had suffered, she had not been broken by her sufferings. She had the old look that Pauline had always thought of as heroic, a look of calm self-possession, of intrepidity. After the first embraces, Madame de Tessé tactfully took her two young nieces by the hand and led them away so that the two sisters could be alone. For a long time they stood looking at one another, unable to speak.

Pauline broke the silence. "Did you see them?" she asked, her breath catching in a sob.

"No," Adrienne said gravely, "I did not have that happiness." As Pauline clung to her, she told a little of what she had heard from Grelet and Father Carrichon.

They couldn't remain alone too long with their sorrow, so intimately shared; they both knew that the others were waiting impatiently to question Adrienne. The talk that afternoon in the salon was not of metaphysics. Adrienne retailed all that had happened to her in the past four years, in Auvergne and in Paris, all that she knew of the conditions that existed in the mother country, where a new constitution had been adopted and a new form of government, consisting of a legislative body and an executive board of five directors, had been instituted. When the question was asked of why she had come to Hamburg, Adrienne replied almost casually, as if it was a matter of course, that she was on her way to Olmütz to live with her husband.

Madame de Tessé and Monsieur de Mun protested loudly and eloquently. She might never reach Olmütz, even if she reached Vienna all sorts of obstacles would face her there. Hadn't she had enough of brutal jailers and stinking, verminous cells? She shouldn't expose herself again—or her daughters—to the hardships of prison life.

Adrienne put aside their arguments gently. She didn't stand in awe of her aunt, or her aunt's elderly gigolo. What they said showed their affection for her, and no lack of consideration for Lafayette. On the contrary, Lafayette was their political hero; Madame de Tessé had been one of his most ardent admirers from the very outset of his career.

Adrienne said that she had foreseen that there would be difficulties, but she thought they could be overcome. While she was talking, Pauline sat close beside her sister on the sofa, looking up at her admiringly and every once in a while putting an arm out to hug her sister close. She would treasure every word that Adrienne said against the time when Adrienne was gone—all too soon.

Adrienne had warned her that her stay at her aunt's house would be only long enough to make preparations for the trip to Austria. She did not try to get in touch with the many friends of Lafayette in Hamburg who had tried to rescue him while he was in Magdebourg, but from the American Consul, Mr. John Parish, whom she went to see immediately about her passport, she got much information.

Recently, only a few weeks earlier, the heroes of the abortive rescue attempt at Olmütz, Dr. Bollmann and the American, Francis Huger, had passed through the town on their way to England after having been prisoners themselves since last November. A year ago, Bollmann, with the backing of Americans in London, had gone to Olmütz. He had gotten in touch with Lafayette through the prison doctor, who was duped into carrying secret messages, written in lemon juice, to and from the fortress.

Somewhat reluctantly, Bollmann had fallen in with a plan of Lafayette's to spirit him away when he was taken for a drive outside the walls of the town, a special concession that had been made to Lafayette's poor health. Bollmann had gone to Vienna to get horses for the adventure and there he had enlisted Huger, a medical student and, by an almost incredible coincidence, the son of the man in whose house Lafayette had stayed when he first landed in America in 1777. Though the plot had misfired and the two young men had been arrested, they were released in August. After his brief taste of freedom—Lafayette had actually mounted a horse and almost reached the frontier—he was closely guarded and nothing had been heard from him.

All of this was of consuming interest to Adrienne. The consul made out a passport for her and her daughters under her new name of Mrs. Motier. Since her real nationality must be kept hidden, she engaged a French servant to go with her as far as Vienna, a man who could speak German and who would attend to all the business of the trip while she remained silent in the background. She also bought, as cheaply as possible, a postchaise and a few necessities.

While she was with Madame de Tessé, Adrienne could not help meeting many of the large colony of émigrés who lived in the vicinity. News traveled fast in this community of exiles; all wanted to see someone who had just come from France. Adrienne could give some of her visitors word of their relatives at home and though most of them, she knew, had gloated over Lafayette's downfall, she showed no resentment. This was an object lesson in Christian forgiveness that was not lost on her two daughters.

Within a week, Adrienne, Anastasie, and Virginie said goodbye to their relatives and left for Vienna.

CHAPTER XVIII

The Canticle of Tobit

They had none of them traveled outside of France before—or so far from home. A whole new world, seen only through the peephole of a carriage window, passed before their eyes. In public they were mum and tried to be as inconspicuous as possible; in the inns along their way they hid themselves behind closed doors. The German-speaking servant was well worth his hire as courier, but there were some anxious moments as they pressed on from posthouse to posthouse, from frontier to frontier of the checkerboard of Central Europe. At last, in mid-October, they reached the beautiful city on the Danube that was the heart and center of the Austrian Empire.

Here, too, they had little chance for sightseeing and tried to avoid attention. One of Adrienne's uncles had been Ambassador at Vienna for many years before the war between France and Austria began in 1792. He had made many Austrian friends. To one of them, a Countess Rumbeck, Adrienne had a letter of introduction.

The Countess was very kind. She advised Adrienne to go

to see Prince von Rosemberg, the Grand Chamberlain of the Austrian court. He, too, had been a friend of the Noailles family.

The Prince was a little puzzled at first to know who this Mrs. Motier of Hartford, Connecticut was and what she wanted. He seemed to be a benevolent old gentleman, however, and when the servant who had let her in was gone, Adrienne revealed her identity and her mission. Von Rosemberg said that he would get her an audience with the Emperor Francis II, without the Emperor's ministers knowing anything of it.

Adrienne, Anastasie, and Virginie went to the great, sprawling jumble of buildings that make up the Hofberg and were led into a room in the inner royal apartments. The Emperor appeared. He was a young man, still in his twenties, a nephew of the slaughtered Marie Antoinette. His manner was coldly polite, but one felt that this was due more to shyness than lack of sympathy. He courteously listened while Adrienne asked very simply and directly for permission to share her husband's captivity.

"I give you my permission," the Emperor said, without any show of surprise; he had been told, apparently, what she would ask. "As for his liberty"—Adrienne had not mentioned liberty—"that would be impossible. His case is very complicated. My hands are tied."

Adrienne, breathless with emotion, murmured her thanks for the great favor he had shown her. She said that the wives of her husband's two friends who were with him at Olmütz, Monsieur de la Tour Maubourg and Monsieur Bureau de Pusy, would envy her.

"They have only to act as you do," the Emperor said, with a stiff little inclination of the head. "I would do the same for them."

Adrienne said tentatively that she had heard there were certain inconveniences in Prussian prisons—she had indeed heard that there were worse than inconveniences at Wesel and Magdebourg! If she found anything wrong at Olmütz and had any requests to make, might she write directly to the Emperor?

"I consent," Francis said, still rigidly polite but obviously anxious to make the interview as brief as possible. "You will find, however, that Monsieur de Lafayette is well-fed and well-treated. I hope you will give me credit for that. Your presence will give him yet another reason for feeling well-satisfied. What is more, you will be pleased with the commanding officer at Olmütz. In the fortress the prisoners are distinguished only by number, but your husband's name is well-known."

As they left the imperial presence, Adrienne was dizzy, reeling with happiness. She wanted to leave Vienna that very day, but she knew that that was impossible. She would have to wait at least a week for the order admitting her to the prison to pass through various hands and for word to be sent ahead of her to Olmütz. She wrote to Hamburg; she wrote to George in America, urging him to ask President Washington to communicate with the Emperor; she wrote also to James Monroe in Paris, telling him that she had arrived safely.

There was a strong temptation to luxuriate in the certainty that she would soon be with Gilbert and to do nothing more herself, but she couldn't forget that her secondary, but none the less cogent, reason for coming to Austria was to work for Lafayette's freedom. She would have to see the Emperor's chief adviser, Baron von Thugut. He was the power behind the throne, she had been told. When the Emperor had said that his hands were tied, he might have been referring to Thugut.

Adrienne did not look forward to the interview. Thugut was unpopular even in Austria and was known to be rabidly anti-French, anti-Revolution, anti-Lafayette. At the moment an exchange was being arranged of certain Jacobin prisoners for the daughter of Louis XVI and Marie Antoinette, who was still in France—the only survivor of the French royal family. It seemed to Adrienne ironic that Lafayette, who had tried to save the lives of the King, the Queen and their children, should be held while those who had voted for the King's death should be set free. But she disdained to use such an argument with Thugut, though before they met she drew up a written statement of the injustice of her husband's imprisonment and presented it to him.

She found the Minister to be as hostile as she had expected. He was a fantastically ugly man, a mixture, someone had said, of Punch and Mephistopheles. He refused to respond to any of her advances, though she tried her best to put a little warmth, a little friendliness into their conversation.

"Surely, Monsieur Thugut," she said, "the coalition lays too much stress on the importance of a single man."

"Too much importance!" Thugut repeated venomously, his ugly face contorted.

She knew that it had been useless to come to see him and was only glad that Prince von Rosemberg had arranged for her to speak with the Emperor first, without the knowledge of his evilly-disposed counselor.

While she was waiting for her permit, Adrienne renewed acquaintance with two women whom she had met formerly in France. Madame d'Ursel and Madame de Windischgratz were relatives of the Comtesse de la Marck, one of the best friends Adrienne had ever made outside of her own family. Both of them were warmhearted and were ready to help her in any way they could. At the end of the week, they invited her to come to their house to meet the Minister of War, Count Ferraris, who would deliver her the permit.

"I think it is my duty to warn you, Madame," the Minister said disapprovingly as he handed her the paper, "that you should think twice before you take this step. You will be very

uncomfortable; life in prison may have some serious conse-
quences for you and your daughters."

Adrienne thanked him mechanically. She had not really
listened to what he was saying. She was only aware that she
was holding the open sesame to Olmütz and that before she
slept that night, she would have left many miles behind her.
In a matter of hours, of minutes, she would be on the last
stage of the journey she had dreamed of for three long years.

*　　　　*　　　　*

The carriage that Adrienne had bought in Hamburg
had broken down before she reached Vienna and she had had
to hire an open wagon to make the three day trip to Olmütz.
She and the girls traveled late and early. As they neared the
end of their route, the rolling country through which they
had been passing flattened out and they entered a wide, fer-
tile plain, which stretched for miles in all directions and
through which flowed a sluggish river. They had moved along
so fast that it was only eleven o'clock in the morning of the
third day when the driver turned around on his seat and
pointed his whip towards the horizon, "Olmütz," he said.
One could see in the distance the outlines of the high wall
that surrounded the city, the tapering points of steeples
pricking up above it.

The vision blurred. Tears filled Adrienne's eyes and rolled
down her cheeks as she began to recite one of her best loved
canticles, the prayer of the blind patriarch from *The Book
of Tobit,* that romantic tale of a journey, a miraculous marriage, and heavenly guidance. When each of her daughters
married, Henriette d'Ayen had read them the words that the
old Tobias spoke in praise of God after he had heard the
wonders that accompanied his son's quest.

"Thou art great, O Lord, forever, and thy kingdom
is unto all ages.

"For thou scourgest, and thou saveth: thou leadest down to hell, and bringest up again: and there is none that can escape thy hand.

"Give glory to the Lord, ye children of Israel: and praise him in the sight of the Gentiles.

"Because he hath therefore scattered you among the Gentiles, who know not him, that you may declare his wonderful works: and make them know that there is no other almighty God besides him."

The night before, Adrienne had said that she wondered how she, how anyone, could survive the overpowering happiness that lay ahead of her. Her heart sank a little, however, as they approached the city.

It was not surrounded, as was Vienna and Paris, by suburbs; its fortifications, which had been remodeled and strengthened during the wars between Frederick the Great and Maria Theresa, rose up sheer from the plain. On the battlements, cannon were mounted; one could see the gleaming bayonets of sentinels above the ramparts. In Vienna, Adrienne had almost succeeded in convincing herself that her stay—and her husband's—here would be short, but now she was not so sure.

They entered the city through a guarded gate. They drove through the winding streets and squares of the town to the house of the Commandant, General von Shroeder. Adrienne sent in her name.

The officer who appeared was not the Commandant, but his deputy, Major von Germack, who was in charge of the military barrack where the prisoners were housed. The Major drove with Adrienne and her daughters to the southern end of the town, where the barrack stood—a great gaunt building which had at one time been a Jesuit college. With its blank facade and rows of narrow, pointed windows, it still had a monastic look.

The cells of the prisoners were at the rear of the building on the first floor. A guard unlocked a wicket to let them in and locked it behind them. Adrienne was once more a prisoner. If she had had any misgivings—she had none!—it would have been too late now to turn back. She was trembling with impatience to press forward.

But there was a tantalizing, excruciating delay while the luggage was examined. Everything was turned out and thoroughly pawed over; some table knives and forks that Adrienne had brought with her were confiscated. She and the girls were told also to hand over their purses; there would be no bribing of jailers here, as at Le Plessis.

They were led down a long series of somber passages. They came to a halt before two padlocked doors. The guard selected a key from the bunch that hung at his wrist.

The door opened on a narrow, bare room at the end of which was a single, barred window; the upper half being closed by a solid shutter. The man who, with the light behind him, looked up in surprise, might have been a stranger. His ragged clothes hung loose; his skin had the bluish pallor of an invalid. Adrienne's moment of supreme joy came to her with a stab of pity and horror.

Lafayette did not know that she was coming! The letter that Adrienne had written aboard *The Little Cherub* and dispatched from Hamburg had never reached the prison. The prisoner was bewildered, incredulous that his wife should be here, that these two big girls who put up their faces to be kissed were the little daughters he had last seen four years ago at Chavaniac.

For almost a year now, ever since the Bollmann-Huger rescue attempt last November, Lafayette had not been outside of his cell or the equally small and bare room that adjoined it. He had seen no one but his jailers and for weeks at a time had been ill with his old chest complaint. How

completely he had been cut off from all news was evident in
the questions that he asked. From where had they come?
Where had they been? He had thought that they were in
Switzerland or perhaps in England with Pauline. He knew
vaguely that there had been a terror in France—he had heard
of the King's execution before leaving Prussia—but he had
had none of the details.

Adrienne, as she realized that he also knew nothing of
the personal tragedies for which she had thought to prepare
him in advance, waited for him to ask a question and dreaded
the answer she must give. There seemed to be constraint on
his part as well. They spoke of many people, of many things,
but he failed to ask for her mother or Louise, the two members of her family to whom he had been particularly devoted.

Several hours passed. It began to grow dark. The Major
returned, bringing a squad of soldiers with him. It was time,
he said, for the young *fraüleins* to be locked up for the night.
They could spend the day with their parents, but they were
to sleep next door. The locking up process was performed
with full military ceremony. As though they were desperados
who might at any moment make a dash for freedom, Anastasie and Virginie were marched from one room to the other
under the naked, crossed swords of the guard.

When they were alone, Adrienne told Gilbert what he had
sensed, what he had avoided forcing her to say until she
could find full comfort in his arms.

CHAPTER XIX

Prison Idyl

THE FOLLOWING DAY, Adrienne began to discover that the Austrian war minister had been right when he predicted discomforts for her and her daughters. She began to see how misleading—or how misinformed—the Emperor had been when he said that her husband was well-fed and well-lodged.

The two rooms in which Lafayette had paced restlessly back and forth for eighteen months, when he was not prostrated by fever, were bare of all furniture except a stove—which was fueled from without and frequently failed to give any heat—a bed, a commode, a table, and four or five straight-backed wooden chairs.

The outlook from the rooms was dreary, though far-reaching, the barrack being set so high on a rise of ground that one could see over the walls of the city and catch a glint of the river that flowed around this southern end of the town. Beyond, lay marshlands, diapered with bands of fog on these chilly October mornings. In the foreground was a jumble of outbuildings, used as arsenals and storehouses.

Immediately below the windows was an empty space

through which flowed an open sewer, its slimy contents flavoring the rooms with a sickening smell even when the windows were tightly closed. The barrack latrines were located here. Dead bodies from the military hospital next door were sometimes carried out and deposited by the sewer until they could be coffined; almost daily, soldiers were brought here to be flogged, the thud of the whip and the shrieks of the victims plainly audible.

Three times a day, the prisoners' meals were carried in by a soldier and dumped down upon the table. They were sufficient, but unappetizing. The dishes were often dirty and had been left standing so long in the guardroom en route from the kitchen that their contents were well-seasoned with tobacco smoke. Since neither fork nor knife was provided, one ate with one's fingers—"a custom," Lafayette commented, "that I have seen among the aborigines of North America."

On the first Sunday after her arrival, Adrienne asked the Major if she and her daughters could go to Mass at the nearest church, but the only answer was a vigorous shake of the head. She thought that she should complain of this in writing to the Commandant—for hadn't the Emperor said that the Commandant would be obliging? She put it off, however, thinking that General von Shroeder might come to see her himself.

The very thought of complaining of anything—anything at all—was distasteful to her. In spite of the squalor of her surroundings, in spite of being frustrated in her religious inclinations, she was happy—happy as she had never been before in her life, except at brief intervals. After twenty years and more of infatuated love, she had her husband entirely to herself; he could not escape her now. There was no career of adventure to beckon him across the seas, no dangerous duties to the state to call him out at all hours, no mistress, no friends or henchmen clamoring for their share of his attention. He was hers, and hers alone.

And, as always when he was with her, he seemed content that this should be so. He had lost none of his responsiveness, his skill in the give and take of affection. She had been afraid that his bitter experiences might have warped him, but he still possessed the quality that she had always adored in him, of detached judgment on human beings and events. He made no effort, as she did, to forgive his enemies, because hatred —personal hatred—seemed entirely absent from his make up. Gleefully she noted that, though he was still haggard and gaunt, his physical condition seemed to improve a little from day to day and this could only be accounted for by her being there with her children.

The strange life that they led soon fell into a pattern. In the mornings, Adrienne was locked into the room next door with the girls until noon. She gave Virginie, poor little Virginie whose education had been so neglected, lessons, as best she could in the absence of all schoolroom equipment. At dinner time, all three went back to Lafayette's room and stayed there until evening.

They talked—how much they had to say to one another! They were busy in various ways. Anastasie took over the housework. She mended her father's clothes, which were in a fearful state of dilapidation after four years' wear without replacements. One old coat that was beyond repair, she cut up to make him a pair of quilted shoes. As a present for her father, Anastasie drew a sketch on her thumbnail—later transferred to paper—of the chief jailer, a detestable little man whom she and Virginie had nicknamed Cataquois. A round bullet head, a meager whisp of pigtail curled over his left shoulder—Cataquois was represented carrying a small hand lamp to light him down the dark passages to the cells, a switch swinging from his wrist by a thong. In the evenings, much to Virginie's delight, Lafayette read aloud to his family from the battered miscellany of books in the cell.

Much daylight time was spent in writing. The pens that

Adrienne had brought with her were confiscated along with
the tableware, but a small slab of India ink had escaped the
luggage inspection. Lafayette had a toothpick, a very valuable toothpick, worth to him its weight in rubies. With it he
had written all the secret letters he had smuggled out of the
prison at Magdebourg. Now it was put to use again. Anastasie wrote, at her father's dictation, a memorandum to his
friends and followers; if not written in his familiar, easily
recognized hand, there might be a chance some day of sending it out of the prison. For paper, Anastasie used the fly
leaves of books; they were much too precious—the India ink,
also—for Virginie to scribble on or to do her sums.

Adrienne too, toothpick in hand, spent long hours bent
over a volume by Buffon, the French naturalist. It had wide
margins and many blank pages, on the reverse of which were
printed engravings. She had wanted for more than a year to
compose a tribute to her mother in the form of a memoir.
While she was in Vienna, she had opened a book by Pascal
and had come upon a passage that seemed to express so perfectly her mother's creed that she thought she could actually
hear her mother's voice speaking softly in her ear. Adrienne
intended not only a brief biography but a psychological portrait. To do so, she must go back to the beginning and see
her mother as a child.

Slowly, delicately, her work took shape.

"Anne-Louise-Henriette d'Aguesseau, my mother," Adrienne wrote, "was born on the 12th of February, 1737. Madame de Fresnes, her mother, having died a few days after
her birth; her father, son of Chancellor d'Aguesseau, handed
her over to the care of a nurse, with whom she was sent,
when she was three years old, to the Convent of the Visitation
of Saint Denis. There she was particularly entrusted to one
of the nuns, Madame d'Héricourt, a most accomplished person, who had great talent as a teacher. She knew how to make

virtue attractive to her pupils. But to virtue my mother's heart was naturally inclined; to its practice she applied herself from her earliest childhood with that rectitude which was her special characteristic. With an irresolute, but superior mind, with a physical and moral inclination to be troubled and alarmed in all circumstances, she had one aim that was superior to all others. To her could always be applied the words of the *118th Psalm*, 'My soul is continually in my hands, yet do I not forget Thy law.' "

Adrienne felt that what her mother had shared with the psalmist and with Pascal to an unusual degree, was the sense of divine guidance and, at the same time, of personal moral responsibility.

The serious, anxious little girl whom Adrienne had conjured up, refrained from playing chess because she found herself thinking of gambits during Mass; she carried on a stately correspondence with her grandfather, the Chancellor. Having read—at the age of five—a book about the fathers of the Church, who wrestled with demons in the desert, Henriette d'Aguesseau was frightened to think that God might have chosen her to be a saint and that she might see terrible, soul-searing visions. She did not find her true vocation until, at eighteen, she was married and had children of her own, for—"to be a mother God had formed her."

"A mother—*my* mother;" as she wrote the words over and over again with pride, Adrienne relived her own childhood and her sisters' in the Hotel de Noailles. Scenes that she had never forgotten and could never forget came back to her. With her sisters, she was standing once again in the garden of the hotel, her face pressed against the windowpane of a dim-lit room on the ground floor. The Duchess had been very ill and for weeks the children had not been allowed to see her. Looking in, they began to whimper, to sob, for the woman lying in the great bed was a stranger. Their mother's face had been so scarred by smallpox that for a moment they did not recognize her!

There was little fear however, little shock in most of what Adrienne could recall so vividly. Peace and security had been her earliest heritage. She tried to analyze the confidence that her mother had inspired.

"It was not the kind of confidence which I think many mothers strive for and seldom obtain from their children, the confidence one feels in a companion of one's own age. It was intimate and limitless; it was born of the innate craving to be directed and approved . . . It was the confidence that always brings one back to a support, to a guide on whose wisdom and tenderness one may lean. . . . Even when one did not agree with her decisions, even when one was sure of her disapproval, one turned to her and the idea of hiding what had been done, or said, or even thought, was unthinkable. Such were the feelings that I had for my mother, when, as often, she let me discuss my problems with her."

Adrienne, when she wrote these words, had come in her account to the time of her own marriage, and, in the shabby room at Olmütz, with Lafayette beside her, she poured out her gratitude for all that her mother had done to make the marriage perfect. She remembered little things, not fully appreciated at the time perhaps, that had smoothed her way —and his; the gayeties that the Duchess arranged for the newly married couple, the dinner parties, the balls at Versailles, the time when Gilbert was inoculated for smallpox and Madame d'Ayen rented a little house at Chaillot where she could nurse him and keep him amused during the tedious weeks of convalescence.

How loyally she had come to his defence when he went to America for the first time and the elders of the Noailles clan grumbled! How constantly she tried to keep Adrienne's courage up during the long years when he was overseas! It was loyalty also that had bridged the gap between his political

ideas and hers during the Revolution. Even at the last, when
he was an exile and all the nation was against him, she had
had the courage to work for him, trudging to see people in
Paris who might help him, or to collect any scrap of news
that she might send to Chavaniac.

Of the end of her mother's life, of what Grelet and Father
Carrichon had told her, Adrienne could not bring herself to
speak but she set down a few details she had learned from a
Madame Lavet, one of the prisoners who was at the Conciergerie on the night before the execution, one of the few
who survived.

The three Noailles women were exhausted when they arrived at the prison. They had only enough money to buy a
little gooseberry wine to slake their thirst. Neither Madame
d'Ayen, nor the Maréchale fully realized that death lay ahead
of them. The Maréchale sat up in bed and read over and
over her act of accusation, saying that she couldn't possibly
be put to death for a conspiracy of which she had never
heard. At times she would break off to worry about her cap,
which she thought was too elegant, too aristocratic to be
worn before a Revolutionary committee. Madame d'Ayen
lay down on a cot and kept begging Louise to lie down beside
her and get some rest, which Louise did occasionally to
humor her mother. Louise knew that it was useless to save
her strength, since this was her last night on earth.

In the morning, the Duchess seemed to see the inevitable
more clearly, and she, who was so timid physically, so apt
"to be troubled and alarmed in all circumstances" showed
great courage. She talked very tenderly of her grandchildren
and tried to leave a watch for them as a final keepsake, with
her fellow prisoners. But the women in the cell were afraid
to take it, nor would they take a lock of hair, a miniature,
and an empty pocketbook that Louise wanted to give them.
For the last time Louise, who had spent the night reading her
prayer book helped her mother and grandmother dress and

said with a smile to Madame Lavet as she thanked her for her kindness, "Your face is happy; you will not die—I am sure!"

Father Carrichon, who had given her mother and Louise Absolution on their way to the scaffold, had told Adrienne—when she saw him in Paris—that as he came away from the Barrière du Trône, he thought of the centurion who stood at the foot of the cross. It would not be irreverent to see, in that cruel death outside the walls of Paris, a reenactment, an imitation of the death in which "all Christians find their second birth."

"That is the consolation which remains to us and which sustains us," Adrienne wrote on the final page of the volume by Buffon. "To follow in the footsteps of those so dear, I think, would have made easy the horrors of such an end.

"I have rejected silence, though what I have had to say is beyond expression."

PART SIX

November, 1795—November, 1799

CHAPTER XX

Freedom Campaign

PEACEFULLY, almost imperceptibly—each day was like the one before, the one that followed after—two months went by. Christmas was not far off and still there had been no call from the Commandant of Olmütz, General von Shroeder, though Adrienne had asked to see him and had written to him, not with the toothpick pen, but with one supplied her by Major von Germack.

Every four weeks the Major had visited the cell so that Adrienne could write to Mr. Parish, the Consul in Hamburg, for money to pay for her board and lodging in the prison. Unlike Lafayette, she and the girls were not to be guests of the Austrian government. The first time Germack came, he brought Adrienne a letter from her father in Switzerland, the second time, letters from Pauline and Madame de Tessé. Under the officer's watchful eye, she was allowed to reply briefly.

When Germack came in December, Adrienne wrote to the Minister of War, Count Ferraris, whom she had met in Vienna. Again she asked to go to Mass, hoping that the minis-

ter would reply promptly and favorably so that she could
be in church on Christmas Day. She asked also that she and
Lafayette might see Lafayette's friends, de Maubourg and
de Pusy, whose cells were in the same block, who were only
a few yards off and yet so far.

It would only take three days for mail to go to Vienna,
three for a return, but Christmas came and went and the
New Year of 1796 had come in before Adrienne heard from
Ferraris. He was concise and frigidly courteous. He told her
that it was the War Department's duty to guard the prisoners
of His Imperial Majesty, not to decide the conditions under
which they were being held; he could do nothing for her.
He took obvious satisfaction in reminding her that he had
warned her in advance and that it was by her own choice that
she and her daughters were in the barrack.

Again Adrienne made use of the writing materials Germack brought her. She thanked Ferraris pointedly for his
politeness in answering her letter. She complained of Von
Shroeder's neglect and repeated the demands that she had
made; to go to Mass, to see de Maubourg and de Pusy, and
also Lafayette's servants, Chavaniac and Félix Pontonnier.
As to his reminder that she had come here of her own free
will, she felt that she could speak for herself, Anastasie, and
Virginie when she said that they none of them had changed
their minds; they were all three much happier here in prison
with Lafayette than they could possibly be anywhere else.

But she had yet another request to make. Since Christmas,
Adrienne had begun to feel wretchedly ill. Her health, which
had survived so many privations, so many long, jolting journeys, so much sorrow, had cracked under the strain of a
sedentary life. Her head ached, she had begun to run a fever,
her arms and legs felt heavy and were swollen. At first she
had hidden her symptoms, and was so cheerful and serene
that neither Lafayette nor the girls noticed that anything was
wrong.

When they discovered her condition, the doctor was sent for, Dr. Kreutschke, who was in charge of the military hospital. He could speak no French. He had, however, received his dose of Latin in medical school and Lafayette could remember enough of the Latin he had learned as a small boy from the curé of Chavaniac to tell the Doctor Adrienne's symptoms and question him. Kreutschke was baffled; a disorder of the blood was as near as he could come to a diagnosis. He could suggest nothing effective in the way of treatment.

Urged on by Lafayette, Adrienne asked Ferraris in her January letter if she could go to Vienna for a week to consult a competent physician, leaving her daughters with their father while she was gone. This time the reply was less slow in transit. On January 27th, Ferraris informed her that neither he nor the War Department could give her permission to leave the prison; for that she must apply to the Emperor himself.

Adrienne wrote at once to Francis, the result being a wait of many weeks and then, in March, a visit—his first—from the Commandant. General von Shroeder told her verbally what was the Emperor's pleasure; she could go to Vienna if she wished, but on one condition, that she should never return to Olmütz.

Adrienne's recoil was definite. For Von Shroeder's benefit, she put into writing a statement that she preferred to stay where she was, no matter what the effect might be on her health. After all that she had been through, she couldn't face "the horrors of another separation."

It was a cruel disappointment to her, however, for she had intended to do much more in Vienna than to let a doctor examine her and listen to her medical history. She would have seen again the friends she had made at the time of her first visit; she would have tried to get close to someone at the top level of authority, other than Baron von Thugut, and to investigate the hidden as well as the obvious reasons for Lafayette's imprisonment. All her complaints and petitions for privileges had been made with the underlying idea of furthering her campaign for freedom.

There was nothing for it now but to make light of her miseries so as not to worry her family. Adrienne put up with the poor comforts of the cell, though there was not even an easy chair in which she could rest her aching body. She was particularly distressed that she could do so little for the other Olmütz prisoners, who had been so self-sacrificing, who had always put Lafayette's welfare first, and had made no move toward their own individual liberties.

Although it was true that Lafayette had not seen any of them since he had been in Austria, he had been able to communicate with de Maubourg and de Pusy after a fashion, thanks to Félix Pontonnier, the coachman's son, Lafayette's youthful secretary.

Félix was a talented and ingenious lad. He could play the recorder and had worked out a shorthand code based on the words of certain popular airs which was known both to Lafayette and to the servant of César de la Tour Maubourg. This man was watched much less closely than Félix and could see his master frequently. De Maubourg had been allowed to receive outside letters when they were denied to Lafayette and, by means of Félix's plaintive tootlings, a few rudimentary messages were relayed from one cell to another. Before Adrienne came to Olmütz, for instance, Lafayette had learned through Félix that she was still alive—but nothing more.

After their arrival in October, Anastasie and Virginie lost no time in developing a simpler, more efficient means of correspondence. When they were locked up for the night, the girls would let down from their window at the end of a cord, a small package and dangle it beneath the nose of the guard below. In the package might be a piece of cheese, or some other tidbit they had saved from their supper. After pleasant relations had been established, they ventured to let down letters addressed to de Maubourg or de Pusy along with their bribe. A night or two later a return letter would be tied to the string before it was drawn up through the bars.

This was well enough for the time being, but in March something of great importance happened, something that compensated for Adrienne's having to abandon her plan to go to Vienna.

Anastasie had been feeling poorly. She was feverish and Adrienne was concerned lest Virginie might catch the infection; the two sisters had to share a single narrow bed. Dr. Kreutschke, who had taken to paying regular professional visits, one day asked the guard to see the room where the young ladies slept; he was afraid that it might be damp; dampness was a mighty breeder of fevers.

Kreutschke was in the room for only a short time, but when Anastasie and Virginie returned to it in the evening they found that the bed had been rumpled. A fat bundle had been stuffed beneath the coverlet, a bundle of mail which had come from Hamburg. It had been brought to Olmütz by a person unknown, who signed himself "Feldmann."

After that, at fairly frequent intervals, Kreutschke came to and went from the prison with his pockets loaded. He was apparently being well-paid for his services. "Whoever you are, Monsieur Feldmann," Adrienne wrote, "we thank you with all our hearts." Now she could write fully and frankly to her family and to many others! Now she and Lafayette could know all that their friends were doing and had done for them!

*   *   *

There were friends, it seemed, no farther away than the encircling walls of Olmütz, that one could see from the barrack window. Even here in the heart of the Austrian empire there were liberals who sympathized with Lafayette's democratic aims and who had learned that he was in the barrack. The rector of the local university was one; a prosperous merchant, Herr Hirsch, was another.

Months ago, Hirsch had received a packet of letters for the Lafayettes, forwarded by James Monroe from Paris. He kept them for sometime and, despairing of getting them into the prison, burned them. In April of 1796, Hirsch was summoned to *The Golden Swan* in the Bachesgässe, the best inn in Olmütz, to meet a Baron Feldmann who had come to the town on business. Hirsch was rather surprised when Feldmann, a total stranger, embraced him affectionately in the public room of the inn and whispered in his ear, "Pretend that you know me! I am a friend of Gilbert!"

Feldmann was actually a French army officer, H. L. V. Ducoudray-Holstein, who had been educated at Leipzig and spoke perfect German. While on leave in Hamburg, he met several of Lafayette's friends, among them Mr. Parish, the American Consul, who sent him to Austria with all the trappings of an affluent business man—fine clothes, a fine carriage to ride in, and a servant to wait upon him. He intended to travel around to other commercial centers in Austria and Silesia to put the authorities off the scent, but as long as he was needed to carry mail his main route would be between Hamburg and Olmütz.

In Hamburg and elsewhere, pro-Lafayette activities had never ceased in the past three and a half years, but that spring and summer of 1796 much was being done in England. Some of Lafayette's Magdebourg letters had been copied and sent about to private individuals, but the letters that began to trickle out of Olmütz via Feldmann got an even wider audience. Their substance was incorporated into articles that appeared in liberal English newspapers and also in Holland, over the signature "Eleuthère," the Greek word for "freeman." Some of them purported to have been written by an ex-officer of the guard at Olmütz to his brother, giving an inside, firsthand account of what went on within the prison. All the grimy details, all the humiliating restrictions were described—and nothing was lost in the telling. The fact that Adrienne had come as an angel of mercy to Olmütz, and that now she and her daughters were being as barbarously persecuted as Lafayette himself, was featured.

The "Eleuthère" articles continued to be printed at intervals for many months and eventually got under the leathery skin of the Austrian government. Protests were sent through the Imperial Ambassador at the Court of St. James and, since nobody in England seemed to know who "Eleuthère" was, spies were sent from Vienna to try, unsuccessfully, to nose him out and silence him. At the same time the Whig leaders in Parliament, Fox, Sheridan, and Fitzpatrick, who as early as 1794 had spoken for Lafayette in the House of Commons, kept up their sniping tactics.

The friends of Lafayette were convinced that the chief obstacle to freedom was not in Vienna, but in Whitehall. The Tory government of William Pitt was pushing the war against France in spite of apathy and resistence at home— and the Tories had never forgotten Lafayette's part in the American Revolution.

As for Austria, she was sick of being forever beaten by the French. She could gain little by victory and was dependent on her ally, England, for military supplies. Baron von Thugut, the malevolent, ugly man whom Adrienne had interviewed in Vienna, was the slave of Pitt. Fox one day in Parliament quoted the very words that the Emperor had spoken to Adrienne: "My hands are tied." It was Pitt, Fox suggested, who had tied them.

This brought a rolling, polysyllabic riposte from the Tory benches. "Those who start revolutions will always be in my eyes the object of an irresistible reprobation," the speaker intoned. "I take delight in seeing them drink to the dregs, the cup of bitterness that they have prepared for the lips of others."

The exchanges in Parliament had publicity value in the campaign for freedom, but of more practical importance for the future, were certain military events that were taking place far to the south of Vienna. In Paris, the five members of the recently elected Directory spent most of their time in plotting against one another and in picking the public purse; on the Rhine the French armies were making little headway; but in March of 1796 a young, untried General, Napoleon Bonaparte, was put in command of the Army of Italy, chiefly because his charming, newly-acquired wife, Josephine Beauharnais, was a good friend of one of the Directors.

Soon news of astounding victories, of towns taken, of Austrian armies brushed aside, came back to France and thence by slow degrees to Olmütz. The significance of the Italian campaign was not grasped at first by the prisoners, for their hopes lay elsewhere. All of them, de Maubourg and de Pusy as well as the Lafayettes, and even Félix Pontonnier, who was studying English in his cell, intended to go to America, if they were freed.

One of the first uncensored letters that Adrienne wrote was to Lafayette's would-be rescuer, Dr. Bollmann, who, with his colleague, Francis Huger, had set sail for the United States about the time Adrienne was arriving in Austria. The American coterie in London had encouraged the adventurous Bollmann to make another effort for Lafayette; he had been given letters of introduction that would bring him to the attention of President Washington. Adrienne thought that by this time, May 22nd, Bollmann would be back in England with instructions of some sort from the President. She wanted not only to thank the Doctor for all that he and Huger had done and suffered, but to ask for news of her son

George, whom he must surely have seen. From George himself, Adrienne had heard nothing since she parted from him
more than a year ago in Paris. Only from Pauline had she
heard of her son's safe arrival in the United States.

CHAPTER XXI

Release

FORTUNATELY, considering the uncertain heating system in the cells, the winter had been mild, but with the return of warm weather the windows had to be kept open. The sun beat into the dingy little rooms, in which no cross draft was possible—and the smell of the sewer was the smell of death. Swarms of flies buzzed about the prisoners' ears.

Adrienne's illness increased and could no longer be disregarded. She was continually feverish. Abscesses formed on her swollen arms and legs. She had difficulty in moving about and even found writing for any length of time painful. Anastasie became her amanuensis. She and Virginie were the only ones who were still healthy, for the letters from de Maubourg and de Pusy told a depressing tale of sickness. De Maubourg could no longer stomach the rancid prison food. De Pusy could survive it better, but he was steadily losing weight and strength.

The following autumn, Major von Germack—who, de Maubourg had quipped, was "born to be a jailer, just as Voltaire was born to be a poet"—disappeared from the prison

staff and his place was taken by a Captain MacElligott, a
Scotchman who had taken service in the Imperial army. He
was very obliging, came to the cells often and tried to make
them a little more comfortable, though what he could do
was severely limited by his lack of authority.

Adrienne and the others also noted a change for the better
in the manners of the jailers. Even the underlings, even the
turnkey, Cataquois, and the men who paced back and forth
at night beneath the girls' window, had heard of the tri-
umphs of General Bonaparte. Each victory raised a trifle
higher, the respect in which the prisoners were held.

And throughout another damp and foggy winter, that
brought no relief to Adrienne's illness, the victories continued. By spring, every fortified town in Italy had fallen to
the French. An army was advancing on Vienna itself. In
April of 1797, a truce was called and the preliminaries to
peace discussions were begun.

In Paris, the Directory was being bombarded by Lafayette
petitions, for some of the Constitutionalists had come out
of hiding and were making themselves heard. Instructions
were sent to Bonaparte that a demand for Lafayette's release
should be made at once. Another general, General Clarke,
was sent to Italy to sit in on the negotiations and with him
went a young man, Louis Romeuf, who had served under
Lafayette and rode into exile with him in 1792. At the same
time, Victor de la Tour Maubourg, César's brother, and
Florimond, César's son, went to Vienna with Ducoudray-
Holstein, alias Baron Feldmann. Disregarded there, they
went on to the castle near Milan where Bonaparte was living
with Josephine.

The victorious General had little sympathy with the prisoners of Olmütz, but he allowed Romeuf to go back to
Vienna to talk with Thugut. As a direct result of these talks,
a visitor was ushered into Lafayette's room on July 24th by
Captain MacElligott—an Austrian officer, whose polished

boots and smart uniform were in sharp contrast to the ragged clothes and the homemade cloth shoes of the man who ceremoniously received him.

MacElligott did not need to introduce the two, for they had met before. The Austrian officer was the Marquis de Chasteler, who had taken Lafayette into custody almost five years ago in Belgium. He had traveled fast to Olmütz, making the trip from Vienna in a single day. He had been commissioned to report to the Emperor on the conditions in the Jesuit barrack and to deliver an offer of freedom to the French prisoners. Its most important proviso was that Lafayette and his friends should promise never to set foot on Austrian soil again.

There were bows, excessive politeness, and dignity on either side. Lafayette was too proud to draw attention to the state of his clothes or the room; he left that to the eyes and nose of his visitor. The only complaint he made was that he had been kept so long without news of his family. He showed a chilly lack of enthusiasm for Chasteler's proposal, said that he needed time to think it over, and that first he would have to consult with his two friends. To this de Chasteler consented.

The next morning, at the early hour of seven o'clock, the key grated in the lock, the door swung back, and de Maubourg and de Pusy walked into the room. The three comrades, so long apart, looked sorrowfully at one another. No one of them realized, perhaps, how much he himself had changed. De Maubourg had lost several of his teeth; he and de Pusy, still in their forties, were old men before their time. As they embraced Lafayette, feeble, invalid tears were trickling down their cheeks.

There was little time to talk privately, however, and there was little to be said. All three quickly and unanimously agreed that the offer must be rejected.

In a very short time, Captain MacElligott again appeared with the Marquis de Chasteler. The prisoners drew themselves up to greet him. Imaginary epaulettes sprouted from their shoulders; imaginary swords dangled at their sides as they explained that, though none of them had the slightest wish to see Austria again, they might, as Frenchmen, be ordered by their government to do so in some military capacity.

De Chasteler expressed his regret. At his request, they drew up a statement of their joint decision and any comments they wished to make on their imprisonment. After the three documents had been looked over, signed, and dated, de Chasteler and the others withdrew, leaving Adrienne and Lafayette alone again.

Adrienne had no fault to find with the way in which her menfolk had behaved. It would be dishonorable, she thought, to sneak out of Austria like branded criminals. When they left, it would be as prisoners of state, whose importance to France had been fully recognized. But that they would leave sooner or later seemed at the moment certain.

As days and weeks went by, however, the certainty began to fade. In August a letter—they were delivered openly now —came from Louis Romeuf in Vienna. He respected the stand that Lafayette had taken, but he was beginning to be discouraged. The Emperor was pigheaded and indifferent. Thugut was furious. At each interview with Romeuf, he poured out his hatred for Lafayette and for Lafayette's "insolence."

The only feature of the situation that was in Romeuf's favor was that Thugut was disgusted with the whole affair and wanted to be rid of it. When, at a moment of comparative calm, Romeuf suggested that Lafayette should be handed over to the American consul at Hamburg, Thugut yielded. Romeuf wrote to Olmütz, hoping, yet doubting, that the arrangement would be satisfactory and reported that he was off for Hamburg to consult with the Consul, Mr. Parish.

More weeks went by. The prisoners had signified their acquiesence but nothing happened, no word came from Vienna. Had Thugut gone back on his word? Was he playing with them?

Adrienne, ill though she was, her sufferings redoubled by the fetid air and the heat of yet another summer, wrote letters to everyone she could think of who might appeal to Thugut or to the Emperor, making drafts of the appeals to be copied and signed. She advised Romeuf as to what he should do and say that would neither compromise him nor run contrary to the stand that Lafayette had taken.

At last, on September 19th, 1797, five years and a month after Lafayette's capture in Belgium, the order for release arrived at the prison. Adrienne was so ill that Lafayette and the others wanted to put off leaving the town for a short time, until she was in better condition to travel, but she wouldn't hear of it. A single day, a single hour longer in this hated spot would be too much!

There were few preparations to be made for the journey, little to be packed. The Lafayettes were reunited with Félix Pontonnier and Chavaniac. Félix had grown to man's estate in the past five years and looked sickly; the valet also.

All the company drove to *The Golden Swan* in the Bachesgässe, which Feldmann had made his headquarters when he was in Olmütz. He was there to greet them in person and to reveal his identity as Ducoudray-Holstein. He would travel with them, he said, as far as Hamburg.

During the dinner that was eaten at the *Swan,* there was a good deal of hysterical laughter, a good many bad jokes made about the awkwardness that everyone showed in handling knife and fork. No time was lost in sitting over table. Before the sun was low, a caravan of carriages drove out of the west-

ern gate of the city. Soon the high walls of Olmütz dwindled
down into the distance behind it.

In the last unit of the caravan rode a single traveler to
whom no one had been more than coldly polite. He was an
Austrian Major, who had been given the thankless task of
seeing that his charges got to Hamburg and were properly
disposed of.

All were anxious to reach the seaport city as soon as possible, but knew that they would have to travel by easy stages
because the jarring motion of the carriage was painful to
Adrienne. In spite of the mild autumn weather, all the windows were at first kept closed. After having spent so many
months—and years—indoors, the prisoners of Olmütz were
almost overpowered by the glare of the sun and the rushing
currents of free air that blew about them.

Several days after they left, but while they were still in
Austrian territory, they saw across some fields, at a bend of
the road, a solitary rider, who had wheeled his horse about
and was looking at them. They recognized Louis Romeuf.
So much of the valiant work he had done for them had been
done in secret that he thought it unwise to approach them.
With a wave of the hand, he rode away. They knew, however,
that he had come all the way from Hamburg just to catch a
glimpse of them and that they would see him soon again.

In the Austrian towns through which they passed, the
travelers were often stared at curiously, but the gentleman in
the last carriage prevented anyone from coming near enough
to speak to them. What a change when they crossed the frontier! They were surrounded by friends. Romeuf was waiting
for them at Dresden, and also the wives of de Maubourg and
de Pusy who, with their children, had been living in sight
of Austria for weeks, expecting the arrival of the Olmütz
party daily. There were two de Maubourg girls, who were

older than Anastasie and Virginie. Madame de Pusy had a little five-year-old daughter, whom her father had never seen.

The caravan was enormously increased. Now began a series of receptions that brought to mind the triumphal progress that the Lafayettes had made six years ago from Paris to Auvergne. Crowds flocked to the inns at every stop. In Leipzig and Halle, university towns, the student corps turned out *en masse* in their caps and sashes. There were torchlight processions and the fine, deep-throated roar of young male voices shouting *Kommerslieder,* followed by *The Marseillaise.*

Ducoudray-Holstein was ecstatic. He had been a student himself at Leipzig, he knew these songs. Lafayette had never heard them, nor had he heard the great anthem of the Republic, but he, who always enjoyed popularity, was uplifted by the cheers and applause.

Adrienne, too, ill though she was, was somewhat revived. Much of the cheering was for her; all these good people knew how she had come to share her husband's prison. She was bewildered when one day a young man, who had just been introduced to her, stood speechless before her and then fell on his knees. He would have kissed the hem of her dress, if she had not laughingly twitched it away and told him to stand up. "I am not a goddess," she exclaimed.

When she saw that her worshiper was crestfallen, she asked Virginie to give up the chair beside her to him so that she could chat with him and make amends.

She was very tired when they reached Hamburg, but apparently no worse for the trip. If anything, she had begun to gain a little strength, though hardly enough to meet the whirlwind welcome staged by Lafayette's admirers. Many American ships were lying in the mouth of the Elbe; all their flags were flying when the Lafayette party approached. The wayfarers were about to cross the river in a ferry when an American sea captain came to invite them on board his ship for dinner and offered to row them ashore to the city in the afternoon.

It was five o'clock when they finally arrived at the house of the American Consul, John Parish. Such masses of people had gathered about it that a way had to be cleared for the Lafayettes to enter. Once they had been squeezed inside, both Adrienne and Lafayette collapsed from exhaustion. They wept. Adrienne was led to a sofa by Mr. Parish, almost in tears himself. In thanking the Consul, Lafayette found that he had forgotten how to speak proper English. He could only stammer out a crude translation of what he might have said in French.

"My friend, my dearest friend, my deliverer! See the work of your generosity! My poor, poor wife, hardly able to support herself!"

They had barely recovered and wiped their eyes when the room began to fill. The Austrian Minister, Baron Buol von Schäuenstein, appeared with the Austrian Major who had come with the caravan from Olmütz, and with an old friend, who must be thanked for his services, Gouverneur Morris. Morris had been in Hamburg all summer and had been dining that day with Baron Buol.

The Baron made a florid speech in which he said how happy he was to deliver Lafayette to Parish, "who seemed to love and respect him so much." He added, however, that the ex-prisoners could only stay in Hamburg for twelve days and the release must be looked upon as a courtesy to the United States; it had nothing to do with any demand that might have been made by France.

This was a bit of face-saving that deceived no one and of which Lafayette politely expressed his doubts in his reply to Von Schäuenstein. He must give full credit, he said, to General Bonaparte. As soon as the ceremony was over, Lafayette, de Maubourg, and de Pusy went to call on the French Minister.

In the twelve days that they remained in Hamburg, Adrienne rested as best she could, though there were constant visitors and constant invitations that had to be accepted. Adrienne met the dramatist Klopstock, to whom she had once written so desperately from Chavaniac and all the friends who had tried to rescue Lafayette from Magdebourg.

Lafayette himself wrote letters to those he could not thank in person, among others to Francis Huger in America and to "Eleuthère" in England. "Eleuthère," he learned, was a French journalist, Josephe Masclet, whom he had never met —an unknown, but enthusiastic fayettist.

Though Lafayette thanked Bonaparte and one of the members of the French Directory, Barras, who had been active in his behalf, he did not write to the Directory as a whole. Before reaching Hamburg, while he was still at Dresden, the newspapers reported that three of the Directors—Barras was one of them—had seized the executive power for themselves. The two ousted officials, Carnot and Siéyès, sent a secret emissary to Lafayette, urging him to come back to Paris at once to join them in a counter move, but he refused, not wanting to take part in yet another lawless *coup d'état.*

There was no hope, therefore, of a return to France at present. Where else could they go—America? It was now October and Adrienne was in no condition to make a winter voyage across the Atlantic. Besides, they learned from their American friends that diplomatic relations had become strained between the United States and France and that James Monroe had been recalled from Paris.

They were somewhat puzzled by the cool attitude towards them of Gouverneur Morris, who had been so helpful when help was needed most. He had slipped back into his pre-Revolutionary attitude of monitor and critic. For this, there was a personal reason. Morris was miffed by the reply Lafayette made to Baron Buol's speech at the American Consul's, but even more by the fact that the Lafayette party was staying at an expensive inn in Hamburg instead of finding cheaper lodgings in the suburbs. Morris could not forget that Adrienne had borrowed 100,000 *livres* from him in 1793 and he was beginning to wonder when he would see his money again.

Return to the world had exacted its penalty. Just as the sun and wind had been too much at first for the liberated prisoners, it was at first a shock to re-discover the complexities of human relationships and the animosities, great and small, that govern them. Adrienne was glad when it was decided shortly before their time in the city was up, that they should all go with the de Maubourgs, the de Pusys, and two other friends who had attached themselves to their group to a little town named Ploen in Holstein, not very far from Hamburg.

CHAPTER XXII

By the Waters of Ploen

THERE WAS NOT ONLY a town of Ploen, there was a lake of
the same name and on the farther shore Madame de
Tessé last summer had found the farm of her dreams. Witmold was the name of the estate. It had vast fields, in which
flax, wheat, and hops were grown; there were barns for the
cattle, chicken runs, and a house large enough to accommodate all of Madame de Tessé's entourage. In the daytime, the
gentlemen ranged the woods in search of game and fished in
the lake; in the evenings they gathered in the salon for cards,
literary discussions, and the verbal fireworks in which Madame de Tessé delighted.

Before she left Altona, she had provided herself with a
chaplain, a superannuated French priest, the Abbé de Luchet,
who was without visible means of support. As far as she was
concerned, Madame de Tessé said, his position was a sinecure. "But," she added with one of her grimacing smiles, "I
think that my niece will manage to keep him busy."

Pauline, as always, was well-occupied from cockcrow until
late into the night. She and a valet of the Marquis de Mun

were the only attendants at the early Mass that the Abbé celebrated daily in his room at the top of the house. Pauline would then visit the stillroom, where the dairy maids were at work. She didn't know how to make the excellent butter and cheese that were sold at a good price in the Hamburg market, but she could act as her aunt's deputy in seeing that all was going smoothly. Part of each day was set aside for her devotions, part for her correspondence. Pauline had organized a charitable fund on a large scale for needy émigrés and this involved a great deal of letter writing. She had also written many letters in behalf of the prisoners of Olmütz, among them one to Gouverneur Morris and one to the Emperor.

Pauline still visited the sick indefatigably, knitted stockings for the poor, and made layettes for newborn babies. She even had had time, during the past year, to produce a baby herself, begotten during one of several visits that Joachim had made at Madame de Tessé's invitation. The baby, a boy, who had been christened Attale, was lusty and seemed more likely to survive than any of the four other children whom Pauline had brought into the world.

Pauline fretted all during the long delay that preceded the liberation from Olmütz. When she heard that Adrienne was in Hamburg, that she was actually coming to Witmold, her schedule was disrupted. She felt the same frenzy of excitement as when her sister had arrived at Altona two years ago. She tried to work, to keep calm, but it was more than flesh— Pauline's quivering, hypersensitive flesh—could bear.

On the morning of October 10th, Pauline was upstairs in her bedroom praying for patience when she heard the squeal of a bugle far away across the lake. She knew what that meant. It was a good old German custom for the postillion, who went on ahead of a convoy of carriages, to announce their arrival by a fanfare. Travelers from a distance seldom came to sleepy Ploen. Adrienne must be nearing the town.

Pauline ran downstairs, out of the house, and down to the lake where a number of small-masted rowboats were docked. The Marquis de Mun was sitting in one of them, about to push off for a quiet, meditative fishing expedition. The old man was startled when Pauline suddenly leapt down into the boat and hysterically demanded to be taken across the lake to meet her sister. Neither of them was an experienced navigator, but somehow, between them, they managed to get up the sail. The day was fine; a breeze, fortunately a gentle breeze, was blowing. They were soon bobbing across the water and as they looked back, they saw that a whole fleet of tiny craft was following them. The others had seen Pauline dash out of the house and were on their way to Ploen also.

On the opposite shore, a group of people were standing, five tall males and eight females, one of whom was a small child. As the boat's nose bumped the shore, Pauline scrambled out without waiting for assistance and flung herself into Adrienne's arms. She embraced Lafayette—she had always loved him in spite of his insanely radical ideas—then Anastasie and Virginie, who seemed a little embarrassed by their aunt's fervor. The strangers were introduced, the de Maubourgs and de Pusys and their children. The two unattached men were a Monsieur Pillet, who had also been a member of Lafayette's military family in 1792, and a Monsieur Théodore de Lameth, a fellow prisoner at Wesel. After a meeting in Hamburg, neither could bear to be separated from their friend and former chief.

By this time the fleet from Witmold was in. All the party was accommodated in the flotilla of boats. Lafayette and Anastasie embarked with Joachim de Montagu; Adrienne, Pauline, and Virginie entrusted themselves to Monsieur de Mun. During their zigzag way across the lake, Adrienne clasped Pauline's hand and murmured the verses from *The Canticle of Tobit* that she had recited when she first caught sight of the walls of Olmütz. On the Witmold shore, Madame de Tessé, the only one who had been left behind, was standing waiting, with outstretched arms.

That was a gala day at Witmold and many gala days of rejoicing followed it. There was not room for all to stay in the farmhouse—or rather, in the farm-mansion—but somehow the four Lafayettes were squeezed in. The others found themselves accommodations in the village and there was a constant going and coming across the lake.

After dinner—what mighty conversations in the drawing-room! Madame de Tessé was in her element. The subject was politics; past, present, and future. The battles of the Revolution were fought over again. Pauline, to her amazement and sorrow, discovered that these men, who had been in the thick of the fight, had no regrets that the Revolution had taken place. They had less to say against the Convention, which had persecuted them, than against the royalists who, by fleeing the country, had failed to support them. Lafayette, as usual, kept his temper, but his friends and, in particular Théodore de Lameth, were caustic.

Pauline could hardly contain herself. One day, when Lafayette was calmly explaining to a visitor the abuses that had caused the Revolution, she exploded. "It is certainly wonderful," she cried, springing up from her chair, "how some people can take their minds off the dreadful things that have happened by all this petty faultfinding with the shortcomings of the old regime!"

But later she was ashamed of herself and did penance in her diary and in the long letters to Rosalie de Grammont that she wrote every night before going to bed. Peace, family peace, was more important than politics.

"Gilbert," she confided to Rosalie, "is just as good, just as unaffected, just as affectionate, just as gentle spoken, as you remember him. He loves his children tenderly, and, in spite of his cold exterior, is devoted to his wife. . . . He has lovely manners and a calm way with him that doesn't deceive me. I know that he would like to play an active part again. I avoid as much as possible discussing directly with him anything that touches the Revolution. . . . I am afraid of blowing up! . . . Poor Gilbert! God preserve him from ever again being called upon the stage of public life!"

Thinking of her young nieces' spiritual welfare, forgetting perhaps how constantly they had been exposed to revolutionary talk, Pauline would lure Anastasie and Virginie away from the salon to another room. While the girls sewed, she read aloud to them the sermons of Fénelon, *The Book of Job,* and Bossuet's *Funeral Orations.* Adrienne was often with them, but she was at home in both camps. As Madame de Tessé had once said, Adrienne was one of the few people who was able to reconcile completely the catechism with the Rights of Man.

*   *   *

But the house party at Witmold could not go on forever. For a month the Lafayettes enjoyed Madame de Tessé's talkative hospitality and then looked about them for a place to spend the winter. With the de Maubourgs they rented a house at Lemkuhlen, a few miles from Witmold, near enough for constant visiting back and forth.

To finance this venture Adrienne had to go to Hamburg to borrow money. She alone had any collateral on which to borrow. When Lafayette left Olmütz, some of his property, the rich lands in Brittany he had inherited from his mother, was still unsold, but the Directory, taking a mean revenge on him for his failure to recognize the legality of their present status, disposed of this last portion of his estate. What with the expenses of the past three years, the long journeys, the money given to Madame de Chavaniac to buy back the chateau, the Lafayette exchequer was again bare. There was the large debt to Gouverneur Morris still hanging over

Adrienne and the interest to be paid regularly on a sizable sum that she and Gilbert had seen fit to settle on Dr. Bollmann, who, unlike his American comrade, Francis Huger, was not a man of property.

Bollmann was still in America. The German adventurer had failed to persuade President Washington to commission him as an agent of the United States in freeing Lafayette. Settled in Philadelphia, he had gone into business with his brother and was courting an American girl, all of which called for more capital than he had been able to raise. Adrienne and her husband thought that it would be a graceful way of showing their gratitude to help along his marriage plans by their gift and had arranged the matter through some friends of Bollmann in Hamburg.

The two families, the de Maubourgs and the Lafayettes, had hardly taken root at Lemkuhlen when George arrived from America, via France. George was in his nineteenth year. To his father, who had not seen him since the winter of 1791, who remembered him only as a boy of eleven, he was an entirely new personality. Even his mother found it hard to realize that this far traveled and mature young man, in whom both she and Gilbert could take such pride, was their son.

George's years in America had not been happy. He had accomplished nothing for his father; he had been desperately homesick. It was five months after his arrival in Boston before he even saw his illustrious godfather and namesake, for that summer of 1795, the political situation in the states was so tense, the rivalry between the pro-French and pro-British parties so keen, that Washington hesitated to receive the son of Lafayette. When at last he invited George and Frestel to Philadelphia, he made up for his earlier coldness.

George was adopted as a son of the house, as his father had been before him. The letter that George brought with him from Mount Vernon praised both visitors—for Washington had taken a great liking to Frestel also—to the skies. No excuse was made, however, for the President's doing nothing for Lafayette during his captivity except to write to the King of Prussia and the Emperor of Austria unofficially. Washington's duties as a private individual were never allowed to impinge upon his duties as chief of state.

In Paris, George had said goodbye to Frestel and gone to call on General Bonaparte to thank him for his father's deliverance. The General, that day, was not at home. Madame Bonaparte was cordial and said that she hoped that her husband and George's father might cooperate. But that had been a mere passing politeness. There was no sign in Paris that the ban might be lifted on a return to France. For the present, at least, the Lafayettes must resign themselves to exile.

Exile was quite bearable for Adrienne, now that her family was once more, after so many years, sheltered under the same roof. The Holstein winter was long and cold, the roads were often blocked with snow, but many guests came to Lemkuhlen.

One who came the most frequently and stayed the longest was César de la Tour Maubourg's younger brother, Charles. He, too, had been a very junior member of Lafayette's staff in 1792. He was a very handsome young man, and—something quite unusual in a Frenchman—had very little to say for himself. Charles' reticence was something of a joke in the family, but Anastasie stood up for him. A great admirer of her father, she liked to talk politics and argue herself, but it was better, she said, to hold your tongue than to say a lot of foolish things for which you were sorry later.

At twenty, Anastasie was an odd mixture of innocence and sophistication. She had had a strange and traumatic girlhood; she had had no companions of her own age except little Virginie. In spite of all that she and her sister had been through, the relatives at Witmold took note that the Lafayette girls looked and seemed younger than their years. Anastasie had long ago lost her prison pallor. She was as pink-cheeked and pretty as if she had been well-fed and had led the most pampered, the most sheltered of lives.

One day Charles de la Tour Maubourg sought a private interview with Lafayette. Lafayette was spending much time these days in his study where he was trying to write his memoirs as a possible source of future income. Charles spoke of his personal prospects. They were practically nonexistent; he was a soldier without a commission and he was poor, except for the promise from his brother of thirty thousand francs when he, Charles, should settle down. Charles wanted to settle down at once. He wanted to marry Anastasie.

Lafayette was charmed; so was Adrienne when she was told of the offer. They had nothing to give their daughter as dowry, but Charles was well aware of that. This was a true love match, something unheard of in their own early days, when each noble marriage was preceded, as theirs had been, by months and even years of sordid dickering over settlements and inheritances. Charles was, also, the brother of their friend, the friend who had shared so many of their trials. They could ask for nothing better than an alliance between the Lafayette and Maubourg families.

When the news was taken to Witmold, however, there were outcries, the lifting of hands, the rolling of eyes. Monsieur de Mun said that only savages in the American wilderness married in this offhand fashion. Madame de Tessé said that there had been nothing like it since Adam and Eve mated in the Garden of Eden. She continued to be very disparaging and outspoken until she saw that her niece and nephew were completely unimpressed by her comments. At least Anastasie and Charles knew what poverty was and were not afraid of being poor, Adrienne said.

Madame de Tessé then offered to provide the trousseau and the wedding.

After Easter, when the lease was up on the Lemkuhlen house, the whole family moved back again to Witmold. Just before the wedding, Lafayette's still beautiful, still fascinating friend, Madame de Simiane, arrived from France for a few weeks visit. Lafayette had been cut off from all direct communication with her during his captivity, but he knew from friends that she had survived the perilous years, and as soon as possible he had begun to write to her, she to him. Madame de Simiane had had to fascinate an ex-Jacobin and get a forged passport to leave the country and to reach Holstein.

"I thought I would find you all very low-spirited here," she said, "but you do nothing but talk about weddings and christenings!"

For Pauline was expecting another baby at any moment, and, round as a ball, was full of excitement and bustle in preparing the trousseau. Madame de Simiane prophecied that Pauline would be brought to bed in one of the big clothespresses she was forever diving into headfirst.

Adrienne had to leave most of the arrangements and the active work to others, for her old sickness, which had remitted for several months, came back on her full force. Again her arms and legs were swollen and abscessed. She could no longer walk. There was talk of putting off the wedding, but she refused as flatly as she had refused to delay in leaving Olmütz last autumn. Abbé de Luchet was to celebrate the Nuptial Mass, and on the wedding day, May 9th, 1798, Adrienne was carried into the improvised chapel at Witmold in an armchair, borne on one side by George and on the other by her future son-in-law.

"When I think," she said, "of the fearful situation my children were in a short time ago, when I see them all three about me and find myself on the point of adopting a fourth child according to the wishes of my heart, I feel as if I couldn't thank God enough."

Ten days after Anastasie's marriage, Pauline's baby, a girl, was born and immediately after birth was christened by Madame de Tessé in one of her atavistic returns to religious ritual. In her hurry to make the little stranger a Christian, Madame de Tessé picked up a bottle of cologne and poured it over the baby as she made the sign of the cross.

※

CHAPTER XXIII

Another Separation

ADRIENNE RECOVERED SLOWLY from her second illness. By midsummer she was very much better, though not entirely well—not as well as she wanted to be, for she must gird herself for yet another effort. If there were to be any sort of financial security for the Lafayettes, something must be done about settling the inheritance from the Duchesse d'Ayen and that would necessitate a visit to France. Adrienne was obviously the one to cross the border, since her name did not appear on any of the list of émigrés.

How strange it seemed that it should be she who was leaving Gilbert—he who had left her so often, so cavalierly. He was very nervous now at the prospect, very much afraid that her strength would not be equal to all that she would have to do and the many miles she would have to cover. He showed plainly that he had come to depend upon her being constantly with him; this, for Adrienne, was something new, something to be savored.

In July the entire family went to Hamburg. Charles and Anastasie would go with Adrienne as far as Holland, where

the de Maubourgs were settled near Utrecht. Virginie would
go all the way to France with her mother. After Lafayette
had seen them off he and George returned, very much depressed, to Madame de Tessé's house at Witmold.

Adrienne had arranged to stay with the Beauchets in
Paris, in the Rue de l'Université. She could not afford any
but the most modest lodgings and she was glad to be with
such good and faithful friends as her former maid and former confidential messenger during the anxious years at Chavaniac.

The matter of the inheritance, Adrienne found, was complicated. Some of the heirs of the Duchess were far away and
some were minors. One of them was the daughter of Clo-
thilde de Thésan, the third d'Ayen sister, who had died so
long ago in 1788, just before the Revolution. Little Jenny
de Thésan was living with her father in Germany. Louis de
Noailles, the father of Louise's children, was in America. All
of Pauline's presumed share, she being officially an outcast,
belonged to the state. Adrienne arranged for a friend of the
family, a lawyer, to buy this portion with the expectation
that it could be bought back if, and when, Pauline was re-
instated as a citizen.

Adrienne was able to consult not only with lawyers but
also with Rosalie de Grammont, who had come from Franche
Comté, bringing with her Monsieur Grelet, Alexis, Alfred,
and Euphémie. Unfortunately, the de Grammonts were living on the opposite side of the city and meetings were rare.
Adrienne felt that she could spare no money for cab fares
and because her legs were still swollen, walking was painful
for her.

Not all of her trudgings about Paris with a cane were on
behalf of the inheritance. She was trying to get the names of
all the family—the names of all their friends as well—erased
from the rolls of the proscribed. She had to deal with corrupt

and disgusting politicians, for the administration of the Directory was venal from top to bottom.

Sometimes it seemed as if her burden was more than she could bear and criticism from those in Holstein made it none the easier. Once when Lafayette reported what the denizens of Madame de Tessé's salon said and what they thought she should or should not have done in a particular case—it happened to be that of Charles de Maubourg—she lost patience and replied sharply.

A contrite letter sped back to her. "I am deeply sorry, my dear heart," Lafayette wrote, "that I have inadvertently wounded you. . . . I admit, however, with pleasure and all my heart, that it was I who was wrong and you who were right . . . Of all this there remains to me only the sorrow of having tormented you with our speculations on the Lake of Ploen and so to have provoked you."

He had complete confidence, Lafayette said, in all that she did, in all that she was. The only thing that he couldn't trust her for was giving a truthful account of her health; that was more important to him than anything else. He implored Rosalie to watch over her. He, who had had such a close view of her illnesses, could tell Rosalie that the worst possible thing for Adrienne was to get overtired or overworried. Virginie too, must pretend that she was a strict little schoolmarm and lecture her mother whenever necessary.

Adrienne, through Lafayette's letters, was kept abreast of the gossip of Witmold; nothing was too large or too small to interest her. Pauline had gone for a visit to a Protestant family, the Stolbergs, whom she had converted to Catholicism—and was troubled by a fever blister on her lip; George was longing to hear from Frestel, whom Adrienne had seen in Paris; Madame de Tessé was thinking of selling her farm, for it seemed as if Holstein would be drawn into the anti-French coalition. Always adventurous, she wanted to go to America and was taking English lessons from George. Lafayette himself was outlining a book, a great book about the legal benefits to mankind of the Revolution, but he didn't think that he was capable of writing it himself and wanted Adrienne to find just the right author, perhaps his old friend, Thomas Paine, and just the right publisher in Paris—yet another task.

She intended to go to Chavaniac before her return and the very idea filled Lafayette with excitement. Since their liberation, he had heard regularly from his aunt. She was still vigorous; the only concession she had made to age was taking a lady companion to live with her. The only serious trouble recently in Lafayette's home village had been a sheep killing she-wolf that Dr. Guitandry, the Mayor, had at last gotten rid of; with all the world in ferment this seemed an ideal state of affairs. Adrienne, Lafayette wrote, must be sure to thank the good doctor when she saw him, for all his services in the past.

But when would he, Gilbert, see *her?* That was the question that Lafayette asked over and over. When they were reunited, he promised her, they would never part again.

The weeks and months went by, however, and Adrienne against her will remained in France. She accomplished her trip to Auvergne, but she could not seem to accomplish a just and satisfactory apportionment of her mother's estate in the absence of so many of the legatees. She and her husband were sinking deeper into debt day by day. All of Adrienne's inheritance might be swallowed up in clearing away these encumbrances and then there would be nothing left to live upon.

In his letters, Lafayette spoke constantly of going to America to start life anew, though his American friends, Washington among them, had discouraged the idea. Relations between the two countries had almost reached the breaking point, chiefly because of the stupid arrogance of the present French government. There was bitter irony for Adrienne in the thought that Lafayette might not be well-received in America merely because he was a Frenchman.

At last she realized that she could do nothing more at present in France. In February of 1799, she had a good reason for turning her back on Paris. Anastasie was going to have a baby and, though Lafayette assured her that a good doctor was in charge of the case, Adrienne wanted to be present when her first grandchild was born.

She and Virginie would only have to go as far as Holland on their return trip. Holstein had become enemy territory, and Lafayette and George had taken refuge in the Batavian Republic, which was willing to shelter them in spite of its alliance with France. They were living in a pretty little cottage which Charles and Anastasie had rented at Vianen, not far from Utrecht. Lafayette could report how happily the de Maubourg's marriage was turning out—Charles was actually talkative! He himself had renewed an old friendship with a General Van Ryssel, who had headed the Dutch Republican troops in 1787. When he and his young folk went to dine with the General in Utrecht, they took with them Charles' brother, Victor de la Tour Maubourg, who was in love with Van Ryssel's daughter. While a lively game of cards was being played by the youngsters in the evening, the two old soldiers would sit over a quiet game of chess in a corner of the salon.

When Adrienne at last arrived, Lafayette was relieved to find that she looked better and stronger than when she left in July, though she was now in her fortieth year and threads of white were beginning to appear in her dark hair. Sixteen-year-old Virginie had grown tall in France and had such a glowing, pink and white complexion that she was often mistaken for an "English miss."

Anastasie's baby appeared promptly after her mother's return—and proved to be twin girls, only one of whom survived. The baby, Celestine, was less than a month old when the little house at Vianen became crowded to capacity. Adrienne, as business head of the family, had called a conference of her sisters. Pauline and Joachim came from Witmold, Madame de Tessé providing the funds for their journey. The de Grammonts came from France.

It was on March 17th, 1799, that they all assembled—Easter Even; the first time in eight years that the three surviving daughters of Henriette d'Ayen would be able to go to Mass together on Easter Day. Pauline and Rosalie had not seen one another since that snowy December morning in 1791, when Rosalie came to the Hotel de Beaune to say goodbye.

Pauline and Rosalie, knowing how impoverished Adrienne was, made common purse with her in meeting the expense of feeding the hungry crowd that sat down every day to dinner at Vianen. Even so, they ran into difficulties. An economical egg dish, *oeufs à la neige,* kept appearing with monotonous regularity on the table. Later Joachim de Montagu, who liked substantial vittles, complained that the only decent dinner he ate in Holland was in the house of General Van Ryssel.

Each evening, after the skimpy supper had been cleared away and the rest of the household had gone to bed, the three sisters held conferences in the chilly little parlor of the cottage. Fires were at a premium; each conferee was wrapped in an overcoat, three pairs of slippered feet were perched on a tiny foot stove set in the middle of the room. The talk was in whispers so as not to disturb the sleeping husbands and children, and the talk was not of business; that could be discussed when the others were present.

Adrienne, Pauline, and Rosalie spoke of the past. They had slipped back again into the red tapestried bedroom of the Hotel de Noailles and felt that their mother was again present, watching over them. They decided to compose a prayer in honor of their dead, to be said daily; if possible at the hour when the Duchess, Louise, and their grandmother had died. It took the form of a litany.

"Lord, Thou hast made Thy light and Thy truth to shine upon them; Thou hast led them to Thy holy hill and allowed them to enter into Thy sanctuary—
"Have mercy on us!
"Lord, who was their strength, their salvation and their guide—
"Have mercy on us!"

Midway in the prayer, to which each contributed a portion, Pauline holding the pen, the others dictating, the petitions for mercy changed to amens and alleluias.

"Thou hast made them pass through fire and water, Lord, and hast brought them into a place of refreshment—
"Alleluia!
"The source of all life is in Thee, oh Lord, and in Thy light they see all light—
"Alleluia!"

Pauline and Rosalie took up again an old game they had played as children of analyzing one another's characters, faults as well as virtues. They were full of mutual admiration, but decided that Pauline was too excitable, she ought to read and meditate; Rosalie was almost too withdrawn from this world, too much of a nun. The younger sisters found a shining example in Adrienne; her faith was strong; she was wise and, as Pauline phrased it, she had a "ravishing" way of giving you her whole attention when you talked to her; but wasn't Adrienne perhaps a little too outgoing? Was she sufficiently introverted? To this pair of pietists, Adrienne seemed to count too heavily on the joys and consolations that she could find this side of heaven.

For a month the sisters were very short of sleep. After their midnight whisperings they had to be up early in the morning to go to Mass. They would have been glad to stay together longer, but they heard that some of the unpleasant characters Adrienne had encountered in Paris had been informed of their meeting and thought they might be plotting mischief.

It had been decided to the satisfaction of all parties how the Duchess' property should be divided. Adrienne would inherit the chateau and demesne of La Grange-Bléneau, Pauline would inherit Fontenay, and Jenny de Thésan lands that lay between the two estates. Rosalie would receive Tangri in the Pas de Calais. Some valuable farms in the Seine-et-Marne district would go to Louise's children.

Early in May the de Grammonts and de Montagus left Vianen, Pauline taking with her a trunkful of clothing that George had brought from America for his aunts and some antique garments of the Vicomte de Beaune, Pauline's troublesome father-in-law, that Adrienne had collected at Plauzat on her recent trip to Auvergne.

A few days later Adrienne went back to France to continue her labors. Again Virginie went with her and this time George as well. While his mother and sister stayed in Paris, he would go to Chavaniac to gladden the eyes of his aunt.

*   *   *

Once more abandoned, Lafayette waited for news, for letters, as Adrienne had so often waited for them in the past. Hardly had his wife left than he began counting the days till her return. He wrote her often out-of-doors in the tiny cottage garden, where a ring dove was sitting on her nest. He kept thinking of La Grange, their future home. She must tell him all about it—the house and farm. How many animals, big and little, were there? How much did it cost to feed and care for them? What was the state of the forest land?

Lafayette had borrowed some English books on agriculture and was deep in their study, for he assured Adrienne that he had no greater ambition than to spend the rest of his life with her in retirement as a gentleman farmer. In June, he told her that he had had a visit from a French officer sent by Carnot, one of the Directors, who hinted at yet another *coup d'état* in Paris—as if there had not been enough already! Would General Lafayette be interested in a leading role? The answer was no.

But this was a moment of great suspense and uncertainty. The skies were darkening over Holland now. An invasion by Britain and Russia, the most recent member of the coalition, was rumored. France was sending in troops to defend her Dutch ally. Lafayette saw again the French uniform and tears came to his eyes.

One day in August, George suddenly burst in upon him, bringing with him an ancient trophy. While in Chavaniac, he had dug up the two swords of honor that Adrienne had buried in the garden when she was expecting the chateau to be attacked in 1792. The United States sword had rusted away, all but the golden hilt, but George thought that it could be affixed to the blade of the other trophy, the one which had been presented to Lafayette on his retirement from the National Guard.

George could give *viva voce* all the news of Paris. The political situation there was changing from hour to hour. It seemed as if the impotent and disorganized Directory would not last much longer but it was hard to say what would replace it. The Jacobin Club had been revived—a menacing circumstance. The foreign war had taken an alarming turn, the French having been driven from Italy—and General Bonaparte was in Egypt.

Adrienne, George said, was very much frightened by the

threatened invasion of the Low Countries. Again she might be cut off from her husband by a barrier of war. She heard that Napper Tandy, the Irish patriot in exile in Hamburg, had been handed over to the British and she could picture Lafayette being surrendered to the allies by the defeated Dutch.

In her anxiety, she had gone to call on one of the Directors. It was difficult to choose among them but she selected the one who seemed to represent most nearly the point of view of the constitutionalists of 1789. This was a former churchman, Abbé Siéyès. He had trimmed his sails to every political wind; he was a clever man with liberal leanings, but without the moral fortitude to live up to them. When someone asked him what he had done during the Terror, he replied simply, "I lived."

Adrienne asked Siéyès if it would be a good idea for her husband to come back to France in case Holland should fall.

The Abbé didn't think so. It would be imprudent, he said. If Lafayette had to seek asylum anywhere, he had better go to one of the states controlled by the now neutral King of Prussia.

"The King of Prussia, who held him prisoner!" Adrienne exclaimed indignantly. "My husband would prefer a prison in France if the worse came to the worst! At least he has a little more confidence in his own countrymen!"

Lafayette had shrugged his shoulders when he first read the report of Adrienne's talk with Siéyès that Virginie, who was also present at the interview, had written out for him. He refused to think of politics then; he refused to think of politics now. Instead, he and George talked about a farm in America that would support the whole family, though George had a more immediate end in view. He and Victor de la Tour Maubourg wanted to enlist in the Dutch army. Lafayette, speaking like any staid and cautious *père de famille*, dissuaded them, saying that it would be unwise politically.

When the invasion began, however, and the lines of defense were driven back, he could restrain them no longer and the two young men went off to Haarlem to join up under assumed names.

Lafayette knew that this would be yet another worry for George's mother. He was glad before long to reassure her. On September 19th, 1799, the second anniversary of their leaving Olmütz, all the church bells in Vianen were ringing to celebrate a victory over the British and Russians at Bergen op Zoom. George came home crestfallen because he had seen no action.

And a few weeks later there was even greater news from France. On October 9th, Napoleon Bonaparte landed in the South at Frejus. His exploits in Egypt had been far from brilliant, but the country as a whole had heard little of Nelson's victory at the Nile and knew by heart the grandiloquent speech that the General had made to his troops in the shadow of the pyramids. Napoleon's march to Paris was a triumph. Within a month of his landing, he was master of the entire country. The Abbé Siéyès was his fellow conspirator in ousting the other members of the Directory who might prove troublesome. On the 18th of Brumaire, the 9th of November, 1799, Bonaparte surrounded the Assembly with a cordon of his troops, had himself appointed supreme military commander, and swiftly wrote a new constitution under which he, as First Consul, would be the chief executive.

Adrienne had acted swiftly also. Even before Bonaparte had taken the Assembly by surprise she went to one of his levees. He spoke vaguely, but favorably, of Lafayette. She wrote at once to Vianen, saying that the time was ripe for return. As a first step, Lafayette must write a letter of congratulation to the General.

Lafayette, interrupted in the middle of a game of chess with General Van Ryssel, wrote somewhat reluctantly, for Bonaparte had never replied to his letter from Hamburg two years earlier. He felt, however, that Adrienne, the master strategist, his commanding officer now, knew best. He sent her the letter to Bonaparte to pass upon and deliver. He set her mind at rest on a subject that he knew was deeply troubling her. Back in France, would he again enter politics or public service? Would the miseries she had suffered when they lived in the Rue de Bourbon be repeated?

"Nothing," Lafayette wrote, "nothing in this world—I swear it on my honor, on my love for you, and on the shades of those for whom we weep—shall ever persuade me to renounce the plan of retirement that I have formed for myself and according to which we shall spend tranquilly the rest of our lives. . . . I can read your heart, my dear, beloved Adrienne, and none of its good, tender and generous impulses escapes me. I have an inexpressible impatience to see you—here or there—and to seize at last the happy moment when we shall be separated nevermore!"

Ten days after the 18th of Brumaire, Alexandre Romeuf, Louis Romeuf's brother, rushed into the cottage at Vianen with a passport that Adrienne had taken out under a pseudonym for Lafayette. Two hours later Lafayette was on his way to France.

PART SEVEN

November, 1799—Christmas Eve, 1807

CHAPTER XXIV

The Garden of Picpus

LAFAYETTE FOUND that they were all there to greet him—
Anastasie and Charles, as well as Adrienne. Adrienne
had managed to get the de Maubourgs a permit to return
under police surveillance in October. They were staying in
a house that belonged to Adrien de Mun, the son of Madame
de Tessé's old admirer, the facetious young man whom
Pauline had found such a tease.

Lafayette wrote at once to Bonaparte and Siéyès to announce his arrival and to present his compliments. He was
summoned to the ministry and told curtly that he should go
back to Holland. The First Consul was enraged. He had no
wish to see a rival to his popularity appear at this critical
moment. No one dared to mention the name of Lafayette in
his presence.

Lafayette shrugged his shoulders—and disobeyed the order.
He would rather, he said, be arrested than go skulking back
to Vianen. Again it was Adrienne who must save the day.
She went alone to call on Bonaparte. This took as great
courage as any of the disagreeable and perilous interviews

she had undertaken in the past. The Corsican was notoriously rude to women. At a dinner party he was quite likely to say to the lady next to him, "My God, what red arms you have!" or "What an ugly way you have of doing your hair!"

But like many a parvenu of the moment, Bonaparte had a sneaking admiration for a great lady of the old regime. He received Adrienne courteously. He listened while she bravely explained the ideas her husband symbolized, the good effect that she thought his return would have on public opinion. The little man with the beautiful, pale face and quick, restless eyes seemed impressed, but when she rose to go he paid her a dubious compliment.

"I am charmed, Madame," he said, "to have made your acquaintance. You are very intelligent—but you don't understand public affairs."

Nevertheless, Lafayette was notified that he could remain in France if he went to the country and lived there quietly while the legality of his status was reviewed. This would take some time.

That the Consulate was determined that he should remain in the background was made plain when, shortly after the new year—and a new century—had begun, the news of the death of Washington was announced in France. In an order of the day, the First Consul decreed that the standards of the army should be hung with black crepe for ten days of mourning. An address was delivered by a major general in the Temple of Mars, praising Washington's glorious deeds, but there was no mention of Washington's adopted son, nor was he invited to be present. George, who went merely as an onlooker, reported to his father that Bonaparte's victories in Egypt were more to the fore than the victory of Yorktown.

The Lafayettes went first to Fontenay and then to La Grange-Bléneau, which would soon be theirs. The old chateau, about thirty miles from Paris, had been built in the thirteenth century. It had come to Henriette d'Ayen from her mother. A big, irregular building, with five massive towers, it looked like the castle of Sleeping Beauty when its future inhabitants saw it first under a somber winter sky. No one had lived here for many years. The avenues were overgrown. The moat that surrounded the blackened walls was thick with sludge. But this, at last, was home, a home for them all. There was good farming land that could be reclaimed and made productive. Lafayette set to work with a will to put his recent studies in agriculture to the test and wrote to his one time farm superintendent, British John Dyson, for advice.

Adrienne was back and forth continually between La Grange and Paris that winter at her old task of getting her friends and family back from exile; it seemed as if the corvée would never end. She also had to see what she could do for George, who should be given the chance that he wanted to enter the army. She got him a commission in a regiment of hussars, and in the spring, to his father's pride and joy, he went off to fight the Austrians in Italy.

Gradually the names of the outcasts were erased, one by one. Pauline was among the first of the Noailles family to return. She arrived in February of 1800, and set to work, with Adrienne's help, on the cases of her husband, her father-in-law, Madame de Tessé, and the Duc de Noailles. Pauline and Adrienne's father wanted to come from Switzerland, bringing with him, of course, his new wife, the former Countess Golovkin, to see if he could salvage anything from the wreck of his immense fortune. He would like to regain possession of the Hotel de Noailles, which had not yet been sold by the government, but there seemed little chance of that. Napoleon had taken exclusive possession of the Tuileries and one of his fellow Consuls, Lebrun, who had formerly lived in the palace, moved into the mansion of the Rue St. Honoré.

Pauline walked in fear during her first days in Paris. She

would tremble at the sound of a cart, rumbling down the street behind her. Some churches were open, where Mass was being said by priests who had taken the required oath—but this Pauline could not abide. Madame de Duras, the cousin with whom Adrienne had passed those agonizing months in Le Plessis, showed Pauline the way to a secret chapel, concealed behind a dressmaker's shop, where she could get the kind of religious sustenance that she craved.

One day Pauline visited an émigré who had been arrested and was an inmate of the Temple where the royal family had been imprisoned. Free to wander where she would, she climbed to the empty rooms where poor Marie Antoinette had once shed so many tears. Rummaging about in a closet, she found a blue-and-white salad bowl that surely had been used by royalty. Pauline reverently carried it home with her as a relic to be handed down to her children and grandchildren.

She was amazed and for some reason a little depressed by the vigor with which her sister and brother-in-law were building for the future at La Grange. Even after the last detail of the inheritance was completed in the spring of 1801, and Fontenay was legally hers, Pauline did not go to live on her estate. She, Joachim, and the children—another baby was on the way—set off to visit Rosalie de Grammont in Franche Comté and from there made a melanchoy pilgrimage to Plauzat to gaze on the scene of former splendors. From the windows of Plauzat in the old days, one could see five manor houses, all belonging to the de Montagu family, all of which had passed, like Pauline's wedding diamonds, into other hands.

When she returned to Paris, Pauline became absorbed in a project that had been decided upon during the meeting of the three sisters at Vianen. They had talked then of finding the place in France where their mother, Louise, and the

Maréchale were buried and of building a tomb for them.
They had made many inquiries. Father Carrichon, the first
to be consulted, did not know where the bodies he had seen
go down into the cart on that July day, were taken after the
execution. No one else could give them any information.
The Terror was a subject that most people preferred to forget and that the Consulate officially ignored.

At last Pauline discovered a clue. She heard that there was
a girl named Mademoiselle Paris, a lacemaker, who was living in a garret in one of the suburbs and who might be able
to tell her something. After making many fruitless expeditions, after having knocked at many doors and climbed up
and down many flights of stairs, she found Mademoiselle
Paris on the fourth floor of a miserable building, not far
from the Barrière du Trône. At first the girl—but one could
hardly call her that, she looked as if she had never been
young—was unresponsive; she seemed to be afraid of timid
little Pauline. When Pauline had told her errand, however,
the lacemaker burst into tears. She was glad that she had
someone to whom she could tell her story.

In July of 1794, Mademoiselle Paris was living with her
father, who had been a groom to the de Brissac family for
thirty years, and with her brother, who was clerk in the
office of a major of the National Guard. The brother was
the only breadwinner. Since the Revolution no one wore
lace any more and Mademoiselle Paris was out of work. A
pension that her father had received was also cut off by the
financial ruin of the de Brissacs.

One day the brother, a steady, reliable boy, who brought
home all his earnings, did not come home at his usual time.
Mademoiselle Paris went to look for him and failed to find
him. When she came back to her apartment it was empty.
Neighbors told her that her father, who could hardly walk,
had just been dragged off to prison, the same prison where
her brother had been under arrest since early morning.

What was the accusation brought against them, by whom
it had been lodged, Mademoiselle Paris never learned, nor
did she see her father and brother again until they were in
the tumbril being taken to the guillotine. She followed the
cortege, as Father Carrichon was to follow it only a few days
later. She watched her father and brother die, as if in a
trance, hardly aware of what she was seeing, murmuring a
prayer over and over without knowing precisely what she
was saying.

When she came to herself, the grisly spectacle was over.
The Place du Trône was almost deserted and the wagon,
with the bodies of the victims in it, was going off in the
direction of Saint Mandé. Still half-dazed, Mademoiselle
Paris followed at a distance. The wagon turned off the road
into a field near the ruins of an Augustinian monastery, the
Monastery of Picpus. It was almost dark but she saw that all
the bodies were thrown pell-mell into a big pit, about thirty
feet square, that was already well-filled. They were quickly
shoveled over with dirt. She was sure of the location, for she
went there often on Sunday to pray by the mound under
which lay the remains of thirteen hundred people, all of
whom had been executed in the six weeks that the guillotine
was in operation at the Barrière du Trône.

Pauline went back to tell Adrienne that their search was
over. The following day, guided by Mademoiselle Paris, the
two sisters visited the monastery ruins. It was a very lonely
place. The fields were uncultivated; the road leading into it
was a mere track. The grave itself was plainly marked, for
a wall had been built about it.

As the three women stood there, looking at the mound,
sorrow seemed to rise from the very ground. How evanescent
life was, how vast and all-embracing the community of death!
Some of the beings who were buried here were mourned, but
many had already been forgotten. There was no one left to
remember that they had ever lived or to say a single prayer

for them. The idea that Adrienne and Pauline had cherished of an individual tomb for their dead seemed petty and insufficient.

They learned something of the history of Picpus. In mediaeval days, the monastery maintained a hospital, and in time of pestilence the monks developed a primitive therapy, which consisted of lancing the boils of their patients and draining off the pus—hence the odd name. Until the Revolution, a community of religious women was located here, but in 1792 it disappeared and all that was left of the establishment was the chapel, which had been partially destroyed by fire. Since then the property had passed through several hands. After the Directory came to power, the fields were put up for sale and the one containing the grave was bought by a Princess Hohenzollern, whose brother, Prince Salm-Kyrbourg, was one of the victims.

Adrienne and Pauline wrote to the German Princess and asked her to unite with them in consecrating the ground to the memory of all who lay beneath it. The Princess refused to give up her property rights.

They then considered buying the surrounding fields as a cemetery, but wondered how they could manage to do so. It was Mademoiselle Paris who suggested that they should raise a subscription from all relatives of the dead. She offered to set aside ten *sous* a week from her meager earnings for the fund.

That was the small—but brave—beginning of a mighty undertaking. The first subscriptions, from the Noailles sisters and their friends, were easy to get, but seeking out the relatives of all who had passed through the Conciergerie during the last six weeks of the Terror was a complicated, time consuming affair. Many had disappeared completely; many, like Louis de Noailles, Louise's husband, were out of France. All —even those who had once been rich—were poor.

Adrienne and Pauline persuaded Abbé Beudot, the priest

of the Parish of Sainte Marguerite, to head the fund, though
they took upon themselves much of the labor of investigation
and letter writing. The ruins of the monastery were bought
in 1802, the rest of the property later. The chapel was rebuilt
and in time enlarged into a church, where Abbé Beudot
came every Sunday to celebrate Mass. Each year, in April or
early May, a solemn Requiem was sung, after which a procession of mourners, headed by the priest, issued from the
church, chanting the *Miserere* and moved through what had
once been the garden of the monastery to the grave. The
grave itself was planted with cypresses and poplars and sur-
mounted by a cross. For a time, the activities at Picpus were
watched by Napoleon's secret service agents, until it was discovered that Eugène Beauharnais, Napoleon's step-son, was
one of the subscribers to the fund.

The wall of the church's transept came slowly to be covered with small marble plaques, each giving the name, the
age, and the occupation of a victim, as it had appeared on
the rolls of the Conciergerie. Men and women were there,
old and young; boys of seventeen—one was discovered who
was only fourteen—and octogenarians. Some were famous
folk—there were poets, generals, and high dignitaries of the
church—but most were obscure. Only a small fraction was of
noble blood, the majority having followed some humble calling, such as that of Mademoiselle Paris' father and brother.

In time, also, a portion of the ruins was transformed into
a retreat for an order of nuns, devoted to the perpetual
adoration of the Blessed Sacrament. To the church, Adrienne
came often to pray behind the white-veiled figures that, day
and night, knelt, immobile as though they had been carved
from marble, before the altar. The road that led by The
Garden of Picpus, as it was called, was the road that took
her to and from La Grange.

CHAPTER XXV

Years of Grace

A<small>T LA GRANGE</small>, Adrienne was finding those joys this side of heaven of which Pauline and Rosalie thought she was a little bit too fond.

Sooner perhaps than he had expected, Lafayette was told that he was *persona grata* in France. When, in the early summer of 1800, Napoleon came back from his campaign in Italy, Lafayette asked for and obtained an audience. The First Consul was surprisingly friendly. They chatted informally then and later. Lafayette was invited to private functions at which Bonaparte was present; whenever he was in Paris he went to the receptions that Josephine held at the Tuileries.

A curious relationship grew up between the two men. Napoleon, the great opportunist, was fascinated by this man of principle, though his admiration was well-mixed with contempt. He couldn't understand how anyone could have had so many chances of seizing power and let them slip through his fingers for a mere nothing, an abstract ideal. Sometimes he envied Lafayette. "Lafayette," he said wistfully, "has the talent for making friends." If he, Napoleon, should fail no one would stand by him, except his wife—"for one always has the person with whom one sleeps"—and perhaps his brother Joseph.

Lafayette, on the other hand, was more than a little attracted by Napoleon's personal charm, his brilliance, and his military genius. At their very first interview, however, Lafayette sniffed the air and scented a despot. Various offers were made that would bind him to Napoleon's chariot wheel. Lafayette accepted reinstatement in the army as a General on the retired list—this brought him a small pension—but he refused a seat in the Senate, a seat on departmental councils, and the post of Minister to the United States. He couldn't picture himself appearing there in knee breeches instead of in a uniform and he didn't want to represent a government that he mistrusted.

"I am like the child," he said quizzically, "who, when they tried to teach him the alphabet, obstinately refused to say 'a' for fear that they would afterwards oblige him to say 'b.' "

When, in 1803, a plebiscite was held that would give Napoleon the First Consulship for life, Lafayette wrote on the register of his commune: "I cannot vote for such a magistracy until the public liberty is sufficiently guaranteed; then I shall give my vote to Napoleon Bonaparte."

That there should be no misunderstanding, he wrote a personal letter to the Consul, thanking him again for the release from Olmütz, but telling him how he had voted. After that Lafayette was ignored and no longer visited the Tuileries.

For Adrienne, how comfortable, how satisfying it was to know that he could not be lured away from her and that honor forbade his cooperating with Napoleon! She had been happy in the squalid cell at Olmütz, she had been happy at Lemkuhlen, she was even happier now, knowing that they were at rest and that the trees and grass that surrounded them were growing on the soil of France.

La Grange was slowly, but steadily, made more habitable and more productive. Lafayette bought some fine rams and ewes at the fairs at Rambouillet and built up a handsome flock. There was a hospital for sick animals in one of his barns, but it was usually empty. Félix Pontonnier, who had played his Panpipe to such good effect at Olmütz, was put in charge of the farm. Monsieur Vaudoyer, the architect who had done so well at Chavaniac, drew up plans for transforming the interior of the chateau.

Adrienne was particularly anxious to restore a small chapel on the ground floor. On one of its walls, she placed a tablet on which was engraved *The Canticle of Tobit*. A circular room in one of the towers Lafayette took for his library—it was "the prettiest thing imaginable," Adrienne said. There was a suite of rooms for Anastasie, Charles, and their babies —Celestine had acquired a little sister—and another suite for George. There were many guest rooms for the friends who dropped in and must be put up for the night, and often for very much longer.

As in the old days in the Rue de Bourbon, Americans were often entertained. Félix Frestel, now married, came with his family; and Josephe Masclet, the "Eleuthère" who had written those biting articles in Lafayette's behalf; and, of course, Madame de Simiane, who had become as close a friend of Adrienne as of Lafayette. Madame de Tessé came so often that a special room was reserved for her use.

There were English visitors, too. One was the novelist, Fanny Burney, who had married Alexandre d'Arblay, one of Lafayette's staff officers. The author of *Evelina* could not say that Madame de Lafayette was beautiful; she was too worn and frail for that—but what "speaking eyes!"

The Whig leaders in Parliament, Charles James Fox and General Fitzpatrick, were also guests whom Lafayette espe-

cially enjoyed at La Grange. Fox agreed with his host's esti-
mate of Napoleon and said that the kind of democracy they
both had tried to promote with small success in their re-
spective countries would not come in their own time, nor
perhaps in George's time, but it would be a living reality for
George's children. Fox planted some English ivy that flourished on the weather-beaten walls of the chateau, saying, in
compliment to Adrienne, that it symbolized constancy.

None of this hospitality and none of the improvements to
the house would have been possible if the Lafayettes' financial situation had not taken a turn for the better. The American government had been asked by Louis Romeuf to
reimburse Lafayette for the large sums he had spent in the
American war, of which his man-of-business, Monsieur Morizot, had kept account. In 1803, a land bonus was being distributed to American veterans and Thomas Jefferson, now
President, saw to it that Lafayette was given some valuable
property, at first in Ohio and later, after the Louisiana Purchase, near New Orleans. It would be years before title could
be taken, but this, like the liberty Fox had promised, was
something to anticipate.

With an eye to the future, income and outgo at La Grange
were carefully watched. The family economized on clothes
and on trips to Paris, which they visited only when absolutely
necessary. Adrienne held the purse strings. In all money
transactions she cast the deciding vote. She knew how care-
less Gilbert could be and how open-handed he was. Once,
when she consulted him about giving some wood to a peasant neighbor who was laid up with a broken leg, he said,
"No, darling, I won't let you give them a quarter of a cord.
Give them half. Then the poor things won't have to come so
often."

She was charitable herself, but at this time she was strug-
gling to pay off some of the older debts, among them the
debt that she had owed so long to Gouverneur Morris. This

was a painful experience. The Lafayettes' last meeting with Morris at Hamburg had not been altogether cordial and he had long since gone home to America. The value of French money had fallen in the past ten years. Morris' notary in Paris, with whom Adrienne negotiated, haggled over principal and interest. Morris himself was indignant that he should not get the full buying power of the 100,000 *livres* he had laid out in 1793. But Adrienne stood firm. To pay the augmented amount, she thought, would be unjust—and even ruinous—to herself, her husband, and her children.

Her children had to be thought of now, for her family was increasing. In 1802, George, who had been wounded at the Battle of Mincio, came home on sick leave from the army. He was twenty-three and it was high time that he should be married. Dutiful son that he was, George would only marry someone of whom his parents thoroughly approved. He found a charming wife in Emilie de Tracy, the daughter of one of Lafayette's ex-officers and a member of the Constituent Assembly in 1789.

The wedding took place in June. Immediately after, the family left *en masse* for Auvergne, so that Aunt Chavaniac could meet and inspect the wife of her beloved George. Each summer since their return, the Lafayettes had visited the old lady, the only drawback to these stays being her passionate grief when they left. The old cry, "I will never live to see you again," was always raised and had lost none of its resonance.

*　　　　*　　　　*

While the Lafayettes were at Chavaniac in 1802, Pauline de Montagu, ever restless, was in Limousin, at Brives-la-Gaillarde, which was once the center of the Noailles estates, seeing if something could be saved for her father from the ruins. All of the property had been confiscated and most of it had been sold, but under a new law, that granted indemnity to former owners of the land, a few crumbs might be garnered.

At Brives, Pauline met an elderly gentleman, a Monsieur de Lasteyrie, who drove about with her on the trips that she had to make in the surrounding countryside, inspecting farms and vacant manor houses. Sometimes the old man's nephew, Louis de Lasteyrie, went with them.

Pauline began to have designs on Louis. He was good-looking and twenty-three years old; he was of noble blood, a Marquis Lasteyrie du Saillant. Titles might have been voted out of existence in 1789, but not for Pauline! She was further interested to discover that the young man was a very distant relative and that he was much to be pitied. He had spent his childhood at Malta and when the island was besieged by the British, escaped by the skin of his teeth to France. Recently his mother, to whom he had been much attached, had died. It seemed to Pauline that here was just the husband for her niece, Virginie.

Virginie was twenty and she too should have been married long ago, though her relatives said kindly that she didn't look a day older than sixteen. The only fault that they could find with her was that she didn't have the stately, erect carriage of a court lady. "But what can you expect of a child who was brought up in a prison?" was Adrienne's comment. At the time when her father was being wooed by the Bonapartes, Josephe Bonaparte suggested that Virginie would make a good wife for his brother Lucien, but this idea was never seriously considered by her parents and Pauline, had she known of it, would have held it in horror.

Before leaving Brives, she consulted Monsieur de Lasteyrie. He was willing to promote what seemed to him a distinguished, if not a rich, alliance for Louis. Pauline wrote that she was bringing some friends to Chavaniac, one of them a candidate for son-in-law.

All went as she had planned. The young people took to

one another. The de Lasteyries were invited to visit La Grange after the Lafayettes had gone home from Auvergne in the autumn and the marriage was scheduled for the spring.

Again Madame de Tessé, long since repatriated, insisted on providing the trousseau. The bride could not be showered with diamonds, as once was the custom, but the relatives banded together to present her with a purse of two thousand francs; they had not been able to do as much for her sister when she was married at Lemkuhlen.

The May wedding was a small one and, Father Carrichon officiating, was held, not in the chapel, but in a room adjoining Lafayette's bedroom, for in February the father of the bride had slipped on an icy pavement in Paris and broken his hip. He allowed two young doctors to experiment with a traction device in setting the fracture. The procedure was exquisitely painful—both for him and for Adrienne—and a complete failure. For the rest of his life Lafayette would walk, as his wife still did at times when she had a recurrence of her old malady, with a cane.

After the wedding, Madame de Tessé invited the entire bridal party, including the invalid in a wheelchair, to the country house at Aulnay she had acquired as soon as she returned to France. She still had a farm, she still kept cows, but she was no longer in the dairy business. All of her milk, cream, and butter was needed for her guests, who were even more numerous than at Witmold.

The stout-hearted disciple of Voltaire spent her mornings in bed, reading, with a pencil in her hand to mark quotable passages. At noon she got up, dressed, and descended to an elegant little *kiosque,* which she had had built in her garden, a different vista from each of its many windows. There she received her court until dinner time and after dinner there was, as anciently, a game of picquet in the salon, followed by reading aloud, and conversation that went on until far into the night.

Nothing had changed in Madame de Tessé's habits, but her nieces felt that she had mellowed a little with the years. She was not as witty as formerly, they noticed, at the expense of religion and religious people. She went regularly to Mass in the village church and insisted that her docile, taciturn old husband should go with her. To him she was more attentive than of old. Being married to him was a habit she had acquired almost half a century ago and she was looking forward soon to celebrating a golden wedding anniversary by yet another fête at Aulnay.

Adrienne and Gilbert themselves had been married for almost thirty years. She was forty-three, he forty-five. With all of their children paired off, they felt that they definitely belonged to the older generation. That summer and the next, they went to take a cure at a spa in Auvergne as well as to visit at Chavaniac.

When the Louisiana Purchase was in prospect in 1803, Jefferson offered Lafayette the governorship of the new territory, and the commissioners who came to Paris to clinch the bargain—one of them was James Monroe—urged their old friend to come where he could do useful work and be sure of making a fortune. He declined, however, giving the uncertain health of his wife as the chief reason.

Jefferson, when he left France in 1789, had worried about Lafayette's being in danger from royal autocracy in France; he worried now as he foresaw a still greater concentration of power in the hands of a single man. In 1804 the subservient Senate, which Lafayette had refused to join, voted the Imperial crown for Napoleon. An Imperial court of princes, dukes, and barons was hastily created. Surprisingly, perhaps, overtures were again made to Lafayette. He was suggested as a candidate for the Legion of Honor by Josephe Bonaparte, now Prince Josephe; another offer of a seat in the Senate was made. Again Lafayette refused, saying firmly, but gently, to Josephe, whom he had always liked, that he preferred to be nothing—in other words, a private citizen.

He seldom left La Grange. While Adrienne was never completely well, Lafayette soon again was vigorous and active, in spite of his lameness. Always till now a lean man, he began to put on weight. Since he was no longer able to mount a horse, he saved himself unnecessary steps by keeping a megaphone in his tower room with which he could carry on shouted conversations with his men in the grounds. His agricultural experiments were so successful that he was able to buy bits of property to round out the estate.

Adrienne was much interested in a little school that she had started at Courpalais, a village near the chateau. She found it hard to find a teacher that would satisfy her, for, the itch for education being in her blood, her standards were high. Celestine, Anastasie's child, was old enough now for informal lessons and to her granddaughter Adrienne began to read some of the books, the classic poems, and plays, that Madame d'Ayen had once read to her children in the red tapestried bedroom of the Hotel de Noailles.

The years that were passing so gently, so delightfully, were not all serene, for the world outside the gates of La Grange was a world at war. Adrienne and Lafayette were saddened by the death in 1804 of Louis de Noailles, who, when they all were very young, used to walk in the garden at Versailles with Gilbert, Adrienne, and Louise.

Noailles had never returned from America. He was a banker for some time in Philadelphia and after the Terror rejoined the French army in Santo Domingo. For five months, with only a small garrison, he held Fort St. Nicholas, which was being besieged on one side by native troops and on the other by the British fleet. He was able to evacuate his men successfully, sail to Cuba, and capture a number of British ships. He might have come to port in France in triumph, if he had not been mortally wounded in the sea fight.

Louis' sons, Alexis and Alfred—they were now of military age—entered the army of Napoleon. George went back into service and Virginie's husband, Louis de Lasteyrie, enlisted for the campaigns of 1805 and 1806. George was twice-wounded and at the bloody, wintertime Battle of Eylau saved his general's life, pulling the general out from under a fallen horse and giving him his own to ride to safety. All of this, as well as his years of service, should have brought advancement to George, but he still remained a lieutenant after the upgrading of all of his comrades. One day, at a review, Napoleon asked who the junior officer was who seemed somewhat older than the others. When he was told, he said, with a shrug, "Oh, *his* son"—and passed on down the line.

During the peace that followed Eylau in 1807, George and Louis, who had also found that he was being held back because of his connection with the Lafayettes, handed in their resignations. That was a very joyful spring for Adrienne. Her son and son-in-law would soon be home. They would all be together again—all the family, to which a new member had been added, for Virginie had just borne her first child, a daughter. A happy year, it seemed, a year to crown all others, lay ahead.

Only Pauline, who came to La Grange for a visit before going to see her father in Switzerland and then on to see Rosalie in Franche Comté, was dubious. She felt a presentiment of sorrow, but she did not put it into words; it was only a presentiment and Pauline, who was so prone to premonitions, had learned over the years to keep them to herself.

CHAPTER XXVI

Yours Alone

THE TWO YOUNG MEN came home from the wars in August. A few days later Adrienne was in great pain. The enemy that had first struck her down at Olmütz returned without warning.

After the violence of the first attack had subsided, she improved a little and Madame de Tessé insisted that she should come to Aulnay to be nearer to Paris and its doctors. They had all intended to go to Chavaniac that autumn and it seemed too bad that the old aunt should be deprived of her yearly, revivifying glimpse of George and Lafayette. On October 11th, Adrienne heard Mass said in the chapel of La Grange and, apparently without thinking that she might never return, was driven to Madame de Tessé's villa. Lafayette and his son left for Auvergne.

They felt that they should make this trip a short one and stayed only a few days at the chateau. Just as they were leaving, a letter came from Aulnay, saying that Adrienne was not so well and had been taken to her aunt's house in Paris. Lafayette, who usually was so optimistic, was panic-stricken.

George was less disturbed by the news than by the effect it had upon his father. He had never seen him so unnerved.

They traveled fast to Paris. They found Madame de Tessé's house had been transformed into a hospital—a well-filled hospital, though there was only one patient. All the family from La Grange was there; George's wife, Emilie, the de Maubourgs, Louis de Lasteyrie, Virginie and her baby, who was still at the breast. Lafayette could see that there had been a change for the worse and that Adrienne was very ill; for a few days after his arrival, however, she rallied. Madame di Simiane came to see her, and Adrienne said stoutly, "I am going to have a malignant fever, but I am being so well taken care of that I will recover."

She felt that she was deeply rooted in life. She had been ill before and had survived.

But the respite was short and all the care that the doctors could give her was only to make her a little more comfortable. The medical men of Paris were as baffled as Dr. Kreutschke of Olmütz had been by this mysterious malady. All that they could say of it was—"a dissolution of the blood."

Adrienne's pains remitted somewhat, but as her fever continued and increased she lost contact with reality. She wandered in strange places. Was it because she had recently been reading *Athalie* with little Celestine that she thought she was in Syria and Egypt? Or did the fantasy stem from her own childhood when she first heard the stately verses of Racine read by her own mother?

She knew that this was a time of great trouble and danger for the House of Jacob. There was war between Syria and Judah. Persecutions would soon begin; martyrs would die for their faith. That she was deeply involved in all this turmoil Adrienne was sure, though she was confused as to how and why, so quickly did one vision succeed upon another, so evanescent were the shapes that moved about her.

Bewildered though she was, there was one figure that was

constant and whose identity she never mistook; her husband was always there beside her. He was loved not only by her, but by the House of Jacob, she said. If there were persecutions, he would be sure to defend the oppressed. One day she felt that a crown was resting on her head; she must be an empress. "But if that is so," she said in puzzlement to Lafayette, "then you must be an emperor and I know that that would lie heavy on your conscience. How strange it would be if I should have to sacrifice myself for a king!"

Then the mists would clear and she would realize that she had been talking nonsense. "I must be mad," she said. "Lean closer and tell me if I have lost my wits."

Lafayette, sitting by her bed, holding her hand, murmured that he would be sorry to think that the loving things she had said to him were all absurdities.

"I did say them? But I said a lot of foolishness as well. We have been playing the tragedy of *Athalie*. Here I am married to the most truthful man in the world and I don't know the true from the false!"

Another day she laughed and shook her head. "How tiresome I am and what a nuisance!" she exclaimed. "My children will have to put up with having such a stupid mother since their father seems to be so contented with his stupid wife."

Even in her delirium she knew that her children were there and once when George would have kissed her hand flung her arms about him in ecstasy, thinking that he had just come back from the army. But she couldn't remember whether Virginie was engaged to Louis de Lasteyrie or married to him, nor was she sure that Anastasie had children. "Do you know what mother love is?" she asked Anastasie. "Do you revel in it as I have? Is there anything sweeter, stronger, more intimate?"

In her unclouded moments, she spoke of La Grange and

how delicious it would be to go back there for six more happy years. She and Lafayette at times talked of things that they had never spoken of before. She told him how when he came home to Paris in 1782, she tried to hide her feelings so as not to trouble him. She did not need to restrain herself now!

"If you don't think you are loved enough," she said, "you will have to blame God for my shortcomings, for He made me what I am. What a fate to have been your wife! I have loved you in the Christian sense, in the worldly sense—and passionately."

He told her often that he loved her too and she would ask him to say it again as if she could hardly believe it. He thanked her for her loyalty when he first went to America and she defended him against the criticism of her family, but she put aside the compliment. "That's true," she said, "it *was* rather nice for a child, but how good of you to re-member something that was so very long ago!"

Even their difference in religious outlook was brought into the light. When Adrienne received Communion, the girls thought that it might embarrass her for their father to be present but when he rose to go she would not let him leave her. Each night she asked him to bless her. She recited *The Canticle of Tobit* for him, saying apologetically, "I have to *say* it because I sing so badly."

One day she put the question that she had always forbid-den herself to ask, "You are not a Christian?"

Lafayette was silent.

"Ah, I know what you are," she continued, with a little smile. "You are a fayettist."

"You must think me very egotistical," he said, abashed, "but aren't you something of a fayettist yourself?"

"You are right," she was still smiling, "that is a sect that I would die for!"

Though there were days, such as this, when she seemed better and her hold upon the present and the past seemed so firm, those who watched her saw that she was steadily losing ground. At the end of November, Pauline was sent for and came to join the distraught group that hovered about the sickroom. With Pauline present, Adrienne felt that her mother was there also and frequently spoke of the Duchess as if she were alive.

"I think I will see my mother today," she said.

It was Christmas Eve, George's twenty-eighth birthday and she had been looking forward to the anniversary. She seemed more comfortable. Her mind had cleared—but all felt that the end was close at hand.

Till then only two or three at a time had come into her room for fear of exhausting her, but they all entered now and sat where she could see them. She looked about her with satisfaction, as though they were all gathered again in the living room at La Grange or Chavaniac. "What a delightful circle," she said. She spoke to each affectionately and then fell silent.

The minutes ticked away, the hours. She murmured something indistinctly that Lafayette could not understand. He leaned over her. For a moment life rushed back. Her voice was clear and strong as she cried, "Then you have loved me! How happy I am! Kiss me."

She put her arm about his neck and drew him down to her. "I am yours, yours alone," she whispered in his ear.

After that she made no further effort to speak. Though she kissed the crucifix that Pauline held out to her and put into her hand, it slipped from her grasp as she groped for Lafayette's fingers and clasped them. Presently he felt her hold relax.

* * *

On Christmas Day, Pauline went to the Garden of Picpus and marked the spot where Adrienne was to be buried, close to the wall surrounding the mass grave.

Shortly after Adrienne's death, Lafayette wrote a long letter to César de la Tour Maubourg, who had known her so well, of whom she had been so fond. He described the details of her illness and the long farewell they had been permitted to take of one another, paying tribute to the virtues that had made her "incomparable;" her courage, her high-mindedness, above all her generosity; on the day of her death Adrienne had sent her love to Madame de Simiane.

"Farewell, my dear friend," the letter concluded. "You have helped me surmount some hard and painful misfortunes . . . but this is the greatest misfortune of all—a misfortune of the heart. I will never rise above it."

On that Christmas Eve of 1807, Lafayette felt that he was a broken man, but he could not look into the future. It would be twenty-seven years before his body was laid beside Adrienne's, twenty-seven years during which he lived fully and adventurously. His career, which had caused his wife so much pride and anguish, which for a time he laid aside to please her, was to have a stirring conclusion.

Lafayette was to play a part in the fall of Napoleon and the restoration of the Bourbons. He was to return in glory to America, and, when the Bourbons failed to live up to his ideal of liberalism, he was to lead yet another revolution when he was in his seventies. He would even put on again his general's uniform, as head of the National Guard and, as he walked through the streets of Paris, people would crowd about him to kiss his hand, to kiss his cheek and cheer him.

Throughout these years, Lafayette never lost touch with Adrienne. The door leading into her bedroom at La Grange was walled up so that visitors could not stray into it uninvited. Everything was left there exactly as it was when she

was alive. Each Christmas Eve, Lafayette went there alone
to spend the evening in her company.

There was daily communion as well. In his old age, Lafayette was valeted by an elderly ex-guardsman named Bastien.
Bastien would come to his General's room early in the
morning to draw the curtains and receive his orders for the
day. Then, as Lafayette fumbled for something beneath his
pillow, Bastien would quietly withdraw for a quarter of an
hour. Lafayette, having found the locket in which was Adrienne's miniature and on the back of which were engraved
the words, "I am yours alone," pressed it to his lips and for
a few minutes felt her sustaining presence. If, for some reason, the ritual had to be omitted, those who were about him
noticed that he seemed troubled and unsure of himself. Lafayette had never become a Christian in Adrienne's sense of
the word but he had found his patron saint.

In her children's hearts, she also survived. After they all
came back to France in 1799, the life of her mother that
Adrienne had written on the margins of the volume by
Buffon at Olmütz was put into print, a friend who had a
small hand press running off a limited number of copies.
Virginie wanted to create a similar tribute to her mother.
As audience, she had in mind particularly her own children,
who had never had the privilege of knowing their grandmother.

Virginie set to her task with some misgivings. So many
records, so many precious letters had been lost! Yet another
difficulty faced her at the very outset. How could she describe
adequately the passionate love for her husband that had
dominated Adrienne's life, that surpassed all other feelings,
all other attachments, and yet did no damage to them?

"I don't know how," Virginie wrote, "I can give you an
idea of my mother's way of loving. It was something that
was hers alone."

Bibliography and Comments

IN GENERAL.

Certain works were used so constantly in preparing this book that it would be tedious to cite them in every particular case in the notes on the individual chapters that follow.

This is true for the primary source for Adrienne's life, a memoir that she wrote of her mother, the Duchesse d'Ayen, and a similar brief biography of Adrienne written after her death by her daughter, Virginie de Lasteyrie. Both lives were published at Paris in 1868 as *Vie de Madame de Lafayette, par Madame de Lasteyrie, sa fille, precedée d'une notice sur la vie de sa Mère, Madame la Duchesse d'Ayen, par Madame de Lafayette*. Adrienne's tribute to her mother was written, as described in Chapter XIX, in the prison of Olmütz, probably in the winter of 1795. After the return of the Lafayette family to France in 1799, a few copies were privately printed. They have been exceedingly rare items for book collectors, though six fresh copies were found recently by Count René de Chambrun at La Grange.

Lafayette's writings were published in six volumes after

his death as *Mémoires, Correspondance et Manuscripts du Général Lafayette* (Paris, 1837-1838). Because of length, and perhaps to save the feelings of those of Lafayette's contemporaries who were still alive, the material was severely pruned. On the other hand, most of the letters that Lafayette wrote from prison and exile were collected during his lifetime by his friend, Louis Romeuf, but were left unpublished for more than a century. They were edited by Jules Thomas, *Correspondance Inedite de Lafayette, 1793-1801* (Paris, c. 1930). These letters are uncut and, like the *Mémoires,* have been freely used.

CHAPTER I. *HEROIC HOMECOMING*

A fragment of the Hotel de Noailles, where Adrienne was born and spent the first twenty-two years of her life, is preserved in the Hotel St. James and Albany at 211 Rue St. Honoré. Where the main body of the mansion stood, the Rue d'Alger has been cut through. The house contained many *objets d'art* and a fine collection of paintings by the early Dutch and Italian artists, as well as the work of men who were distinctly modern when the Hotel was in its prime —Watteau, Boucher, and Fragonard. There was also a magnificent library.

The meeting of Adrienne and Lafayette in 1782 is not mentioned in either Adrienne's life of her mother, nor in her own biography by Virginie. Adrienne may have wished to forget her moment of weakness; Virginie may never have heard of it. The incident, however, is described in various memoirs of the day, among them Volume I, page 188, of the Comte de Ségur's *Mémoires, Souvenirs et Anecdotes* (Paris, 1827).

Recently, The American Friends of Lafayette distributed to its members printed copies of the words and music of the popular song cited at the end of this chapter. It was probably one of many that were being sung at this time. Its title is *Adieux de Ventre-à-Terre, Dragon, a Margotton Sa Mie.*

CHAPTER II. *A RED TAPESTRIED ROOM*

Adrienne's childhood and marriage is not only described in the *Vie de Madame Lafayette* but also in a biography of one of her younger sisters, *Anne Paule Dominique de Noailles, Marquise de Montagu,* which was published anonymously at Rouen in 1859. Later editions give Auguste Callet as author.

Lafayette's marriage was arranged by his maternal great-grandfather, the Comte de la Rivière and his great-aunt, the Comtesse de Lusignem. His father, another Gilbert du Motier, died when Lafayette was two-years-old, his mother when he was twelve.

There is no eye witness report of Adrienne's wedding, but it no doubt set the pattern for Pauline's marriage, which is detailed in Chapter I of Callet's book.

CHAPTER III. *THE HOUSE IN THE RUE DE BOURBON*

Lafayette's affair with Aglaé de Hunolstein is the subject of Louis Gottschalk's book, *Lady in Waiting, the Romance of Lafayette and Aglaé de Hunolstein* (Baltimore, 1939). Except for the letter that Lafayette wrote from Chavaniac in 1783, the evidence in the case is slight. Aglaé had another American friend beside Lafayette, John Paul Jones, with whom she corresponded. The little that is known of her life after she left the Palais Royal is told in the *Mémoires* of Madame de Genlis, who was governess to the children of the Duke de Chartres, one of the Duke's many mistresses, and therefore hostile to Aglaé. Madame de Genlis does not give the name of the convent in which Aglaé led the life of a penitent. It was abolished in 1789 and she then boarded with a poor family on the fifth floor of a tenement. After the Terror, she was reunited with her husband, but shortly after died, in 1795.

More about Lafayette's attachment to Madame de Simiane may perhaps be learned after all the documents at La Grange have been published. Many of Lafayette's letters to her are given in abbreviated form in the *Mémoires*. She is mentioned by many of her contemporaries, by Madame Vigée le Brun, who painted her portrait twice, *Souvenirs de Madame Vigée le Brun,* (Paris, 1822) Vol. II, p. 305, and in the *Memoirs of the Comtesse de Boigne,* (New York, 1908) Vol. I, p. 21 and Vol. III, p. 4. Thomas Jefferson was so familiar with her connection with Lafayette that when Madame de Simiane's husband committed suicide in 1787 he wondered, in a letter to his secretary, William Short, whether he should condole with Lafayette or congratulate him.

The Lafayettes' house in the Rue de Bourbon no longer exists and the name of the street itself was changed during the Revolution to the Rue de Lille. A house still standing at No. 121 Rue de Lille, and now occupied by the Institut Neerlandais, was built at the same time as the Hotel de Lafayette and was identical with it, according to an item on page 165 of the catalogue of the exposition held in Paris in 1957 to celebrate the two hundredth anniversary of Lafayette's birth.

The very condensed view of Lafayette's career given here follows that given fully and painstakingly by Louis Gottschalk in his excellent book, *Lafayette between the American and the French Revolutions* (Chicago, 1950) and in Volume I of Brand Whitlock's *Lafayette* (New York, 1929).

CHAPTER IV. *THE KING'S JAILER*

There are many firsthand accounts of the march on Versailles and the riot in the Champ de Mars. Their variations are due to the political outlook of the observers. The report given to the National Assembly after the Champ de Mars affair set the casualties at a dozen killed, with perhaps a dozen more wounded; the radicals, however, said that 600 and even 2000 people fell. In Gaetano Salvemini's *The French Revolution* (New York, 1954), page 231, he cites a dispassionate German observer, who estimated that there were about sixty hurt or killed.

Just how much sinister plotting was done by the Duc d'Orleans has never been accurately determined, but Lafayette was convinced of the Duke's evil intentions and saw that he was sent away on a mission to England after the October 5th outbreak. The sniper who almost killed Lafayette on July 17th, 1791, was a gunman said to be in the Duke's pay.

CHAPTER V. *THE HOUSE IN THE HILLS*

Three books tell something of the history of the chateau of Chavaniac; Henri Mosnier's *Le Chateau de Chavaniac* (Le Puy, 1883), Louis Romeuf's *Au Pays de Lafayette* (Paris, 1921), and *Une Grande Famille d'Auvergne* by George Paul Pierre Bodinet and Marie Louise Le Verrier (Clermont-Ferrand, 1951). The chateau came into Lafayette's branch of the family by the marriage of his grandfather in 1708. Even today the house in the hills seems remote. Part of it is preserved as a Lafayette shrine, part is a preventorium for tubercular children maintained by a Franco-American committee.

Lafayette was brought up by his grandmother, a maiden aunt, Marguerite-Madeleine de Lafayette, and his "Aunt Chavaniac," whose given name was Louise-Charlotte, the only survivor of the trio in 1791.

The meeting with Pauline de Montagu at Vaire and her

departure for England are detailed in Chapter IV of her biography.

CHAPTER VI. *A WAITING TIME*

The account given here of the sack of the Tuileries follows closely that given in Friederich Kapp's *Justus Erich Bollmann, Ein Lebensbild Aus Zwei Welttheilen* (Berlin, 1880). The author used this work extensively in preparing an earlier book dealing with the Lafayette legend, *A Chance for Glory* (New York, 1957). Bollmann, who later was to try to rescue Lafayette from the prison of Olmütz, was in Paris on August 10th, 1792, and followed the crowd to the Tuileries.

CHAPTER VII. *THE BEST OF NEWS*

The material for this and the next chapter is taken from an account written by Anastasie de Lafayette and published in the *Revue Retrospective* in 1900 (Vol. 13, p. 363 ff.). At that time, the manuscript was in the possession of Louis Edmond, the last descendant of Lafayette in the male line. It must have been written soon after the events described, by a girl who had a sense of humor, a keen eye for detail and characterization. All the conversation quoted is reproduced from Anastasie's report.

Though she gives such a vivid picture of the servants at Chavaniac, Anastasie does not mention an American employee of Lafayette whose existence is revealed by a document exhibited at the 1957 Lafayette exposition in Paris. His name was Zamord, he was about thirty-years-old and was baptized by Father Durif on December 26th, 1791. Adrienne was his godmother.

CHAPTER IX. *THE COURT OF PUBLIC OPINION*

Anastasie's account breaks off abruptly before the prisoners reached Le Puy. The editor says that there was more of the manuscript, but that at the time of publication it was lost and the owner was hunting for it. Virginie's less detailed account takes over at this point. In her life of Adrienne, she gives all of the letters quoted here. Aulagnier's report to Roland is given in the Appendix to the *Vie*. The letters to Brissot were found among his papers after he was guillotined in 1793.

Adrienne's letter to Washington and another letter to him mentioned in the following chapter appear in Volume 10 of Jared Spark's *The Writings of George Washington* (Boston, 1838), also the covering letter that Dyson wrote from England in which he says that—"her situation is truly affecting . . . Under these circumstances she relies on your influence." Adrienne could speak a little English, but could not write it perfectly. With the first letter she may have had Dyson's help and Frestel's with the second, Frestel having by that time, March, 1793, returned to the chateau.

CHAPTER X. *A NET OF MANY STRANDS*

The correspondence of the ministers in regard to Lafayette is taken from Gouverneur Morris' *Diary of the French Revolution* (Boston, 1939) and an article by Samuel Flagg Bemis, "Lafayette and America" in *The Magazine of the Daughters of the American Revolution* for June, July, and August, 1924.

Pauline's view of the fortress of Wesel is told in Chapter V of her biography.

CHAPTER XI. *THE LAW OF SUSPECTS*

Lafayette's letter to Adrienne from Magdebourg is given on page 193 of *Correspondance Inedite de Lafayette. La Belle Gabrielle* Plantation was still in his possession when he returned from exile in 1799 and was sold to the French government in 1802, with the proviso that the Negroes should be free.

Adrienne in the life of her mother (p. 131) says that the Duchesse d'Ayen saw in Paris during the winter of 1793 a *valet de chambre* of Lafayette, who had escaped from prison, that she sent him on to Chavaniac, but that little could be learned from him. This, of course, was not Chavaniac, who was with his master all during his captivity. Lafayette, however, mentions in his letter to Adrienne a man named Desmanches who escaped during the removal of the prisoners from Wesel to Magdebourg and asks her to do something for his family in case he had never reached France.

CHAPTER XII. *DETAINED*

Armand Raoul in his *In the Shadows, Three Heroines of the Revolution* (New York, 1928) says that the House of Detention at Brioude was the Hotel Doradour.

CHAPTER XIII. *LE PLESSIS PRISON*

All of this chapter is based on Madame de Duras' account of her prison experiences, *Les Prisons de mon Père, de ma Mère et des Miennes* (2nd. ed., Paris, 1889).

The Hymn to the Supreme Being is quoted from page 191 of Edith Sichel's *The Household of the Lafayettes* (London, 1910).

CHAPTER XIV. *OUTSIDE THE WALLS OF THE CITY*

Grelet's account of the events of July 21st, 1794, is given in Madame de Duras' book; Father Carrichon's is appended to Adrienne's life of her mother. An article by the Duc de La Force, "Une Prisonière sous la Terreur" in the *Revue des Deux Mondes* (Vol. 47, Sept. 1938, p. 361) quotes liberally from the letters that Louise wrote to Grelet and her children from the Luxembourg, more than a hundred of them having been preserved.

CHAPTER XV. *IN THE SHADOWS*

The New York Public Library owns the manuscript letters that Adrienne wrote to Monroe. They have been printed in *Bookman's Holiday* (New York, 1942), edited by Charles Flower McCoombs. Among the Monroe papers, also in the New York Library, is the citizenship certificate written for Adrienne at Aurat by Dr. Guitandry. This must have been one of the papers that Adrienne asked Monroe to take to the Committee. It is not certain from yet another unpublished letter in the Monroe collection just when he visited her, but the editor thinks that it was after she left Le Plessis and therefore probably in the Maison Delmas.

CHAPTER XVI. *MRS. MOTIER*

The author's *A Chance for Glory* deals with the Lafayette-Huger rescue attempt. Adrienne wrote to Dr. Bollmann from Olmütz on May 22nd, 1796, saying that she had heard of his exploit while she was still in prison in Paris. Her information at that time probably came from the Princesse d'Hénin, Lafayette's cousin in London. The letter is given on page 321 of Jules Cloquet's *Recollections of the Private Life of General Lafayette* (London, 1835).

Rosalie de Grammont is said to have written, as did Adrienne, a memoir of her mother; if so, it has never been found. Rosalie was the only one of the sisters to live to a ripe old age. She died in 1853 in her eighty-fifth year and thus witnessed two more revolutions, those of 1830 and of 1848. In 1848, her granddaughter asked her if she wasn't afraid of seeing the guillotine set up in the public square, but she replied characteristically, "Poor darling—we have to die, don't we? The important thing is to be always ready; the manner of death is a mere detail."

Adrienne's letter to Lafayette written on board *The Little Cherub* is quoted from the account of the discovery of the Lafayette letters at La Grange in *The New York Times,* June 19th, 1956. As mentioned in Chapter XVIII, it was not delivered to Lafayette in Olmütz, but it eventually came into his possession and he must have treasured it, for it was found in his wallet after his death.

CHAPTER XVII. *A NEST OF EXILES*

Pauline de Montagu's biography, Chapters V to IX, are drawn upon for this chapter.

Madame de Tessé's pre-Revolutionary Paris salon was one of those where Lafayette was most at home. Madame de Tessé was a friend of Jefferson. They shared an interest in agriculture and exchanged letters to the day of her death. See Chinard's *Trois Amitiés françaises de Jefferson* (Paris, 1927).

The Duc d'Ayen had been intimate with the Countess Golovkin as early as 1790. Pauline met her then when she went for a cure to Switzerland. Madame Golovkin and the Duke were married in 1796.

CHAPTER XVIII. *THE CANTICLE OF TOBIT*

Virginie describes the interview with the Emperor; Adrienne describes, in a letter to Madame de Tessé (Vol. IV, p.

270 of the *Mémoires*), the interview with Thugut. The wives of de Maubourg and de Pusy later tried to reach Vienna and the Emperor unsuccessfully.

The description of the prison of Olmütz given by Virginie is supplemented by that given by César de la Tour Maubourg, whose letters, smuggled out of the prison, appear in *The French American Review* for October, 1948. Another letter of La Tour Maubourg is quoted in Cloquet's *Recollections* (p. 73).

CHAPTER XIX. *PRISON IDYL*

There is no internal evidence of just when Adrienne wrote the life of her mother, but it seems likely that it was soon after her arrival at Olmütz. Madame Lavet, who was with the Duchess and Louise during their last night at the Conciergerie, wrote a brief account that is appended to Adrienne's.

CHAPTER XX. *FREEDOM CAMPAIGN*

How the mail was brought to Olmütz is told in H. L. V. Ducoudray-Holstein's *Memoirs of Gilbert M. Lafayette* (New York, 1835), Chapter XXIII.

There are many quotations from "Eleuthère's" later correspondence with Lafayette given in Cloquet's *Recollections*. The letter, earlier mentioned in the notes on Chapter XVI, that Adrienne wrote to Bollmann was found among "Eleuthère's" papers. Since Bollmann was in America at the time, it was never delivered.

CHAPTER XXI. *RELEASE*

That Adrienne was practically in command of the freedom campaign in its final stages is proved by her letters given on page 300 and following of the *Correspondance Inedite*.

The trip to Hamburg is described in Chapter XXV of Ducoundray-Holstein's *Memoirs*.

Gouverneur Morris' unfriendly criticism of the Lafayettes is given on page 302, Volume II of his *Diary and Letters* (New York, 1888).

CHAPTER XXII. *BY THE WATERS OF PLOEN*

Chapter XIII of Pauline's biography deals with the Lafayettes' stay at Witmold and Lemkuhlen.

Madame de Simiane was an old and intimate friend of Madame de Tessé.

CHAPTER XXIII. *ANOTHER SEPARATION*

Lafayette's letters to Adrienne while she was away from him in France are taken not only from his *Mémoires* (Vol. V), but also from the *Correspondance Inedite* (p. 339 ff.).

Pauline as well as Virginie describes the meeting of the three sisters at Vianen.

CHAPTER XXIV. *THE GARDEN OF PICPUS*

In Virginie's life of Adrienne (p. 410) she says that her mother first heard of Picpus from a priest, but Pauline's biographer gives Pauline the credit for the discovery; both stories may be true.

A book by G. Lenôtre, the pen name of Louis L. T. Gosselin, *Le Jardin de Picpus* (Paris, 1928) gives a history of the cemetery and adds some gruesome details of the burial of victims of the guillotine. The cemetery is now within the city limits. Among those buried in the mass grave are the poet, André Chénier and the Prussian adventurer, Baron von Trenck. A wreath is laid on Lafayette's grave every July 4th by The American Friends of Lafayette.

Gosselin points out that the spectators who took a ghoulish delight in attending public executions represented a minority of the citizens of Paris. The fact that the guillotine was set up in various places, and eventually outside the walls of the city, was due to protests from local inhabitants. A vigorous protest was lodged in 1794, against the Picpus property being used for a burial ground, by a man who had rented the house of the former religious community as a sanitorium. His business venture, he declared, had been ruined. *Le Jardin de Picpus* lists the names of all in the mass grave.

CHAPTER XXV. *YEARS OF GRACE*

Lafayette himself described his relations with Bonaparte in a long letter to his friend, General Van Ryssel, beginning on page 148 of Volume V of his *Mémoires*.

Cloquet's *Recollections* give a careful description of La Grange. He, the family doctor, visited it frequently—though this was after Adrienne's death. His catalogue of the things that were in the chateau—and even their position in the various rooms—is so exact that this book has been invaluable to the Comte and Comtesse de Chambrun in their restoration of La Grange.

Cloquet tells of being called once to La Grange to take care of a son of Félix Frestel who was visiting there and was injured in a hunting accident.

Chapter XVII of Pauline's biography tells of Virginie's marriage and of the death of Louis de Noailles. Louis' sons, Alexis and Alfred, both had military careers. Alfred was killed during Napoleon's invasion of Russia in 1812.

CHAPTER XXVI. *YOURS ALONE*

Lafayette's long letter to César de la Tour Maubourg, describing Adrienne's illness, is given at the end of Virginie's life of her mother.

After Adrienne's death, Pauline came to live, more or less, at Fontenay and kept up her charitable enterprises. She cared not only for her own children but for her orphaned nephews and nieces. She was in close touch with the Lafayettes and with Rosalie de Grammont, also with her father and his second wife, who apparently was a satisfactory and kindly stepmother to the children of his first marriage. The Duke returned from Switzerland after the fall of Napoleon and regained possession of the Hotel de Noailles, though he was so poor that he could only live in a corner of it. He died, aged eighty-five, at Fontenay in 1824. Pauline survived her husband, Joachim, and died in 1839. The most long-lived of all the characters touched upon in this story was Madame de Chavaniac. She reached the age of ninety-three and was constantly visited by Lafayette and George until her death in 1814.